Joachim Breitner

Lazy Evaluation

From natural semantics to a machine-checked compiler transformation

The cover background pattern was created using the substrate algorithm by J. Tarbell, as implemented for the XScreensaver project by Mike Kershaw.

Lazy Evaluation

From natural semantics to a machine-checked compiler transformation

by
Joachim Breitner

KIT Scientific Publishing

Dissertation, Karlsruher Institut für Technologie (KIT)
Fakultät für Informatik, 2016

Tag der mündlichen Prüfung: 25. April 2016
Erster Gutachter: Prof. Dr.-Ing. Gregor Snelting
Zweiter Gutachter: Prof. Tobias Nipkow, Ph.D.

Impressum

KIT Scientific Publishing

Karlsruher Institut für Technologie (KIT)
KIT Scientific Publishing
Straße am Forum 2
D-76131 Karlsruhe

KIT Scientific Publishing is a registered trademark of Karlsruhe Institute of Technology. Reprint using the book cover is not allowed.

www.ksp.kit.edu

Print on Demand 2016

ISBN 978-3-7315-0546-4
DOI 10.5445/KSP/1000056002

Contents

Abstract

High level programming languages, in particular the lazy, pure, functional kind, liberate the programmer from having to think about the low-level details of how his code is going to be executed, and they give the compiler extra leeway in optimising the program. This distance to the actual machine makes it harder to reason about the effect of the compiler's transformations on the program's performance. Therefore, these transformations are often only evaluated empirically by measuring the performance of a few benchmark programs. This yields useful evidence, but not universal assurance.

Formal semantics of programming languages can serve as guide rails to the implementation of a compiler, and formal proofs can universally show that the compiler does not inadvertently change the meaning of a program. Can they also be used effectively to establish that a program transformation performed by the compiler is indeed an optimisation?

In this thesis, I answer this question in three steps: I develop a new compiler transformation; I build the tools to analyse it in an interactive theorem prover; finally I prove safety of the transformation, i.e. that the transformed program – in a suitable abstract sense – performs at least as well as the original one.

My compiler transformation and accompanying program analysis *Call Arity*, which is now shipped with the Haskell compiler GHC, solves a long-standing problem with the *list fusion* program transformation: Accumulator passing list consumers like foldl and sum would, if they were allowed to take part in list fusion, produce badly performing code. Call Arity empowers the compiler to further rewrite such code, by eta-expanding function definitions, into a form that runs efficiently again. The key ingredient is a novel cardinality analysis based on the notion of *co-call graphs*, which can detect whether a variable is used at most once, even in the presence of recursion.

I provide empirical evidence that my analysis is indeed able to solve the problem: Now list fusion can provide significant improvements in these cases. The measurements also show that there are instances besides list fusion where the transformation fires and improves the program. No program in the benchmark suite regressed as a result of introducing Call Arity.

In order to be able to verify these statements formally, I formalise Launchbury's natural semantics for lazy evaluation in the interactive theorem prover Isabelle. As Launchbury's semantics is a very successful and commonly accepted semantics for lambda calculus with mutually recursive let-bindings that models lazy evaluation, it is a natural choice for this endeavour.

My formalisation uses nominal logic, in the form of the Isabelle package Nominal2, to handle the issue of names and binders, which is generally one of the main hurdles in any formalisation work in programming languages. It is one of the largest Isabelle developments using this method, and the first to effectively combine it with the HOLCF package for domain theory. My first attempt to combine these turned out to be a dead end. I explain how and why that did not go well and how I eventually overcame the challenges.

Furthermore, I give the first rigorous adequacy proof of Launchbury's semantics. The proof sketch given by Launchbury has resisted past attempts to complete it. I found a more elegant and direct proof by slightly deviating from his outline.

Equipped with this formalisation, I model the Call Arity analysis and transformation in Isabelle and prove that it does not degrade program performance. My abstract measure of performance is the number of allocations performed by the program; I explain why this is a suitable choice for my use case. The proof is modular and introduces *trace trees* as a suitable domain for abstract cardinality analyses.

Every formal development, whether machine-checked or not, has a formalisation gap between the model and the modelled artefact. I discuss the breadth of the gap, in particular its limits given that Call Arity is but one part in a large, real-world compiler.

All in all I present novel program analyses to solve an open problem with *list fusion* and to generally improve the compiler, and I demonstrate how formal methods can be used to prove an operational property – safety – at this high level.

Zusammenfassung

Höhere Programmiersprachen, insbesondere rein funktionale mit Bedarfsauswertung, befreien den Programmierer von der Pflicht, sich darüber Gedanken zu machen, wie ihr Programm tatsächlich auf der Maschine ausgeführt werden wird. Ebenso hat der Compiler beim Optimieren von Programmen in solchen Sprachen größeren Spielraum. Dieser Abstand zur Maschine macht es allerdings auch schwieriger, vorherzusagen, wie sich die Programmtransformationen des Compilers auf die Leistung des Programms auswirkt. Daher werden solche Transformationen oft nur empirisch untersucht, indem die Leistung von ein paar wenigen Beispielprogrammen gemessen wird. So werden zwar durchaus wertvolle Anhaltspunkte gewonnen, jedoch keine allgemein gültigen Aussagen.

Formale Semantiken von Programmiersprachen können als Leitplanken bei der Implementierung eines Compilers dienen, und formale Beweise können allgemeingültig zeigen, dass ein Compiler die Bedeutung eines Programmes nicht unbeabsichtigt verändert. Können wir mit ihrer Hilfe auch beweisen, dass eine Programmtransformation, wie sie der Compiler vornimmt, in der Tat eine Optimierung ist?

Dieser Frage gehe ich in dieser Arbeit in drei Schritten nach: Ich entwickle eine neue Compiler-Transformation; ich baue die Werkzeuge um sie in einem interaktiven Theorembeweiser zu untersuchen; letztendlich beweise ich, dass das umgeschriebene Programm – in einem geeigneten abstrakten Sinne – mindestens so performant ist als zuvor.

Meine Compiler-Transformation, genannt *Call Arity*, wird inzwischen mit dem Haskell-Compiler GHC ausgeliefert und löst ein schon lange bestehendes Problem mit der Programmtransformation *list-fusion*: Funktionen wie foldl und sum, die Listen verarbeiten und dabei einen Akkumulator verwenden, haben, wenn auch sie von *list-fusion* umgeschrieben würden, zu unerwünscht langsamen Code geführt. *Call Arity* ermöglicht es dem Compiler, solchen Code weiter umzuschreiben und wieder in eine effiziente Form zu bringen, in dem er Funktionsdefinition geeignet eta-expandiert. Die dabei entscheidende Zutat ist eine neue Kardinalitäts-Analyse, die erkennen kann, wenn eine Variable höchstens einmal verwendet wird – und das sogar bei rekursivem Code.

Ich zeige empirisch, dass meine Analyse tatsächlich das Problem löst und nun auch in diesen Fällen *list-fusion* die Leistung der Programme signifikant verbessern kann. Ich zeige auch, dass es Situationen jenseits von *list-fusion* gibt, in denen meine Transformation anspringt und zu Verbesserungen führt.

Um diese Aussagen auch formal überprüfen zu können, formalisiere ich Launchburys Semantik für Sprachen mit Bedarfsauswertung im interaktiven Theorembeweiser Isabelle. Diese verbreitete und allgemein akzeptierte Semantik modelliert Bedarfsauswertung im Lambda-Kalkül mit wechselseitiger Rekursion und ist daher in meinem Fall die Semantik der Wahl.

Um die Problematik von Namen und Bindungen, die generell eine der Hauptschwierigkeiten bei der Formalisierung von Programmiersprachen ist, in den Griff zu bekommen, verwende ich Nominallogik, die für Isabelle im Paket *Nominal2* implementiert ist. Meine Formalisierung ist eine der größten Isabelle-Formalisierungen, die *Nominal2* verwendet, und die erste, die es effektiv mit dem *HOLCF*-Paket, welches Domäntheorie umsetzt, kombiniert. Mein erster Anlauf, diese Techniken zu kombinieren, scheiterte; ich erkläre, wie und warum, und beschreibe, wie ich die Probleme letztendlich überwand.

Darüber hinaus habe ich den ersten rigorosen Beweis, dass Launchburys Semantik adäquat ist, geführt. Launchburys Beweisansatz widersteht bisher jeglichen Versuchen, ihn zu vervollständigen. Ich wich ein wenig von dem Weg ab, den er umrissen hat, und fand so einen eleganteren und direkteren Beweis.

Auf dieser Formalisierung baue ich auf, modelliere die *Call Arity*-Transformation und -Analyse in Isabelle und beweise, dass sie die Leistung der Programme nicht verringert. Als abstraktes Leistungsmaß verwende ich dabei die Anzahl der Speicherzellen, die das Programm anfordert. Ich erkläre, warum dies in meinem Fall eine geeignete Wahl ist. Der Beweis ist modular und führt das Konzept der *trace trees* ein, mit der sich abstrakte Kardinalitäts-Analysen beschreiben lassen.

Bei jeder Formalisierung, ob Computer-geprüft oder nicht, entsteht ein Formalisierungs-Spalt zwischen dem Modell und dem Modellierten. Ich bemesse die Breite des Spaltes, der sich im vorliegenden Fall insbesondere daraus ergibt, dass *Call Arity* nur ein Teil eines großen, produktiv eingesetzten Compilers ist.

Insgesamt führe ich also eine neue Programmanalyse ein, die ein offenes Problem mit *list fusion* löst und auch darüber hinaus den Compiler verbessert. Darüber hinaus zeige ich, wie formale Methoden genutzt werden können um auf dieser hohen Abstraktionsebene Beweise über nicht-funktionale Eigenschaften wie das Performanceverhalten zu führen.

Acknowledgements

I have to thank Prof. Gregor Snelting for giving me the possibility to join his group and to work on this thesis. He expected and allowed me to work with great freedom and latitude, and I could pursue my own ideas without pressure or worries.

I also thank Prof. Tobias Nipkow for serving as the co-referee, but also for creating Isabelle in the first place. Without his work, two thirds of this thesis would not exist.

I am indebted to Simon Peyton Jones, with whom I spent three months as an intern. This was a very fruitful time that heavily influenced my work. He pointed me to the open problem of making foldl a good consumer, which initiated the whole work on Call Arity, and nudged me to go further when I thought my solution was "good enough". Furthermore, I enjoyed the privilege to be his co-author. Finally, without his work on GHC and Haskell, two thirds of this thesis would not exist.

I was able to pursue my research with few constraints, and was able to attend summer schools and conferences, due to a generous scholarship by the Deutsche Telekom Stiftung. I thank Prof. Sigmar Wittig for his commitment as a mentor and for keeping me on track in critical times, and Christiane Frense-Heck for managing the scholarship program so very efficiently, smoothly and friendly. I also thank Gabriela Weitze-

Schmithüsen for helping me to secure the scholarship in the first place, and for not holding a grudge after I left her research group.

The programming paradigms group at the Karlsruhe Institute of Technology has been a great place to work at, and I am happy that I was part of this group. In particular I would like to thank my colleagues for 3-pm-rituals, board game nights and a roughly monthly supply of cake. Special thanks go to my office mate Denis Lohner, who was always available to discuss questions with, and my former office mate Andreas Lochbihler, who initiated me to semantics and interactive theorem proving.

I thank Martin Mohr, Sebastian Buchwald, Denis Lohner, Manuel Mohr, Mareike Schmidtobreick, Ulrike Leyn and Thomas Breitner for proofreading a draft of this thesis.

Finally, I'd like to thank Isabelle for a great many hours of working together in solitude. She is sometimes difficult to work with, but her endless patience and unerring pedantry taught me a lot. She would not take a *sorry*, but when I admitted that she is – as always – right and I made up for my mistakes, she never was resentful.

I also thank the other Isabelle for being so quite different: always available for a little quiz, other games or just a mindless chat.

> Functional programming combines the flexibility and power of abstract mathematics with the intuitive clarity of abstract mathematics.
>
> *Randall Munroe, xkcd #1270*

CHAPTER 1
Introduction

It is a pleasure to create programs in functional programming languages, as they allow for a very high-level style of programming, using abstraction and composition. It suits the human brain that is trying to solve a problem, instead of accommodating the machine that has to implement the instructions.

But such an abstraction comes at a cost: Generally, programs written in such high-level style perform worse than manually tweaked low-level code. Therefore, we reach out to optimising compilers, with the hope that they can amend this overhead, at least to some extent.

An optimising compiler necessarily needs to be conservative in how it changes the programs: We would not be happy if the program becomes faster, but suddenly computes wrong results. Naturally, this limits the compiler's latitude in applying fancy and far-reaching transformations. Conversely, the more declarative the language is – i.e. the less low-level details it specifies – and the fewer side-effects can occur, the more possibilities for optimising transformations arise.

This explains why compilers of pure, lazy functional programming languages, such as Haskell, can pull quite astonishing tricks on the code. A prime example for such a far-reaching transformation is *list fusion*: This technique transforms a program built from smaller components, each producing and/or consuming a list of values, into one combined loop. This not only avoids having to allocate, traverse and deallocate the list structure of each intermediate value, it also puts the actual processing codes next to each other, allowing for local optimisations to work on code that was originally far apart.

Unfortunately, there are many instances of code where the sufficiently smart compiler could do something clever – and often the uninitiated user actually expects that clever thing to happen – but the real compilers out there just do not do it yet. This thesis is about one such instance: A large number of list processing functions, including common combinators such as sum and length, were not set up to take part in list fusion. This is not because including them in the technique is difficult to do, but because the code that results from such a transformation would perform very badly.

I found a new program analysis, called *Call Arity*, which gives the compiler enough information to further transform that problematic code into nice, straightforward and efficient code – code that is roughly what a programmer would write manually, if he chose to program such low-level code. I motivate and describe the analysis and its impact on program performance, determined empirically.

The same language treats – purity and laziness – which make it easier for the compiler to transform programs also ease a rigorous, formal discussion of the artefacts at hand. I therefore evaluate Call Arity not only empirically, but also prove that it is correct (i.e. does not change the meaning of the program) and safe (i.e. does not make the program's performance worse). While the former is common practice in this field of research, the latter is rarely done with such rigour.

What makes me so confident that my proof deserves to be called rigorous? If I just did a pen-and-paper proof, I would not trust it to that extent. For that reason, I implemented the syntax, the semantics and the compiler transformations in the theorem prover Isabelle and performed all proofs therein. Occasionally, this required derivations from the pen-and-paper presentation given in this thesis. I discuss these differences, and other noteworthy facts about the formalisation, in dedicated sections in the following chapters.

Such a formal proof requires a formal semantics for the programming language at hand, and in order to make statements about an operational property, the semantics has to be sufficiently detailed. Launchbury's natural semantics for lazy evaluation [Lau93] is such a semantics, and can be considered a standard semantics in lazy functional programming language research. I implemented this semantics in Isabelle, including proofs of the two fundamental properties: correctness and adequacy (with regard to a standard denotational semantics). As no rigorous proof of adequacy existed before, I present my proof in detail.

I have structured this thesis as follows: This chapter contains a brief introduction to the Haskell compiler GHC, in particular its intermediate language *Core*, its evaluation strategy and list fusion, introduces the central notion of *arity*, describes nominal logic and the interactive theorem prover Isabelle. Chapter 2 lays the foundation by formally introducing the syntax and the various semantics, and contains rigorous correctness and adequacy proofs for Launchbury's semantics. Chapter 3 motivates, describes and empirically evaluates Call Arity. Chapter 4 builds on the previous two chapters and contains the formal proof that Call Arity is safe.

Appendix A contains the Isabelle formulation of the main results and relevant definitions. Appendix B lists the Haskell implementation of Call Arity. The bibliography and an index of used symbols and terms, including short explanations, follow. Figure 1 contains a map to the main artefacts and how they relate to each other. In the interest of readability I omit elaborate definitions and descriptions in the figure; if necessary, consult the index.

The present book is essentially my thesis, which is officially published separately [Bre16]. I have fixed spelling mistakes, adjusted the typography, slightly expanded Section 4.6 and mentioned newer, independet measurements in Section 3.5.4.

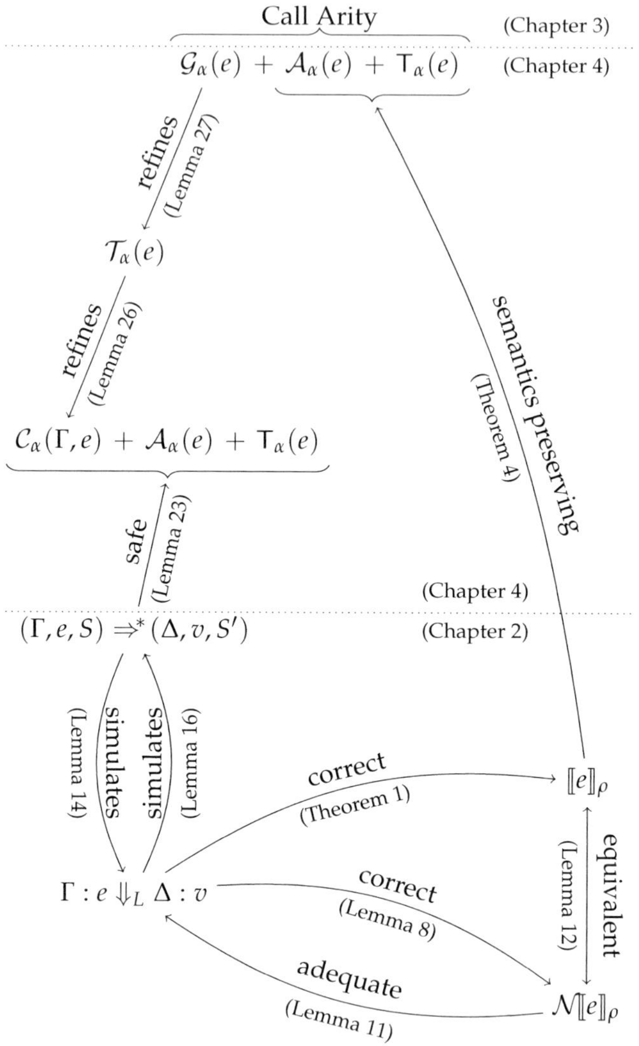

Figure 1: Main artefacts of this thesis and their relationship

1.1 Notation and conventions

I use mostly standard mathematical notation in this text, and any custom notation is introduced upon its first use. The index at the end of the thesis also includes symbols and notations, together with a short description of each entry.

Proofs are concluded by a black square (■), theorems, lemmas, definitions and examples span to the next diamond (◇).

When a function argument is just a single symbol, possibly with sub- or superscripts, I usually omit the parentheses for better readability: $\mathsf{fv}\, e_1$ instead of $\mathsf{fv}(e_1)$.

Variables printed with a dot (e.g. $\dot{\alpha}$) refer to lists whose elements are usually referred to by the plain variable (e.g. α). Variables printed with a bar (e.g. $\bar{\alpha}$) refer to objects that are partial or total maps from variable names to whatever the plain variable usually stands for. The same notation is used to distinguish related functions: If $\mathcal{T}$ is a plain function with one argument of a certain type, then $\dot{\mathcal{T}}$ is a function that expects a list of elements of that type and $\overline{\mathcal{T}}$ expects a map from variables names to values of that type.

Source code listings and code fragments within the text are typeset using a proportional sans-serif font, with language keywords highlighted by heavy type: **if** p a **then** f 1 **else** f 2.

When writing Haskell code, I use some Unicode syntax instead of the more common ASCII representation, in particular a lambda instead of a backslash for lambda abstractions, and a proper arrow instead of ->, e.g. (λx → x) :: a → a.

The Isabelle code snippets are produced by Isabelle from the sources, and printed in the usual LaTeX style of Isabelle's document generation facilities. The name of the Isabelle file containing the snipped is given in the top-right corner, unless it is the same as for the preceding snippet.

There are various schools of writing concerning the use of "we", "I" and "the author". Since a dissertation thesis is necessarily more tied to the person than a paper, even if it was a single author paper, I decided to use the first person singular whenever I describe what I have done or not done, and why I have done so. Nevertheless, large parts of the text, especially the proofs, are an invitation to you, the reader, to follow my train of thoughts. Optimistically assuming that you follow this invitation, I will commonly use "we" in these parts, referring to you and me, just as if we were standing in front of a blackboard where I walk you through my proof.

I do not avoid the passive voice as fundamentally as other authors would: It is used whenever I believe readability is best served this way.

1.2 Reproducibility and artefacts

This thesis describes a few artefacts that cannot be included in their entirety in the document, or that will evolve further in the future and thus diverge from what is discussed here. This includes the Call Arity implementation, which is part of the GHC source tree, and the Isabelle formalisations of Launchbury's semantics [Bre13] and of the safety of Call Arity [Bre15d]. Furthermore, I have conducted performance measurements of which only a summary is included in this text (Section 3.5.3), but neither the raw data nor the tools that produced them.

In the interest of reproducibility and verifiability, I have collected all these artefacts on http://www.joachim-breitner.de/thesis. In particular, there you will find:

- The Isabelle sources of both developments, in precisely the version that is described in this document, in three formats: The plain `.thy` file, a browsable HTML version and the Isabelle-generated LaTeX output.
- Scripts to fetch and build GHC in the version discussed in this thesis (7.10.3).
- Patches to that version of GHC to produce the various variants compared in the benchmark sections.
- Scripts to run the benchmark suite, collect the results and produce Tables 1 and 3 in the benchmark sections.

- Code that I have created to check claims in this thesis, e.g. about the performance cost of unsaturated function calls (Section 1.4.3) and the effect of Call Arity on difference lists (Table 2).
- The LaTeX sources of the thesis document itself.
- Errata, if necessary.

1.3 Lazy evaluation

With the title of this thesis sporting the term *lazy evaluation* so prominently, it seems prudent to briefly introduce it in general terms.

Consider the function

```
writeErrorToLog e =
  writeToLog ("Error " ++ errNum e ++ ": " ++ errDesc e)
```

which turns an error, given as an element of a structured data type, into a readable text and uses a hypothetical writeToLog function to write the text to a log file. In most programming languages, writeErrorToLog e would first calculate the text and only then call writeToLog. But assume that in the application at hand, logging is optional, and actually turned off: writeToLog would have to discard the text passed to it, and the calculation would have been useless. This behaviour is called *strict evaluation* or *call-by-value*.

In a programming language with lazy evaluation, the function writeErrorToLog would not actually assemble the text, but defer this calculation, by creating a *thunk* that serves as a placeholder. If writeToLog decides that no log file is to be written, it will discard the thunk and the useless calculation never happens. On the other hand, if writeToLog does write to the log file, this will eventually require the actual value of the argument and only then trigger the evaluation of the thunk. We also say that its evaluation is *forced*.

The point of lazy evaluation is not just to avoid useless computation: One of its main benefits is that code can be refactored much more easily. Consider the following plausible implementation of writeToLog:

```
writeToLog txt =
  if logLevel >= 1 then appendFile "error.log" txt
                   else return ()
```

This function does two things: It decides whether logging is actually required, and if so, it performs the logging. Likely there are more places where we need to decide whether logging is required, so it is desirable to abstract over this procedure and implement it in a definition of its own:

```
ifLogging action =
  if logLevel >= 1 then action
                   else return ()

writeToLog txt = ifLogging (appendFile "error.log" txt)
```

In a programming language with strict evaluation, this will not work as intended: The argument appendFile "error.log" txt would be evaluated before ifLogging gets a chance to check the log level. Our refactoring just broke the program! Note that even in strict languages, the **if**-**then**-**else**-construct evaluates the two branches lazily, but this is a built-in special case for this syntactic construct, and not available for the programmer to abstract over.

In a programming language with lazy evaluation, however, this refactoring is valid. This way, lazy evaluation allows the programmer to define custom control structures.

Another aspect of lazy evaluation that is crucial to my work is *sharing*: Although the argument to a function is not evaluated until it is used for the first time, it will not be evaluated a second time. For example the code map (2^b *) xs, which multiplies every element of the list xs by a certain power of two, will not actually calculate 2^b if the list xs is empty. But even if xs has more than one element, 2^b is calculated only once, and the result is shared between the various uses. This feature distinguishes lazy evaluation, also called *call-by-need*, from *call-by-name* evaluation. According to the latter scheme, which is of less practical relevance, the calculation of an argument is also deferred until it is needed, but it would be re-evaluated repeatedly if used more than once.

A common way to implement sharing is to add code to every thunk that, after the evaluation of the thunk has been triggered and its value has been calculated, replaces the thunk by this value, so that every existing reference to the thunk now references the value. This mechanism is called *updating*.

1.4 The GHC Haskell compiler

The programming language Haskell has been created in the 1990s by a committee with the aim to overcome the then wild growths of lazy functional programming languages. The committee produced a series of language specifications, including the final Haskell 98 language report [Pey03].[1] This standardisation allowed a number of Haskell compilers to emerge.

These days, still a number of compilers are actively developed, but while most of them are dedicated to special purposes or research, only one compiler is of practical relevance: The Glasgow Haskell Compiler (GHC).

In order for my work to have an impact on actual users using Haskell to solve real problems, I implemented Call Arity within GHC. It was first shipped with GHC-7.10, released on March 27th 2015[2]. GHC's internal structure necessarily influenced the design and implementation of Call Arity, so I will outline its relevant features here.

1.4.1 GHC Core

Speaking in terms of syntax, Haskell is a large language: As of version 7.10.3 of GHC, the data types used to represent the abstract syntax tree of an Haskell expression have over 79 constructors, and 24 more are required to express the Haskell types. Therefore GHC – like most compilers – transforms the source language into a smaller intermediate

1 After a long phase of stability, a revision was published in 2010 and is now the most recent Haskell specification [Mar10]. With regard to this thesis, the differences are irrelevant.

2 The coincidence with my birthday is, well, coincidental.

language. In this case, the intermediate language is *GHC Core* and uses only the 15 constructors given in Fig. 2 to represent expressions.

The translation from Haskell to Core is not just a matter of simple syntactic desugaring, as the type systems differ noticeably: Haskell has features in the type system that have a computational meaning; most prominently type classes. Therefore, GHC has to type-check the full Haskell program, and as a side-effect of type-checking the compiler produces the code that implements these features. In the case of type classes the compiler generates dictionaries[3] for each instance and passes them around as regular function arguments.

```
data Expr b = Var      Id
            | Lit      Literal
            | App      (Expr b) (Expr b)
            | Lam      b (Expr b)
            | Let      (Bind b) (Expr b)
            | Case     (Expr b) b Type [(AltCon, [b], Expr b)]
            | Cast     (Expr b) Coercion
            | Tick     (Tickish Id) (Expr b)
            | Type     Type
            | Coercion Coercion

data AltCon = DataAlt  DataCon
            | LitAlt   Literal
            | DEFAULT

data Bind b = NonRec b (Expr b)
            | Rec [(b, (Expr b))]
```

Figure 2: The data type representing GHC Core expressions

[3] From an operational point of view, these might better be called tuples, as they are single-constructor data types and the members are at fixed, statically known positions. There is no runtime string-based lookup as in "dictionaries" in dynamic languages.

Nevertheless, Core does have a type system, and Core terms are explicitly typed. This is used as an effective quality assurance tool [MP12]: The internal type checker (called linter) would complain if the Core generated from the Haskell source is not well-typed, or if any of the further processing steps breaks the typing. The type system is relatively small (12 constructors) but powerful enough to support all features of the Haskell type system, including fancy extensions like GADTs [PVWW06] and type families [SPCS08].

The theory behind Core is System F_C, an explicitly typed lambda calculus with explicit type abstraction and application as well as type equality witnesses called coercions [SCPD07]. The latter add another 15 constructors to the count. Core and its theoretical counterpart, System F_C, are continuously refined, recently by a stratification of the coercions into roles [WVPZ11; BEPW14].

Most of the published research around Core and System F_C revolves around the type system: How to make it more expressive and more powerful. There is, however, a lack of operational treatments of Core in the literature. The extended version of [BEPW14] contains a small-step semantics of System F_C. It serves not as a description of Core's operational behaviour but rather as a tool to prove type safety of System F_C and punts on let-bindings completely. Eisenberg also maintains a small-step semantics for full Core [Eis15], which is call-by-name. There is no description of how Core implements lazy evaluation besides the actual implementation in GHC, i.e. the Core-to-STG transformation. This lack contributed to the breadth of the formalisation gap of this work (Section 4.5.2).

Almost all of the optimisations performed by GHC are Core-to-Core transformations; Call Arity is no exception. But as not all features of Core are relevant in the description and discussion of Call Arity, the trimmed down lambda calculus introduced in Section 2.1 serves to take the role of Core; I discuss this simplification in Section 4.5.1.

1.4.2 Rewrite rules and list fusion

When we teach functional programming, we often use equational reasoning to explain when two programs are the same, or to derive more specialised or faster programs from specifications or existing programs, e.g. as Bird does [Bir89]. Such equational reasoning is especially powerful in pure, lazy languages, as more equalities hold here: For example, bindings may be floated out of or into expressions, or inlined completely, common code patterns can be abstracted into higher-order functions etc.

But instead of expecting the programmer to apply such equalities, we can actually teach the compiler to do that. This mechanism, called *rewrite rules*, lets the author of a software library specify rules that contain a code pattern (the left-hand side of the rule) and replacements (the right-hand side of a rule), with free variables that will be matched by any code [PTH01].

For example, the code

```
{-# RULES
 "map/map" forall f g xs. map f (map g xs) = map (f . g) xs
 #-}
```

allows the compiler to make use of the functoriality of map and replace code like

```
sum (map (+1) (map (*2) [0..10]))
```

by

```
sum (map ((+1) . (*2)) [0..10]),
```

which calls map only once, and hence avoids the allocation, traversal and deallocation of one intermediate list.

What about the other intermediate lists in that code? Can we get rid of them as well? After all, the code could well be written completely list-lessly:[4]

[4] Due to the excessive use of the stack, this is not an efficient way to sum the elements of a list, and a real implementation would use a strict accumulator and tail recursion. For the sake of this explanation, please bear with me here.

```
go 0
  where go n | n > 10    = 0
             | otherwise = (n*2 + 1) + go (n + 1)
```

This feat is done by *list fusion* [GLP93], which is essentially a set of rewrite rules that tell the compiler how to transform the high-level code with lists into the nice code above. The central idea is that instead of allocating the list constructors (: and []), the producer of a list passes the head of the list and the (already processed) tail of the list to a function provided by the consumer. Thus a list producer is expected to use the following build function to produce a list, instead of using the constructors directly:

```
build :: forall a. (forall b. (a → b → b) → b → b) → [a]
build g = g (:) []
```

The higher rank type signature ensures that g is consistent in using the argument provided by build to produce the result: By requiring the argument g to build a result of an arbitrary type b, it has no choice but to use the given arguments (here (:) and []) to construct it.

A list producer implemented using build is called a *good producer*.

For example, instead of defining the enumeration function naively as

```
[n..m] = go n m
  where go n m | n > m     = []
               | otherwise = n : go (n+1) m
```

it can be defined in terms of build, and thus the actual code in go is abstract in the list constructors:

```
[n..m] = build (go n m)
  where go n m cons nil | n > m     = nil
                        | otherwise = n `cons` go (n+1) m cons nil
```

The build function has a counterpart that is to be used by list consumers; it is the well-known right-fold:

```
foldr :: (a → b → b) → b → [a] → b
foldr k z = go
  where go []     = z
        go (y:ys) = y `k` go ys
```

Any list consumer implemented via foldr is called a *good consumer*.

It is a typical exercise for beginners to write a list consuming function like sum in terms of foldr:[5]

```
sum :: [Int] → Int
sum xs = foldr (+) 0 xs
```

After rewriting as many list producers as possible in terms of build, and as many list consumers as possible in terms of foldr, what have we gained? The benefit comes from one single and generally applicable rewrite rule

```
{-# RULES
 "fold/build" forall k z g. foldr k z (build g) = g k z
 #-}
```

which fuses a good producer with a good consumer. It makes the producer use the consumer's combinators instead of the actual list constructors, and thus eliminates the intermediate list.

Simplifying our example a bit, we can see that sum [0..10] would, after some inlining, become

```
foldr (+) 0 (build (go 0 10))
  where go n m cons nil | n > m     = nil
                        | otherwise = n `cons` go (n+1) m cons nil
```

where the rewrite rule is applicable, and GHC rewrites this to

```
go 0 10 (+) 0
  where go n m cons nil | n > m     = nil
                        | otherwise = n `cons` go (n+1) m cons nil
```

which can further be simplified (by a constant propagation and dropping unused arguments) to

```
go 0 10
  where go n m | n > m     = 0
               | otherwise = n + go (n+1) m
```

which is roughly the code we would write by hand.

[5] As mentioned in the previous footnote, this is *not* a good and practical definition for summation. In your code, please do use sum = foldl' (+) 0 instead!

A function like map is both a list consumer and a list producer, but it poses no problem to make it both a good consumer and a good producer:

```
map :: (a → b) → [a] → [b]
map f xs = build (λcons nil → foldr (λ x ys → f x 'cons' ys) nil xs)
```

With this definition for map, the compiler will indeed transform the expression sum (map (+1) (map (∗2) [0..10])) into the nice list-less code on page 12.

It is remarkable that list fusion does not have to be a built-in feature of the compiler, but can be completely defined by library code using rewrite rules.

List fusion based on foldr/build is but one of several techniques to eliminate intermediate data structures; there is unfoldr/destroy [Sve02] and stream fusion [CLS07]; they differ in what functions can be efficiently turned into good producers and consumers [Cou10]. I focus on foldr/build as that is the technique used for the list data type in the Haskell standard libraries.

1.4.3 Evaluation and function arities

When GHC is done optimising the program at the Core stage, it transforms it to machine code via yet another intermediate language. GHC Core is translated to the Spineless Tagless G-Machine (STG) [Pey92]. Although still a functional language based on the untyped lambda calculus, it already determines many low-level details of the eventual execution: In particular, allocation of data and of function closures is explicit, the memory layout of data structures is known and all functions have a particular arity, i.e. number of parameters. So although it is not machine code yet, together with the runtime system (which is implemented in C), most details of the runtime behaviour are known by now.

The function arity at this stage has an important effect on performance, as a mismatch between the number of arguments a function expects and the number of arguments it is called with causes significant overhead during execution.

```
multA :: Int → Int → Int
multA 0 y = 0
multA x y = x * y

multB :: Int → Int → Int
multB 0 = λ_ → 0
multB x = λy → x * y
```

Figure 3: Semantically equal functions with different arities

Consider the two functions in Fig. 3, which both implement a short-circuiting multiplication operator. The first has an arity of 2, while the second has an arity of 1. This matters: Evaluating the expression multB 1 2 is more than 25% slower than evaluating multA 1 2! Why is that so?

For the former, the compiler sees that enough arguments are given to multA to satisfy its arity, so it puts them in registers and simply calls the code of multA.

For the latter, the code first pushes onto the stack a continuation that will, eventually, apply its argument to 2. Then it calls multB with only the first argument in an register. multB then evaluates this argument and checks that is not zero. It then allocates, on the heap, a function closure capturing x, and passes it to the continuation on the stack. This continuation, implemented generically in the runtime, analyses the function closure to see that it indeed expects one more argument, so it finally passes the second argument, and the actual computation can happen.

This example demonstrates why it is important for good performance to have functions expect as many arguments as they are being called with.

Could the compiler simply always make a function expect as many arguments as possible? No!

Compare the expression sum (map (multA n) [1..1000]) with the expression sum (map (multB n) [1..1000]). The former will call multA one thousand times and thus perform the check n == 0 over and over again, while the latter calls multB once, hence performs the check once, and then re-uses the returned function a thousand times. In this example the check is rather cheap, but even then, for n=0, the latter code is 20% faster. With different, more expensive checks, the performance difference can become arbitrarily large.

More details about how GHC implements function calls, and why it does it that way, can be found in [MP06].

1.5 Arities and eta-expansion

The notion of arity is central to this thesis, and deserves a more abstract definition in terms of eta-expansion. This definition formally builds on the syntax and semantics introduced later, but can be understood on its own.

Eta-expansion replaces an expression e by $(\lambda z.\, e\ z)$, where z is fresh with regard to e. More generally, the n-fold eta-expansion is described by

$$\mathcal{E}_n(e) := (\lambda z_1 \ldots z_n.\, e\ z_1 \ldots\ z_n),$$

where the z_i are distinct and fresh with regard to e.

We intuitively consider an expression e to have *arity* $\alpha \in \mathbb{N}$ if we can replace it by $\mathcal{E}_\alpha(e)$ without negative effect on the performance – whatever that means precisely. Analogously, for a variable bound by **let** $x = e$, its arity x_α is the arity of e.

Example
The Haskell function

```
let f x = if x then λ y → y + 1
                else λ y → y − 1
```

can be considered to have arity 2: If we eta-expand its right-hand side, and apply some mild simplifications, we get

```
let f x y = if x then y + 1
                  else y − 1
```

which should in general perform better than the original code. Note that in a lazy language, x will be evaluated at most once. ◇

In this example, I determined the arity of an expression based on its definition and obtained its *internal* arity. Such an analysis has been part of GHC since a while and is described in [XP05].

For the rest of this work, however, I treat e as a black box and instead look at how it is being used, i.e. its context, to determine its *external* arity. For that, I can give an alternative definition: An expression e has arity α if upon every evaluation of e, there are at least α arguments on the stack.

Example
In the Haskell code

```
let f x = if g x then λ y → y + 1
                 else λ y → y − 1
in f 1 2 + f 3 4
```

the function f has arity 2: Because it is always called with two arguments, the eta-expansion itself has no effect, but it allows for subsequent optimisations that improve the code to

```
let f x y = if g x then y + 1
                   else y − 1
in f 1 2 + f 3 4.
```

The internal arity is insufficient to justify this, as in a different context, this transformation could create havoc: Assume the function is passed to a higher-order function such as map (f 1) [1.1000]. If f were now eta-expanded, the possibly costly call to g 1 would no longer be shared and repeated a thousand times. ◇

If an expression has arity α, then it also has arity α' for $\alpha' \leq \alpha$; every expression has arity 0. The arities can thus be arranged to form a lattice:

$$\cdots \sqsubset 3 \sqsubset 2 \sqsubset 1 \sqsubset 0.$$

For convenience, I set $0 - 1 = 0$. As mentioned in Section 1.1, $\bar{\alpha}$ is a partial map from variable names to arities, and $\dot{\alpha}$ is a list of arities.

1.6 Nominal logic

In pen-and-paper proofs about programming languages, it is customary to consider alpha-equivalent terms as equal, i.e. $\lambda x.\, x = \lambda y.\, y$. The human brain is relatively good in following that reasoning, keeping track of the scope of variables and implicitly making the right assumptions about what names in a proof may be equal to another. For example, in a proof by induction on the formation of terms, it often goes without saying that in the case for $\lambda x.\, e$, the x is fresh and not related to any name occurring outside the scope of this lambda.

Such loose reasoning stands in the way of a rigorous and formal treatment. If the formalisation introduces terms as raw terms where the name of the bound variable contributes to the identity of the object, i.e. $\lambda x.\, x \neq \lambda y.\, y$, then in every inductive proof one would have to worry about the bound variable possibly being equal to some name in the context, and if that poses a problem, one has to explicitly alpha-rename the lambda abstraction, which in turn requires a proof that the statement of the lemma indeed respects alpha-equivalence.

One alternative is to use nameless representations such as de-Bruijn indices. With these, every term has a unique representation and the issue of alpha-equivalency disappears. The downsides of such an approach are the need for two different syntactic constructors for variables – one for the index of a bound name, and one for the name of a free variable – and the relatively unnatural syntax, which stands in the way of readability

A way out is provided by *nominal logic*, as devised by Pitts [Pit03]. This formalism allows us to use names as usual in binders and terms, while still equating alpha-equivalent terms, and it provides induction principles that allow us to assume bound names to be as fresh as we intuitively want them to be.

This section gives a shallow introduction to nominal logic. I took inspiration from [UT05], simplified some details and omitted the proofs.

In the main body of the thesis I present my definitions and proofs in the intuitive and somewhat loose way, without making use of concepts specific to nominal logic. In particular I do not bother to state the equivariance of my definitions and predicates. Having a machine-checked formalisation, where all these slightly annoying and not very enlightening details have been taken care of, gives me the certainty that no problems lurk here.

1.6.1 Permutation sets

A core idea in nominal logic is that the effect of *permuting* names in an object describes its binding structure.

Full nominal logic supports an infinite number of distinct sorts of names, or *atoms*, but as I do not need this expressiveness, I restrict this exposition to one sort of atoms, here suggestively named Var.

We are concerned with sets that admit swapping names:

Definition 1 (PSets)
A pset is a set X with an action $\bullet$ of the group $\mathrm{Sym}(\mathsf{Var})$ on X. ◇

Deciphering the group theory language, this means that there is an operation $\bullet$ that satisfies, for every $x \in X$,
- $() \bullet x = x$ and
- $(\pi_1 \cdot \pi_2) \bullet x = \pi_1 \bullet (\pi_2 \bullet x)$ for all permutations π_1, π_2

where $()$ is the identity permutation, and $\cdot$ the usual composition of permutations.

The set of atoms, Var, is naturally a pset, with the standard action of the permutation group.

Any set can be turned into a pset using the trivial operation, i.e. $\pi \bullet x = x$ for all elements x of the set. This way, objects that do not "contain names", e.g. the set of natural numbers, or the Booleans, can be elegantly part of the formalism. Such a pset is called *pure*.

Products and sums of psets are psets, with the permutations acting on the components. Similarly, the set of lists with elements in a pset is a pset.

Functions from psets to psets are psets, with the action defined as

$$\pi \bullet f = \lambda x. \pi \bullet (f(\pi^{-1} \bullet x)).$$

Note that the permutation acting on the argument has to be inverted.

1.6.2 Support and freshness

Usually, when discussing names and binders, one of the first definitions is that of $\mathsf{fv}\, e$, the set of free variables of some term e. Intuitively, it is the set of variables occurring in e that are not hidden behind some binder.

But this intuition gets us only so far: Consider the identity function $\mathrm{id}\colon \mathsf{Var} \to \mathsf{Var}$. On the one hand, it does not operate on any variables, it just passes them through. On the other hand, its graph mentions all variables. So what should its set of free variables be – nothing ($\{\}$) or everything (Var)?

Nominal logic avoids this problem by giving a general and abstract definition of the set of free variables[6] of an element of any pset:

Definition 2 (Free and fresh variables)
The set of free variables of an element x of some pset X is defined as

$$\mathsf{fv}\, x = \{a \mid \mathrm{card}\{b \mid (a\, b) \bullet x \neq x\} = \infty\}. \qquad \diamond$$

A variable v is *fresh* with regard to x if $v \notin \mathsf{fv}\, x$.

Spelled out, this says that a variable a is free in x if there are infinitely many other variables b such that swapping these two affects x. Or, more vaguely, a matters to x.

From this definition, many useful and expected equalities about fv can be derived:

- $\mathsf{fv}\, v = \{v\}$ for $v \in \mathsf{Var}$.
- $\mathsf{fv}((x, y)) = \mathsf{fv}\, x \cup \mathsf{fv}\, y$.
- $\mathsf{fv}\, x = \{\}$ if x is from a pure pset.
- $\mathsf{fv}(\mathrm{id}) = \{\}$, as $\pi \bullet \mathrm{id} = \mathrm{id}$ for all permutations π.
- If $a, b \notin \mathsf{fv}\, x$, then $(a\, b) \bullet x = x$.

When talking about programming languages, we are used to having “enough” variables, i.e. there is always one that is fresh with regard to everything else around.

This is not true in general. For example, let $f\colon \mathsf{Var} \to \mathbb{N}$ be a bijection, then $\mathsf{fv}\, f = \mathsf{Var}$, as every transposition $(a\, b)$ changes f. If such an object

[6] This is commonly called the *support*. I use the term *free variables* in this introduction, as the notions coincide in all cases relevant to this thesis.

would appear during a proof, we would not be able to say "let x be a variable that is fresh with regard to f"

But in practice, such objects do not occur, and there is always a fresh variable. This is captured by the following

Definition 3 (Finite support)
A pset X is said to have *finite support* if $\mathsf{fv}\, x$ is finite for all $x \in X$. $\diamond$

Since Var is infinite, it immediately follows that for every x from a pset with finite support, there is a variable a that is fresh with regard to x.

The pset Var, as well as every pure pset, is a set with finite support. Products, sums and lists of psets with finite support have themselves finite support.

Sets of functions from psets with finite support, or from an infinite set to a pset with finite support, do in general not have finite support. This can be slightly annoying, as discussed in Section 2.6.2.

1.6.3 Abstractions

The point of nominal logic is to provide a convenient way to work with *abstractions*. Formally, a nominal abstraction over a pset X is any operation $[\_].\_ \colon \mathsf{Var} \to X \to X$ that fulfils
(i) $\pi \bullet ([a].x) = [\pi \bullet a].(\pi \bullet x)$ and
(ii) $[a].x_1 = [b].x_2 \iff x_1 = (a\,b) \bullet x_2 \wedge (a = b \vee a \notin \mathsf{fv}\, x_2)$.

For a pset X with finite support, this implies

$$\mathsf{fv}([a].x) = \mathsf{fv}\, x \setminus \{a\},$$

which further shows that this notion of free variables coincides with our intuition and expectation.

This notion of abstraction can be extended to multiple binders, e.g. to represent mutually recursive let-expressions [UK12].

1.6.4 Strong induction rules

My use case for nominal logic is to model the syntax of the lambda calculus, and to get better induction principles.

Consider this inductive definition of lambda expressions:

$$e \in \mathsf{Exp} ::= x \mid e\, e \mid \lambda x.e$$

where x is a meta-variable referring to elements of Var. This would yield the following induction rule

$$\begin{aligned}
&(\forall x \in \mathsf{Var}.\, P(x)) \implies \\
&(\forall e_1, e_2 \in \mathsf{Exp}.\, P(e_1) \implies P(e_2) \implies P(e_1\, e_2)) \implies \\
&(\forall x \in \mathsf{Var}, e \in \mathsf{Exp}.\, P(e) \implies P(\lambda x.e)) \implies \qquad P(e)
\end{aligned}$$

where in the case for lambda expressions, the proof obligation is to be discharged for *any* variable x, even if that variable is part of the context (i.e. mentioned in P). This can be a major hurdle during a proof.

If one had Exp as a permutation set such that $\lambda x.e$ is a proper nominal induction, then it would be possible to prove a stronger induction rule:

$$\begin{aligned}
&(\forall s \in X, x \in \mathsf{Var}.\, P(s, x)) \implies \\
&(\forall s \in X, e_1, e_2 \in \mathsf{Exp}.\, P(s, e_1) \implies P(s, e_2) \implies P(s, e_1\, e_2)) \implies \\
&(\forall s \in X, x \in \mathsf{Var}, e \in \mathsf{Exp}.\, x \notin \mathsf{fv}\, s \implies P(s, e) \implies P(s, \lambda x.e)) \implies \\
&\qquad P(s, e)
\end{aligned}$$

Here the proposition P explicitly specifies its "context" in its first parameter, which may be of any pset X with finite support. In the case for the lambda abstraction, we may additionally, and without any manual naming or renaming, assume the variable x to be fresh with regard to that context.

The construction of Exp as a permutation set with a nominal abstraction is not trivial and described in [UT05]. Luckily, we do not have to worry about that: The implementation of nominal logic in Isabelle takes care of that (cf. Section 1.7.2).

1.6.5 Equivariance

The last concept from nominal logic that I need to introduce at this point is that of *equivariance*. In order to systematically construct inductively defined types as psets, and then to define functions over terms of such types by giving equations for each of these "constructors", the involved operations and functions need to be well-behaving, i.e. oblivious to the concrete names involved. This intuition is captured by the following

Definition 4 (Equivariance)
A function $f\colon X_1 \to X_2 \to \cdots \to X_n \to X$, $n \geq 0$, between psets is called *equivariant* if

$$\pi \bullet f(x_1, x_2, \ldots, x_n) = f(\pi \bullet x_1, \pi \bullet x_2, \ldots, \pi \bullet x_n). \qquad \diamond$$

Most common operations, such as tupling, list concatenation, the constructors of Exp etc. are equivariant, and this ability to freely move permutations around is crucial to, for example, being able to prove

$$(\lambda x.\, e\ x) = (\lambda y.\, e\ y).$$

1.7 Isabelle

This work has been formalised in the interactive theorem prover Isabelle [NPW02]. Roughly speaking, an interactive theorem prover has the appearance of a text editor that allows the user to write mathematics (definitions, theorems, proofs), with the very peculiar feature that it understands what is written, and either points out problems to the user, or confirms the correctness of the math.

There are a number of such systems in use, with Coq [Coq04] and Isabelle being the most prominent examples. One distinguishing feature of Isabelle is its genericity: It provides a meta-logical framework that can be instantiated with different concrete logics.

I build on the logic Isabelle/HOL, which implements a typed higher-order logic of total functions, in contrast to, for example, Isabelle/ZF, which builds on untyped set theory à la Zermelo-Fraenkel. Although I, like – presumably – most mathematicians, have been taught mathematics assuming set theory as the foundation of all math, all the actual math that we commonly do happens in an implicitly typed setting, and the choice of Isabelle/HOL over Isabelle/ZF is indeed natural. Furthermore, the tooling provided by Isabelle – libraries of existing formalisations, conservative extensions, proof automation – is much more comprehensive for Isabelle/HOL.[7]

This theses builds on and refers to the Isabelle 2016 release.

1.7.1 The prettiness of Isabelle code

One distinguishing feature of Isabelle is its proof language *Isar* [Nip02], which has a somewhat legible syntax with keywords in English and allows for proofs that are nicely structured and readable. Furthermore, Isabelle supports generating LaTeX code from its theory files. So the question arises whether I could have avoided re-writing everything in the hand-written style, by generating the all the definitions, proofs and theorems of this thesis out of my Isabelle theories.

For some parts, this would certainly be a viable option. Consider the hand-written proof and the corresponding fragment of the Isabelle theory in Fig. 4, taken from the case for application in the proof of Theorem 2. To a reader who knows some Isabelle syntax, it is pleasing to see how similar the hand-written proof and the Isabelle formalisation are. However, even this carefully selected fragment still has its warts:

- The syntax does not quite match up. For example, the abstract syntax tree node for an application is written explicitly using the *App* constructor, whereas it is nicer to simply write $e\ x$. This is not possible in Isabelle – juxtaposition cannot be overloaded.[8]

  In some cases, I can define custom syntax in Isabelle that comes very close to what I want. The $\_ \downarrow_{\mathsf{Fn}} \_$ operator is a good example for that. Unfortunately, this often comes at the cost of extra inconvenience when entering these symbols. In antiquotations, where Isabelle is asked to produce a certain existing term, such as the conclusion of a previously proven lemma, Isabelle can make use of such fancy syntax automatically, and hence for free, but regular

7 In Isabelle 2016, the HOL directory is more than 13 times the size of the ZF directory, measured in lines of code.

8 At least not within reasonable use of the system.

Isabelle theories will be converted to LaTeX as they are entered, so in order to get fancy syntax, fancy syntax needs to be typed in.

- An Isabelle formalisation will almost always contain some technicalities that I would like not to pervade the presentation.

  A good example for that is the seemingly stray centre dot after *Fn*: My formalisation uses the HOLCF package [Huf12], which has a type dedicated to *continuous* functions. This design choice avoids having to explicitly state continuity as a side conditions, but it also means that normal juxtaposition cannot be used to apply such functions, and a dedicated binary operator has to be used explicitly – this is the "·" seen in some of the Isabelle listings in this thesis.

- While Isabelle commands are chosen so that a theory is reminiscent of a proper English text, it is not a great pleasure to read. Many Isabelle commands (such as **by** *simp*) are only relevant to the system, but should be omitted when addressing a human reader, and other bits of technical syntax (e.g. invoking the induction hypothesis as *Application.hyps(9)[OF prem1]*) would be out of place.

  There are ways to hide any part of the Isabelle code from the generated LaTeX, but these markers would in turn clutter the Isabelle source code, and defeat the purpose of having a faithful representation of the proof in print.

Other parts of the development are even further away from a clean and easy-to-digest presentation, so I chose to keep most of the Isabelle development separate from the dissertation thesis. Appendix A contains a few snippets of the development, namely the main theorems and all definitions that are involved in them. The full formalisation is published in the Archive of Formal Proof [Bre13; Bre15d].

$$
\begin{aligned}
[\![e\ x]\!]_{\{\!\{\Gamma\}\!\}\rho} &= [\![e]\!]_{\{\!\{\Gamma\}\!\}\rho} \downarrow_{\mathsf{Fn}} \{\!\{\Gamma\}\!\}\rho\ x \\
&\quad \{\text{ by the denotation of application }\} \\
&= [\![\lambda y.\, e']\!]_{\{\!\{\Delta\}\!\}\rho} \downarrow_{\mathsf{Fn}} \{\!\{\Gamma\}\!\}\rho\ x \\
&\quad \{\text{ by the induction hypothesis }\} \\
&= [\![\lambda y.\, e']\!]_{\{\!\{\Delta\}\!\}\rho} \downarrow_{\mathsf{Fn}} \{\!\{\Delta\}\!\}\rho\ x \\
&\quad \{\text{ see above }\} \\
&= [\![e']\!]_{(\{\!\{\Delta\}\!\}\rho)(y \mapsto \{\!\{\Delta\}\!\}\rho\ x)} \\
&\quad \{\text{ by the denotation of lambda abstraction }\} \\
&= [\![e'[y := x]]\!]_{\{\!\{\Delta\}\!\}\rho} \\
&\quad \{\text{ by Lemma 5 }\} \\
&= [\![v]\!]_{\{\!\{\Theta\}\!\}\rho} \\
&\quad \{\text{ by the induction hypothesis }\}
\end{aligned}
$$

CorrectnessOriginal.thy

have $[\![\ App\ e\ x\ ]\!]_{\{\!|\Gamma|\!\}\varrho} = ([\![\ e\ ]\!]_{\{\!|\Gamma|\!\}\varrho}) \downarrow Fn\ (\{\!|\Gamma|\!\}\varrho)\ x$
  by *simp*
also have ... $= ([\![\ Lam\ [y].\ e'\ ]\!]_{\{\!|\Delta|\!\}\varrho}) \downarrow Fn\ (\{\!|\Gamma|\!\}\varrho)\ x$
  using *Application.hyps*(9)[*OF prem1*] **by** *simp*
also have ... $= ([\![\ Lam\ [y].\ e'\ ]\!]_{\{\!|\Delta|\!\}\varrho}) \downarrow Fn\ (\{\!|\Delta|\!\}\varrho)\ x$
  unfolding ∗..
also have ... $= (Fn\cdot(\Lambda\ z.\ [\![\ e'\ ]\!]_{(\{\!|\Delta|\!\}\varrho)(y := z)})) \downarrow Fn\ (\{\!|\Delta|\!\}\varrho)\ x$
  by *simp*
also have ... $= [\![\ e'\ ]\!]_{(\{\!|\Delta|\!\}\varrho)(y := (\{\!|\Delta|\!\}\varrho)\ x)}$
  by *simp*
also have ... $= [\![\ e'[y ::= x]\ ]\!]_{\{\!|\Delta|\!\}\varrho}$
  unfolding *ESem_subst*..
also have ... $= [\![\ v\ ]\!]_{\{\!|\Theta|\!\}\varrho}$
  by (*rule Application.hyps*(12)[*OF prem2*])
finally
show $[\![\ App\ e\ x\ ]\!]_{\{\!|\Gamma|\!\}\varrho} = [\![\ v\ ]\!]_{\{\!|\Theta|\!\}\varrho}$.

Figure 4: A hand-written proof and the corresponding Isabelle code

1.7.2 Nominal logic in Isabelle

I have outlined the concepts of nominal logic in Section 1.6 in general terms. In my formalisation, I did not implement this machinery myself, but rather build on the Nominal2 package for Isabelle by Christian Urban and others [UT05; UK12], which provides all the basic concepts of nominal logic, together with tools to work with them.

Permutation sets are modelled as types within the type class *pt*, which fixes the permutation action $\bullet$. In the context of this type class, the package provides general definitions for support (*supp*), freshness (*fresh*, or written infix as $\sharp$). Type classes that extend *pt* with additional requirements are *fs* for permutation sets with finite support and *pure* for pure permutation sets.

I define the function *fv* as the support, restricted to one sort of atoms:

definition fv :: $'a{::}pt \Rightarrow {'b}{::}at\_base\ set$ Nominal-Utils.thy
  where $fv\ e = \{v.\ atom\ v \in supp\ e\}$

Nominal2 provides the proof method *perm_simp* which simplifies proof goals involving permutations by pushing them inside expressions as far as possible. It maintains a list of equivariance theorems that the user can extend with equivariance lemmas about newly defined constants.

The command **nominal_datatype** allows the user to conveniently construct a permutation set corresponding to a usual, inductive definition with binding structure annotated. See Section 2.6.1 for an example.

The constructors of such a data type cannot be used as constructors with Isabelle tools like **fun**, because they do not completely behave as such. For example, they are not necessarily injective. Therefore, Nominal2 provides the separate command **nominal_function** to define functions over a nominal data type. It is not completely automatic and requires the user to discharge a number of proof obligations, such as equivariance of the function's graph and representation independence of the equations.

Similarly, Nominal2 provides the command **nominal_inductive**, which can be used, after defining an inductive predicate as usual with **inductive**, to specify which free variables of a rule should not clash with the context during a proof by induction. It requires the user to prove that the variable is fresh with regard to the conclusion of the rule, and in return generates a stronger induction rule akin to the one shown in Section 1.6.4. The proof method *nominal_induct*, which can be used instead of the usual *induct* method, supports the additional option *avoiding* and instantiates the strong induction rule so that the desired additional freshness assumptions become available.

1.7.3 Domain theory and the *HOLCF* package

Applications of domain theory, i.e. the mathematical field that studies certain partial orders, pervade programming language research: They are used to give semantics to recursive functions and to recursive types; they structure program analysis results and tell us how to find fixpoints.

As my use of domain theory in this thesis is quite standard, I will elide most of the technicalities and usually state just the partial order used. My domains are of the pointed, chain-complete kind. I consider only ω-chains, i.e. sequences $(a_i)_{i\in\mathbb{N}}$ with $a_i \sqsubseteq a_{i+1}$; completeness of the domain implies that every such chain has a least upper bound $\bigsqcup_{i\in\mathbb{N}} a_i$. A domain is called *pointed* if it has a least element, written $\bot$.

This choice is motivated by my use of the Isabelle package HOLCF [Huf12], which is a comprehensive suite of definitions and tools for working with domain theory in Isabelle. In particular, it allows me to define possibly complex recursive domains such as the domain used by the resourced denotational semantics in Section 2.3.3, with one command:

domain *CValue* CValue.thy
  = *CFn* (**lazy** $(C \to CValue) \to (C \to CValue)$)
  | *CB* (**lazy** *bool discr*)

This will not only define the type *CValue*, but also the two injection functions *CFn* and *CB*, corresponding projection functions and induction principles. The command **fixrec** can then define functions over such a domains.

The type *CValue* is then automatically made a member of a number of type classes that come with HOLCF. Most relevant for us are

- *po* for types supporting a partial order, written with square operators and relations, i.e. $\sqsubseteq$,
- *cpo* for complete partial orders, i.e. types in *po* where additionally every ω-chain has a least upper bound and
- *pcpo* for pointed complete partial order, which extends *cpo* by the requirement that a least element $\bot$ exists.

HOLCF introduces a type dedicated to continuous functions, written *'a → 'b*, which is separate from Isabelle's regular function type, written *'a ⇒ 'b*. Encoding the continuity of functions in the types avoid having to explicitly assume functions to be continuous in the various lemmas.

This is particularly important when some definition is only well-defined if its arguments are continuous, as it is the case for the fixed-point operator *fix* : *('a → 'a) → 'a* (with *'a::pcpo*, i.e. the type *'a* has an instance of the type class *pcpo*). Without this trick, *fix* would not be a total function, and working with partial functions in Isabelle is always annoying to some degree.

The downside of this design choice is that such continuous functions cannot be applied directly. Therefore, HOLCF introduces an explicit function application operator _·_ : *('a → 'b) ⇒ 'a ⇒ 'b*. I advise to simply assume this operator is not there when reading Isabelle code using HOLCF.

The custom type has further consequences: Existing tools to define new functions, such as **definition**, **fun** and the Nominal-specific command **nominal_function** know how to define normal functions, but are unable to produce values of type *'a → 'b*. In these cases, I have to resort to defining the function by using the – again HOLCF-specific – lambda abstraction for continuous functions written *(Λ x. e)* on the right-hand side of the definition. I can still prove the intended function equations, with the argument on the left-hand side, manually afterwards, as long as the function definition is indeed continuous.

The standard proof principle for functions defined in terms of the aforementioned *fix* is *fixed-point induction*: In order to prove that a predicate

P holds for $fix \cdot F$, where the functorial F is of type $'a \rightarrow 'a$ with $'a{::}pcpo$, it suffices to prove that

- the predicate P is admissible, i.e. if it holds for all elements of a chain, then it holds for the least upper bound of the chain,
- P holds for $\bot$ and
- P holds for any $F \cdot x$, given that P holds for x.

A derived proof principle is that of *parallel fixed-point induction* which can be used to establish that a binary predicate P (usually an equality or inequality) holds for $fix \cdot F$ and $fix \cdot G$. This requires a proof that

- the predicate P, understood as a predicate on tuples, is admissible,
- $P \bot \bot$ holds and
- $P\ (F \cdot x)\ (F \cdot y)$ holds, given that $P\ x\ y$ holds.

Both principles are provided by HOLCF as lemmas, and an extensible set of syntax-directed lemmas helps to take care of the admissibility proof obligation.

I mean, ostensibly, yes. Honestly, we hacked most of it together with Perl.

Randall Munroe, xkcd #224

CHAPTER 2

Formalizing Launchbury's natural semantics

Formal semantics are the basic building block of all rigorous programming language research. Not only do they force us to think our work through in all details – without a precise definition of the meaning of programs, we cannot conduct any proofs. Therefore, as I do want to be able to prove theorems about my work, I need a suitable semantics, and also implement it in Isabelle.

Furthermore, semantics provide a common ground for the research community: If the same semantics are used, then results can easily be compared and combined. Therefore, I should not just define a semantics that happens to suit me, but preferably choose an existing, well-established semantics to build on.

One such semantics is John Launchbury's "Natural Semantics for Lazy Evaluation" [Lau93], which has several important traits: It is simple, as it has only four rules. It is detailed enough to model lazy evaluation. It is abstract enough to not model unnecessary details. And it is widely accepted as a standard semantics.

Using a standard denotational semantics, Launchbury underpins his natural semantics by claiming correctness (evaluation in the natural semantics preserves denotation) and adequacy (all programs with a denotation have a derivation in the natural semantics). While he proves correctness in sufficient detail, he only outlines the adequacy proof – an omission that resisted fixing, despite the popularity of the semantics, and despite serious attempts to follow his proof sketch (e.g. [SHO14]).

In this chapter, I reproduce Launchbury's semantics, including subsequent improvements by Sestoft [Ses97] and modernisations to how names binding is handled. This yields a definition that is suitable for formalisation in Isabelle. The original correctness proof was almost directly usable in the mechanisation and required only minor adjustments, which I discuss. I then provide a full adequacy proof, where I do not follow Launchbury's outline directly, but find a more elegant and direct proof. Parts of this chapter, in particular the adequacy proof, has been submitted to the Journal of Functional Programming [Bre15c].

Dedicated sections explicate the differences to Launchbury's work, serving two purposes: The reasons for deviation can be educational to someone attempting a similar formalisation. Furthermore they are checklists when combining this work with other Launchbury-based developments.

Finally, in preparation of Chapter 4, I extend the semantics and the proofs with a simple base type, and introduce a corresponding small-step semantics.

2.1 Launchbury's semantics

Launchbury defines a semantics for the simple untyped lambda calculus given in Fig. 5, consisting of variables, lambda abstractions, applications and mutually recursive bindings.

The set of free variables of an expression e is denoted by $\mathsf{fv}\, e$; I overload this notation and use fv with arguments of other types that may contain variable names. For example for tuples (or, equivalently, multiple arguments), we have $\mathsf{fv}(\Gamma, e) = \mathsf{fv}\,\Gamma \cup \mathsf{fv}\, e$.

A variable x is *fresh* with regard to an expression e (or a similar object) if $x \notin \mathsf{fv}\, e$. The expression e with every free occurrence of x replaced by y is written as $e[x := y]$.

$$
\begin{aligned}
x, y, z, w &\in \mathsf{Var} \\
e \in \mathsf{Exp} &::= \lambda x.\, e \\
&\quad \mid e\ x \\
&\quad \mid x \\
&\quad \mid \textbf{let } x_1 = e_1, \ldots, x_n = e_n \textbf{ in } e
\end{aligned}
$$

Figure 5: Launchbury's core lambda calculus

I equate alpha-equivalent lambda abstractions ($\lambda x.\, x = \lambda y.\, y$) and the bound variable is not part of the set of free variables ($\mathsf{fv}(\lambda x.\, y\ x) = \{y\}$). **let** bindings are handled likewise. The theoretical foundation used is nominal logic (see Section 1.6). This does impose a few well-formedness side conditions, such as equivariance of definitions over expressions. I skip them in this presentation, and do so with good conscience, as they have been covered in the machine-checked proofs.

Note that the term on the right hand side of an application has to be a variable. A general lambda term of the form $e_1\ e_2$ would have to be pre-processed to **let** $x = e_2$ **in** $e_1\ x$ before it can be handled by my semantics. This restriction simplifies the semantics, as all bindings on the heap are created by a **let** expression and we do not have to ensure separately that the evaluation of a function's argument is shared. This is a standard trick applied by Launchbury [Lau93] and others [Ses97; GS01; HH14]. In some of the less formal parts of this thesis, e.g. in examples, I occasionally use expressions as arguments in the interest of readability. This should be understood as a shorthand for the proper, let-bound form.

2.1.1 Natural semantics

Launchbury gives meaning to this language by way of a natural semantics. I present his semantics with minor adjustments due to Sestoft and myself, and explain these differences in Section 2.1.3.

$$\frac{}{\Gamma : \lambda x.\, e \Downarrow_L \Gamma : \lambda x.\, e}\textsc{Lam}$$

$$\frac{\Gamma : e \Downarrow_L \Delta : \lambda y.\, e' \qquad \Delta : e'[y := x] \Downarrow_L \Theta : v}{\Gamma : e\ x \Downarrow_L \Theta : v}\textsc{App}$$

$$\frac{\Gamma : e \Downarrow_{L \cup \{x\}} \Delta : v}{x \mapsto e, \Gamma : x \Downarrow_L x \mapsto v, \Delta : v}\textsc{Var}$$

$$\frac{\mathsf{dom}\,\Delta \cap \mathsf{fv}(\Gamma, L) = \{\} \qquad \Delta, \Gamma : e \Downarrow_L \Theta : v}{\Gamma : \textbf{let}\ \Delta\ \textbf{in}\ e \Downarrow_L \Theta : v}\textsc{Let}$$

Figure 6: Launchbury natural semantics, as revised by Sestoft

The semantics is given by a relation

$$\Gamma : e \Downarrow_L \Delta : v$$

with the intuition that the expression e within the heap Γ reduces to the value v, while modifying the heap to Δ, while avoiding the names in the set L. The relation is defined inductively by the rules in Fig. 6, which obey the following naming conventions:

$$\Gamma, \Delta, \Theta \in \mathsf{Heap} = \mathsf{Var} \rightharpoonup \mathsf{Exp}$$
$$v \in \mathsf{Val} \quad ::= \lambda x.\, e$$

A heap is a partial function from variables to expressions ($\mathsf{Var} \rightharpoonup \mathsf{Exp}$), and usually represented by Γ, Δ or Θ. The same type is used for the list of bindings in a **let**. The domain of a heap Γ, written $\mathsf{dom}\,\Gamma$, is the set of variables bound by the heap.

In contrast to expressions, *heaps* are not alpha-equated, so we have $\mathsf{dom}\,\Gamma \subseteq \mathsf{fv}\,\Gamma$. I write $x \mapsto e$ for the singleton heap and use commas to combine heaps with distinct domains.

A v represents a *value*, i.e. an expression in weak head normal form. So far, the only values are lambda abstractions; this will change when I add Booleans in Section 2.4.2. I use the predicate $\mathsf{isVal}\, e$ to denote that the expression e is a value.

The first rule, LAM, does not actually "do" anything: Expression and heap on the left and on the right are the same. This rule thus states that to evaluate an expression that is already a value, nothing has to be done.

The second rule, APP, handles evaluation of an application. As we want to model lazy evaluation, first the called expression e is evaluated. The argument x, which by our syntactic restriction is just a variable, is then substituted into the the resulting lambda abstracted expression, and evaluation continues with that. Observe that the argument itself is not necessarily evaluated.

Rule VAR takes care of evaluating a variable x. This is only possible if it is mentioned in the heap.

During the evaluation of the expression e, the binding $x \mapsto e$ is removed from the heap: This way, if the evaluation of e would itself require the evaluation of x, the VAR rule does not apply over and over again, but rather the inference is stuck. An inference algorithm derived from these rules would exhibit the same behaviour as a runtime for lazy functional programs that sports *blackholing*, where a thunk under evaluation is replaced by a so-called blackhole which, if evaluated, aborts the program [Pey92].

This rule also implements *sharing*: After having evaluated e to a value v, this is not only returned as the result of the computation, but also added to the resulting heap as the new binding for x. This *updating* of x ensures that any further evaluation of x will immediately return with its once evaluated value.

The final rule, LET, implements let-bindings, which may be mutually recursive, simply by moving them to the heap. The let-expression itself represents an alpha-equivalency class and hence does not have names for the bound values, so it is the application of this rule that actually determines $\operatorname{dom} \Delta$, and the first assumption of the rule ensures that these variables do not clash with existing ones.

The set L was not present in Launchbury's rules. It was added by Sestoft [Ses97] to keep track of variables that must be avoided when choosing new names in the LET rule, but would otherwise not be present in the judgement any more, because they were blackholed by VAR. I explain this modification in greater detail in Section 2.1.3).

The semantics has a few noteworthy properties, which I describe in the following lemmas.

Evaluation does not forget bindings:

Lemma 1
If $\Gamma : e \Downarrow_L \Delta : v$ then $\mathsf{dom}\,\Gamma \subseteq \mathsf{dom}\,\Delta$.

Proof
by induction on the derivation of $\Gamma : e \Downarrow_L \Delta : v$. ∎

Furthermore, names that appear as new bindings on the heap do not clash with any names in the set L:

Lemma 2
If $\Gamma : e \Downarrow_L \Delta : v$ then $(\mathsf{dom}\,\Delta \setminus \mathsf{dom}\,\Gamma) \cap L = \{\}$.

Proof
by induction on the derivation of $\Gamma : e \Downarrow_L \Delta : v$. In the case for let expressions, we use that the names chosen for the bound variables are fresh with regard to L, as $\mathsf{dom}\,\Delta \cap \mathsf{fv}(\Gamma, e, L) = \{\}$. ∎

I consider a judgement $\Gamma : e \Downarrow_L \Delta : v$ to be *closed* if $\mathsf{fv}(\Gamma, e) \subseteq \mathsf{dom}\,\Gamma \cup L$, i.e. all occurring names are either bound in the heap, or explicitly listed in the set L of names to avoid.

Note that this is preserved by the semantics in the following sense:

Lemma 3
If $\Gamma : e \Downarrow_L \Delta : v$ holds and $\mathsf{fv}(\Gamma, e) \subseteq \mathsf{dom}\,\Gamma \cup L$, then $\mathsf{fv}(\Delta, v) \subseteq \mathsf{dom}\,\Delta \cup L$.

Proof
In light of Lemma 1, this follows from: If $\Gamma : e \Downarrow_L \Delta : v$ holds, and x' is fresh with regard to Γ and e, then x' is either also fresh with regard to Δ and v, or x' appears in $\mathsf{dom}\,\Delta$, in which case $x' \notin L$ must hold. I prove this by induction on the derivation.

Case: LAM
This case is trivial.

Case: APP
By the first induction hypothesis, there are two subcases to consider:

- The variable x' is still fresh with regard to Δ and $\lambda y.\, e'$. In order to invoke the second induction hypothesis, we need to show that x' is fresh with regard to $e'[y := x]$. This is the case, as $x' \neq x$, by the assumption, and either $x' = y$, or x is fresh with regard to e'.
- The variable x' appears in $\mathsf{dom}\, \Delta$ and is not in L. By Lemma 1, it then also appears in $\mathsf{dom}\, \Theta$.

Case: VAR
As x' is fresh with regard to $(x \mapsto e, \Gamma)$ and x, we have $x' \neq x$. Furthermore, x' is also fresh with regard to Γ and e, so we can invoke the induction hypothesis.

- If x' is still fresh with regard to Δ and v, then it is also fresh with regard to $(x \mapsto v, \Delta)$, as $x' \neq x$.
- If $x' \in \mathsf{dom}\, \Delta$ and $x' \notin L \cup \{x\}$, we obviously also have that $x' \in \mathsf{dom}\, (x \mapsto v, \Delta)$ and $x \notin L$.

Case: LET
As this case introduces new names on the heap, this decides what side of the disjunction in the proposition x' ends up in.

- If $x' \in \mathsf{dom}\, \Delta$, then $x' \in \mathsf{dom}\, (\Delta, \Gamma)$, and by Lemma 1, $x' \in \mathsf{dom}\, \Theta$. Also, by the freshness condition on LET, $x' \notin L$.
- Otherwise, x is fresh with regard to (Δ, Γ) and e by the assumption, so we can invoke the induction hypothesis. ■

2.1.2 Denotational semantics

In order to show that the natural semantics behaves as expected, Launchbury defines a standard denotational semantics for expressions and heaps, following Abramsky [Abr90]. The semantic domain Value is the initial solution to the domain equation

$$\mathsf{Value} = (\mathsf{Value} \rightarrow \mathsf{Value})_\perp,$$

in the category of pointed chain-complete partial orders with continuous functions. In this domain, we can distinguish $\bot$ from $\lambda x.\bot$.

The injection

$$\mathsf{Fn}(\_)\colon (\mathsf{Value} \to \mathsf{Value}) \to \mathsf{Value}$$

turns values of type $\mathsf{Value} \to \mathsf{Value}$ into non-bottom values of Value, while the deconstruction

$$\_ \downarrow_{\mathsf{Fn}} \_\colon \mathsf{Value} \to \mathsf{Value} \to \mathsf{Value}$$

does the converse, defined as

$$v_1 \downarrow_{\mathsf{Fn}} v_2 = \begin{cases} f\, v_2 & \text{if } v_1 = \mathsf{Fn}(f) \\ \bot & \text{otherwise.} \end{cases}$$

The partial order $\sqsubseteq$ on Value is the usual, with $\mathsf{Fn}(f) \sqsubseteq \mathsf{Fn}(g)$ if $\forall x.\, f\, x \sqsubseteq g\, x$ for $f, g \in \mathsf{Value} \to \mathsf{Value}$, and $\bot$ below everything.

A semantic environment maps variables to values,

$$\rho \in \mathsf{Env} = \mathsf{Var} \to \mathsf{Value},$$

and the initial environment $\bot$ maps all variables to $\bot$. Environments are ordered by lifting the order on Value pointwise.

With the *domain of an environment* ρ, written $\mathsf{dom}\, \rho$, I denote the set of variables that are not mapped to $\bot$.

The environment $\rho|_S$, where S is a set of variables, is the restriction of ρ to S:

$$(\rho|_S)\, x = \begin{cases} \rho\, x, & \text{if } x \in S \\ \bot & \text{if } x \notin S. \end{cases}$$

The environment $\rho \setminus S$ is defined as the restriction of ρ to the complement of S, i.e. $\rho \setminus S := \rho|_{\mathsf{Var} \setminus S}$.

The semantics of expressions and heaps are mutually recursive. The meaning of an expression $e \in \mathsf{Exp}$ in an environment $\rho \in \mathsf{Env}$ is written as $[\![e]\!]_\rho \in \mathsf{Value}$ and is defined by the equations in Fig. 7.

$$
\begin{aligned}
[\![\lambda x.\, e]\!]_\rho &:= \mathsf{Fn}(\lambda v. [\![e]\!]_{\rho \sqcup [x \mapsto v]}) \\
[\![e\ x]\!]_\rho &:= [\![e]\!]_\rho \downarrow_{\mathsf{Fn}} \rho\, x \\
[\![x]\!]_\rho &:= \rho\, x \\
[\![\mathbf{let}\ \Delta\ \mathbf{in}\ e]\!]_\rho &:= [\![e]\!]_{\{\!\{\Delta\}\!\}\rho}.
\end{aligned}
$$

Figure 7: The standard denotational semantics

We can map this function over a heap to obtain an environment:

$$
[\![\Gamma]\!]_\rho\ x := \begin{cases} [\![e]\!]_\rho, & \text{if } (x \mapsto e) \in \Gamma \\ \bot & \text{if } x \notin \mathsf{dom}\,\Gamma. \end{cases}
$$

The semantics of a heap $\Gamma \in \mathsf{Heap}$ in an environment ρ, written $\{\!\{\Gamma\}\!\}\rho \in \mathsf{Env}$, is then obtained as a least fixed point:

$$
\{\!\{\Gamma\}\!\}\rho = (\mu\rho'.\, \rho +\!\!+_{\mathsf{dom}\,\Gamma} [\![\Gamma]\!]_{\rho'})
$$

where

$$
(\rho +\!\!+_S \rho')\ x := \begin{cases} \rho\ x, & \text{if } x \notin S \\ \rho'\ x, & \text{if } x \in S \end{cases}
$$

is a restricted update operator.

The least fixed point exists, as all involved operations are monotone and continuous, and by unrolling the fixed point once, we can see

Lemma 4 (Application of the heap semantics)

$$
(\{\!\{\Gamma\}\!\}\rho)\ x = \begin{cases} [\![e]\!]_{\{\!\{\Gamma\}\!\}\rho}, & \text{if } (x \mapsto e) \in \Gamma \\ \rho\, x, & \text{if } x \notin \mathsf{dom}\,\Gamma. \end{cases}
$$

◇

The following substitution lemma plays an important role in finding a more direct proof of adequacy, but is also required for the correctness proof, as performed by Launchbury:

Lemma 5 (Semantics of substitution)

$$[\![e]\!]_{\rho(y \mapsto \rho\, x)} = [\![e[y := x]]\!]_{\rho}. \qquad \diamond$$

Proof
We first show $\forall \rho.\, \rho\, x = \rho\, y \implies \{\!\{e\}\!\}\rho = \{\!\{e[y := x]\}\!\}\rho$ by induction on e, using parallel fixed-point induction in the case for **let**. This allows us to calculate

$$\begin{aligned} [\![e]\!]_{\rho(y \mapsto \rho\, x)} &= [\![e[y := x]]\!]_{\rho(y \mapsto \rho\, x)} && \{ \text{ as } \rho(y \mapsto \rho\, x)\, x = \rho(y \mapsto \rho\, x)\, y \,\} \\ &= [\![e[y := x]]\!]_{\rho} && \{ \text{ as } y \notin \mathsf{fv}(e[y := x]). \,\} \end{aligned} \qquad \blacksquare$$

I sometimes write $\{\!\{\Gamma\}\!\}$ instead of $\{\!\{\Gamma\}\!\}\bot$. In an expression $\{\!\{\Gamma\}\!\}(\{\!\{\Delta\}\!\}\rho)$ I omit the parentheses and write $\{\!\{\Gamma\}\!\}\{\!\{\Delta\}\!\}\rho$.

2.1.3 Discussions of modifications

It is rare that a formal system developed with pen and on paper can be formalised to the letter, partly because of vagueness (what, exactly, is a "completely" fresh variable?), partly because of formalisation convenience, and partly because the stated facts – even if morally correct – are wrong when read scrupulously. Launchbury's work is no exception. This section discusses the required divergence from Launchbury's work.

Naming

Getting the naming issues right is one of the major issues when formalising anything involving bound variables. In Launchbury's work, the names are manifestly part of the syntax, i.e. $\lambda x.\, x \neq \lambda y.\, y$, and his rules involve explicit renaming of bound variables to fresh ones in the rule VAR. His definition of freshness is a global one, so the validity of a derivation using VAR depends on everything around it. This is morally what we want, but very impractical.

Sestoft [Ses97] noticed this problem and fixed it by adding a set L of variables to the judgement, so that every variable to be avoided occurs somewhere in Γ, e, or L. Instead of renaming all bound variables in the rule VAR, he chooses fresh names for the new heap bindings in the rule LET.

I build on that, but go one step further and completely avoid bound names in the expressions, i.e. $\lambda x.\, x = \lambda y.\, y$. I still have them in the syntax, of course, but these are just representatives of an α-equivalency class. Nominal logic (cf. Section 1.6) forms the formal foundation for this. So in my rule LET I do not have to rename the variables, but simply may assume that the variables used in the representation of the **let**-expression are sufficiently fresh.

The names of bindings on the heap are not abstracted away in that manner; this follows [SHO12].

Closed judgements

Launchbury deliberately allows non-closed configurations in his derivations, i.e. configurations with free variables in the terms that have no corresponding binding on the heap. This is a necessity, as rule VAR models blackholing by removing a binding from the heap during its evaluation.

With the addition of the set of variables to avoid, which will always contain such variables, the question of whether non-closed configurations should be allowed can be revisited. And indeed, Sestoft defines the notion of *L-good configurations*, where all free variables are either bound on the heap, or contained in L. He shows that this property is preserved by the operational semantics and subsequently considers only L-good configurations. I follow this example with my definition of *closed* judgements. Threading the closedness requirement through a proof by rule induction is a typical chore contributing to the overhead of a machine-checked formalisation.

Join vs. update

Launchbury specifies his denotational semantics using a binary operation $\sqcup$ on environments:

$$\{\!\{\Gamma\}\!\}\rho = (\mu\rho'.\,\rho \sqcup [\![\Gamma]\!]_{\rho'})$$

He does not define it explicitly, but the statements in his Section 5.2.1 leave no doubt that he indeed intended this operation to denote the least upper bound of its arguments, as one would expect. Unfortunately, with this definition, his Theorem 2 is false.

The proposition of the theorem (which corresponds to Theorem 2 in this document) is

$$\Gamma : e \Downarrow_L \Delta : v \implies \forall \rho \in \mathsf{Env}.\ [\![e]\!]_{\{\!\{\Gamma\}\!\}\rho} = [\![v]\!]_{\{\!\{\Delta\}\!\}\rho}$$

and a counter example is given by

$$\begin{aligned} e &= x, \\ v &= (\lambda a.\,\mathbf{let}\ b = b\ \mathbf{in}\ b), \\ \Gamma = \Delta &= (x \mapsto v), \text{ and} \\ \rho &= (x \mapsto \mathsf{Fn}(\lambda\_.\mathsf{Fn}(\lambda x.x))). \end{aligned}$$

Note that the denotation of v is $\mathsf{Fn}(\lambda\_.\bot)$ in every environment. We have $\Gamma : e \Downarrow_{\{\}} \Delta : v$, so according to the theorem, $[\![e]\!]_{\{\!\{\Gamma\}\!\}\rho} = [\![v]\!]_{\{\!\{\Delta\}\!\}\rho}$ should hold, but the following calculation show that it does not:

$$\begin{aligned} [\![e]\!]_{\{\!\{\Gamma\}\!\}\rho} &= (\{\!\{\Gamma\}\!\}\rho)\ x \\ &= \rho\ x \sqcup [\![v]\!]_{\{\!\{\Gamma\}\!\}\rho} \\ &= \mathsf{Fn}(\lambda\_.\mathsf{Fn}(\lambda x.x)) \sqcup \mathsf{Fn}(\lambda\_.\bot) \\ &= \mathsf{Fn}(\lambda\_.\mathsf{Fn}(\lambda x.x) \sqcup \bot) \\ &= \mathsf{Fn}(\lambda\_.\mathsf{Fn}(\lambda x.x)) \\ &\neq \mathsf{Fn}(\lambda\_.\bot) \\ &= [\![v]\!]_{\{\!\{\Delta\}\!\}\rho}. \end{aligned}$$

The crucial property of the counter-example is that ρ contains compatible, but better information for a variable also bound in Γ. The mistake in his correctness proof is in the step $(\{\!\{x \mapsto v, \Delta\}\!\}\rho)\, x = [\![v]\!]_{\{\!\{x \mapsto v, \Delta\}\!\}\rho}$ in the case for VAR, which should be $(\{\!\{x \mapsto v, \Delta\}\!\}\rho)\, x = [\![v]\!]_{\{\!\{x \mapsto v, \Delta\}\!\}\rho} \sqcup \rho\, x$.

Intuitively, such rogue ρ are not relevant for a proof of the main Theorem 1. Nevertheless, this issue needs to be fixed before attempting a formal proof. One possible fix is to replace $\sqcup$ by a right-sided update operation that just throws away information from the left argument for those variables bound on the right. The syntax $\rho +\!\!+_S \rho'$ denotes this operation. If that is used instead of the least upper bound, then the proof goes through in full rigour.

It is slightly annoying having to specify the set S in this operation explicitly, as it is usually clear "from the context": Morally, it is the set of variables that the object on the right talks about. But as environments, i.e. total functions from $\mathsf{Var} \to \mathsf{Value}$, do not distinguish between variables not mentioned at all and variables mentioned, but bound to $\bot$, this information is not easily exploitable in a formal setting.

For the same reason Theorem 2 uses the more explicit equality between restricted environments instead of Launchbury's ordering $\leq$ on environments. I elaborate on this in Section 2.2.1.

2.2 Correctness

The main correctness theorem for the natural semantics is

Theorem 1 (Correctness)
If $\Gamma : e \Downarrow_L \Delta : v$ holds and is closed, then

$$[\![e]\!]_{\{\!\{\Gamma\}\!\}} = [\![v]\!]_{\{\!\{\Delta\}\!\}}. \qquad \diamond$$

A proof by rule induction requires the following generalisation:

Theorem 2 (Correctness, generalized)
If $\Gamma : e \Downarrow_L \Delta : v$ holds and is closed, then for all environments $\rho \in \mathsf{Env}$, we have

$$[\![e]\!]_{\{\!\{\Gamma\}\!\}\rho} = [\![v]\!]_{\{\!\{\Delta\}\!\}\rho} \quad \text{and} \quad (\{\!\{\Gamma\}\!\}\rho)|_{\mathsf{dom}\,\Gamma} = (\{\!\{\Delta\}\!\}\rho)|_{\mathsf{dom}\,\Gamma}. \qquad \diamond$$

The proof follows Launchbury's steps, but differs in some details. In the interest of a self-contained presentation, I give the full proof here. Two technical lemmas used in the proof are stated and proved subsequently.

For clarity, $\rho =_{|S} \rho'$ abbreviates $\rho|_S = \rho'|_S$.

Proof
by induction on the derivation of $\Gamma : e \Downarrow_L \Delta : v$. Note that in such a derivation, all occurring judgements are closed.

Case: LAM
This case is trivial.

Case: APP
The induction hypotheses are $[\![e]\!]_{\{\!\{\Gamma\}\!\}\rho} = [\![\lambda y.\, e']\!]_{\{\!\{\Delta\}\!\}\rho}$ and $\{\!\{\Gamma\}\!\}\rho =_{|\mathsf{dom}\,\Gamma} \{\!\{\Delta\}\!\}\rho$ as well as $[\![e'[y := x]]\!]_{\{\!\{\Delta\}\!\}\rho} = [\![v]\!]_{\{\!\{\Theta\}\!\}\rho}$ and $\{\!\{\Delta\}\!\}\rho =_{|\mathsf{dom}\,\Delta} \{\!\{\Theta\}\!\}\rho$.

We have $\{\!\{\Gamma\}\!\}\rho\ x = \{\!\{\Delta\}\!\}\rho\ x$: If $x \in \mathsf{dom}\,\Gamma$, this follows from the induction hypothesis. Otherwise, we know $x \in L$, as the judgement is closed, and the new names bound in Δ avoid L, so we have $\rho\, x$ on both sides.

While the second part follows from the corresponding induction hypotheses and $\mathsf{dom}\,\Gamma \subseteq \mathsf{dom}\,\Delta$ (Lemma 1), the first part is a simple calculation:

$$
\begin{aligned}
[\![e\ x]\!]_{\{\!\{\Gamma\}\!\}\rho} &= [\![e]\!]_{\{\!\{\Gamma\}\!\}\rho} \downarrow_{\mathsf{Fn}} \{\!\{\Gamma\}\!\}\rho\, x \\
&\quad \{\text{ by the denotation of application }\} \\
&= [\![\lambda y.\, e']\!]_{\{\!\{\Delta\}\!\}\rho} \downarrow_{\mathsf{Fn}} \{\!\{\Gamma\}\!\}\rho\ x \\
&\quad \{\text{ by the induction hypothesis }\} \\
&= [\![\lambda y.\, e']\!]_{\{\!\{\Delta\}\!\}\rho} \downarrow_{\mathsf{Fn}} \{\!\{\Delta\}\!\}\rho\ x \\
&\quad \{\text{ see above }\} \\
&= [\![e']\!]_{(\{\!\{\Delta\}\!\}\rho)(y \mapsto \{\!\{\Delta\}\!\}\rho\ x)} \\
&\quad \{\text{ by the denotation of lambda abstraction }\} \\
&= [\![e'[y := x]]\!]_{\{\!\{\Delta\}\!\}\rho} \\
&\quad \{\text{ by Lemma 5 }\}
\end{aligned}
$$

$$= [\![v]\!]_{\{\!\{\Theta\}\!\}\rho}$$

$$\{ \text{ by the induction hypothesis } \}$$

Case: VAR
We know that $[\![e]\!]_{\{\!\{\Gamma\}\!\}\rho'} = [\![v]\!]_{\{\!\{\Delta\}\!\}\rho'}$ and $\{\!\{\Gamma\}\!\}\rho' =|_{\mathsf{dom}\,\Gamma} \{\!\{\Delta\}\!\}\rho'$ for all environments ρ'.

We begin with the second part:

$$\begin{aligned}
\{\!\{x \mapsto e, \Gamma\}\!\}\rho &= \mu\rho'.\,(\rho \mathbin{++}_{\mathsf{dom}\,\Gamma} \{\!\{\Gamma\}\!\}\rho')[x \mapsto [\![e]\!]_{\{\!\{\Gamma\}\!\}\rho'}] \\
&\quad \{ \text{ by the following Lemma 6 } \} \\
&= \mu\rho'.\,(\rho \mathbin{++}_{\mathsf{dom}\,\Gamma} \{\!\{\Gamma\}\!\}\rho')[x \mapsto [\![v]\!]_{\{\!\{\Delta\}\!\}\rho'}] \\
&\quad \left\{ \begin{array}{l} \text{by the induction hypothesis. Note that} \\ \text{we invoke it for } \rho' \text{ with } \rho' \neq \rho! \end{array} \right\} \\
&=|_{\mathsf{dom}\,(x \mapsto e, \Gamma)} \mu\rho'.\,(\rho \mathbin{++}_{\mathsf{dom}\,\Delta} \{\!\{\Delta\}\!\}\rho')[x \mapsto [\![v]\!]_{\{\!\{\Delta\}\!\}\rho'}] \\
&\quad \{ \text{ by the induction hypothesis; see below } \} \\
&= \{\!\{x \mapsto v, \Delta\}\!\}\rho \\
&\quad \{ \text{ again by Lemma 6 } \}
\end{aligned}$$

The second but last step is quite technical, as the $|_{\mathsf{dom}\,(x \mapsto e, \Gamma)}$ operator needs to commute with the fixed-point operator. This goes through by parallel fixed-point induction if we first generalise it to $|_{\mathsf{Var} \setminus \mathsf{dom}\,\Delta \cup \mathsf{dom}\,(x \mapsto e, \Gamma)}$, the restriction to the complement of the new variables added to the heap during evaluation of x.

The first part now follows from the second part:

$$\begin{aligned}
[\![x]\!]_{\{\!\{x \mapsto e, \Gamma\}\!\}\rho} &= (\{\!\{x \mapsto e, \Gamma\}\!\}\rho)\, x \\
&= (\{\!\{x \mapsto v, \Delta\}\!\}\rho)\, x \\
&\quad \{ \text{ by the second part and } x \in \mathsf{dom}\,(x \mapsto e, \Gamma) \} \\
&= [\![v]\!]_{\{\!\{x \mapsto v, \Delta\}\!\}\rho} \\
&\quad \{ \text{ by Lemma 4. } \}
\end{aligned}$$

Case: LET
We know that $[\![e]\!]_{\{\!\{\Delta,\Gamma\}\!\}\rho} = [\![v]\!]_{\{\!\{\Theta\}\!\}\rho}$ and $\{\!\{\Delta,\Gamma\}\!\}\rho =|_{\mathsf{dom}\,(\Delta,\Gamma)} \{\!\{\Theta\}\!\}\rho$. For the first part we have

$$\begin{aligned}
[\![\textbf{let}\ \Delta\ \textbf{in}\ e]\!]_{\{\!\{\Gamma\}\!\}\rho} &= [\![e]\!]_{\{\!\{\Delta\}\!\}\{\!\{\Gamma\}\!\}\rho} && \{\text{ by the denotation of let-expressions }\}\\
&= [\![e]\!]_{\{\!\{\Delta,\Gamma\}\!\}\rho} && \{\text{ by the following Lemma 7 }\}\\
&= [\![v]\!]_{\{\!\{\Theta\}\!\}\rho} && \{\text{ by the induction hypothesis }\}
\end{aligned}$$

and for the second part we have

$$\begin{aligned}
\{\!\{\Gamma\}\!\}\rho &=|_{\mathsf{dom}\,\Gamma} \{\!\{\Delta\}\!\}\{\!\{\Gamma\}\!\}\rho && \{\text{ because dom}\,\Delta\text{ are fresh }\}\\
&= \{\!\{\Delta,\Gamma\}\!\}\rho && \{\text{ again by Lemma 7 }\}\\
&=|_{\mathsf{dom}\,(\Delta,\Gamma)} \{\!\{\Theta\}\!\}\rho. && \{\text{ by the induction hypothesis. }\} \quad \blacksquare
\end{aligned}$$

In the case for VAR, I switched from the usual, simultaneous definition of the heap semantics to an iterative one, in order to be able to make use of the induction hypothesis:

Lemma 6 (Iterative definition of the heap semantics)

$$\{\!\{x \mapsto e, \Gamma\}\!\}\rho = \mu\rho'.\,\big((\rho \mathbin{++}_{\mathsf{dom}\,\Gamma} \{\!\{\Gamma\}\!\}\rho')[x \mapsto [\![e]\!]_{\{\!\{\Gamma\}\!\}\rho'}]\big). \qquad \diamond$$

A corresponding lemma can be found in Launchbury [Lau93], but without proof. As the proof involves some delicate juggling of fixed points, I include it here in detail:

Proof
Let

$$L = \lambda\rho'.\,(\rho \mathbin{++}_{\mathsf{dom}\,(x\mapsto e,\Gamma)} [\![x \mapsto e, \Gamma]\!]_{\rho'})$$

be the functorial of the fixed point on the left hand side, and

$$R = \lambda\rho'.\,\big((\rho \mathbin{++}_{\mathsf{dom}\,\Gamma} \{\!\{\Gamma\}\!\}\rho')[x \mapsto [\![e]\!]_{\{\!\{\Gamma\}\!\}\rho'}]\big).$$

the functorial of the fixed point on the right hand side.

By Lemma 4, we have

$$\begin{aligned}
(\mu L)\, y &= [\![e']\!]_{\mu L} && \text{for } y \mapsto e' \in \mathsf{dom}\,\Gamma, && (1)\\
(\mu L)\, x &= [\![e]\!]_{\mu L}, && && (2)\\
(\mu L)\, y &= \rho\, y && \text{for } y \notin \mathsf{dom}\,(x \mapsto e, \Gamma). && (3)
\end{aligned}$$

Similarly, by unrolling the fixed points, we have

$$\begin{aligned}
(\mu R)\, y &= [\![e']\!]_{\{\!\{\Gamma\}\!\}(\mu R)} && \text{for } y \mapsto e' \in \mathsf{dom}\,\Gamma, && (4)\\
(\mu R)\, x &= [\![e]\!]_{\{\!\{\Gamma\}\!\}(\mu R)}, && && (5)\\
(\mu R)\, y &= \rho\, y && \text{for } y \notin \mathsf{dom}\,(x \mapsto e, \Gamma), && (6)
\end{aligned}$$

and also for $\rho' \in \mathsf{Env}$ (in particular for $\rho' = (\mu L)$ and $\rho' = (\mu R)$), again using Lemma 4,

$$\begin{aligned}
(\{\!\{\Gamma\}\!\}\rho')\, y &= [\![e']\!]_{\{\!\{\Gamma\}\!\}\rho'} && \text{for } y \mapsto e' \in \mathsf{dom}\,\Gamma, && (7)\\
(\{\!\{\Gamma\}\!\}\rho')\, y &= \rho'\, y && \text{for } y \notin \mathsf{dom}\,\Gamma. && (8)
\end{aligned}$$

We obtain

$$\{\!\{\Gamma\}\!\}(\mu R) = (\mu R) \tag{9}$$

from comparing (4)–(6) with (7) and (8). We can also show

$$\{\!\{\Gamma\}\!\}(\mu L) = (\mu L), \tag{10}$$

by antisymmetry of $\sqsubseteq$ and using that least fixed points are least pre-fixed points:

- $\sqsubseteq$: We need to show that $(\mu L) +\!\!+_{\mathsf{dom}\,\Gamma} [\![\Gamma]\!]_{(\mu L)} \sqsubseteq (\mu L)$, which follows from (1).

- $\sqsupseteq$: We need to show that

  $$\{\!\{\Gamma\}\!\}(\mu L) +\!\!+_{\mathsf{dom}\,(x \mapsto e, \Gamma)} [\![x \mapsto e, \Gamma]\!]_{\{\!\{\Gamma\}\!\}(\mu L)} \sqsubseteq \{\!\{\Gamma\}\!\}(\mu L).$$

  For $\mathsf{dom}\,\Gamma$, this follows from (7), so we show $[\![e]\!]_{\{\!\{\Gamma\}\!\}(\mu L)} \sqsubseteq (\mu L)\, x = [\![e]\!]_{(\mu L)}$, which follows from the monotonicity of $[\![e]\!]_{\_}$ and case $\sqsubseteq$.

To show the conclusion of the lemma, i.e. $(\mu L) = (\mu R)$, we again use antisymmetry and the leastness of least fixed points:

$\sqsubseteq$: We need to show that $L\,(\mu R) = \mu R$, i.e.

- $\rho\, y = (\mu R)\, y$ for $y \notin \mathsf{dom}\,(x \mapsto e, \Gamma)$, which follows from (6),
- $[\![e']\!]_{\mu R} = (\mu R)\, y$ for $y \mapsto e' \in \Gamma$, which follows from (4) and (9) and
- $[\![e]\!]_{\mu R} = (\mu R)\, x$, which follows from (5) and (9).

$\sqsupseteq$: Now we have to show that $R\,(\mu L) = (\mu L)$, i.e.

- $\rho\, y = (\mu L)\, y$ for $y \notin \mathsf{dom}\,(x \mapsto e, \Gamma)$, which follows from (3),
- $[\![e']\!]_{\{\!\{\Gamma\}\!\}(\mu L)} = (\mu L)\, y$ for $y \mapsto e' \in \Gamma$, which follows from (1) and (10), and
- $[\![e]\!]_{\{\!\{\Gamma\}\!\}(\mu L)} = (\mu L)\, x$, which follows from (2) and (10). ■

The final lemma required for the correctness proof shows that the denotation of a set of bindings with only fresh variables can be merged with the heap it was defined over:

Lemma 7 (Merging the heap semantics)
If $\mathsf{dom}\,\Delta$ is fresh with regard to Γ and ρ, then

$$\{\!\{\Delta\}\!\}\{\!\{\Gamma\}\!\}\rho = \{\!\{\Delta, \Gamma\}\!\}\rho. \qquad \diamond$$

Proof
We use the antisymmetry of $\sqsubseteq$, and the leastness of least fixed points.

$\sqsubseteq$: We need to show that $\{\!\{\Gamma\}\!\}\rho \mathrel{++}_{\mathsf{dom}\,\Delta} [\![\Delta]\!]_{\{\!\{\Delta,\Gamma\}\!\}\rho} = \{\!\{\Delta, \Gamma\}\!\}\rho$, which we verify pointwise.

- For $x \in \mathsf{dom}\,\Delta$, this follows directly from Lemma 4.
- For $x \notin \mathsf{dom}\,\Delta$, this holds as the variables bound in Δ are fresh, so the bindings in $\{\!\{\Gamma\}\!\}\rho$ keep their semantics.

$\sqsupseteq$: We need to show that $\rho \mathrel{++}_{\mathsf{dom}\,(\Delta,\Gamma)} [\![\Delta, \Gamma]\!]_{\{\!\{\Delta\}\!\}\{\!\{\Gamma\}\!\}\rho} = \{\!\{\Delta\}\!\}\{\!\{\Gamma\}\!\}\rho$.

- For $x \in \mathsf{dom}\,\Delta$, this follows from unrolling the fixed point on the right hand side once.

- For $x \mapsto e \in \mathsf{dom}\,\Gamma$ (and hence $x \notin \mathsf{dom}\,\Delta$), we have

$$
\begin{aligned}
& (\rho \mathbin{++}_{\mathsf{dom}\,(\Delta,\Gamma)} [\![\Delta,\Gamma]\!]_{\{\!\{\Delta\}\!\}\{\!\{\Gamma\}\!\}\rho})\, x \\
= {} & [\![e]\!]_{\{\!\{\Delta\}\!\}\{\!\{\Gamma\}\!\}\rho} \\
& \{\text{ by Lemma 4 }\} \\
= {} & [\![e]\!]_{\{\!\{\Gamma\}\!\}\rho} \\
& \{\text{ because } \mathsf{dom}\,\Delta \text{ is fresh with regard to } e \,\} \\
= {} & (\{\!\{\Gamma\}\!\}\rho)\, x \\
& \{\text{ by unrolling the fixed point }\} \\
= {} & ([\![\Delta]\!]_{\{\!\{\Gamma\}\!\}\rho})\, x \\
& \{\text{ because } x \notin \mathsf{dom}\,\Delta \text{ and Lemma 4. }\}
\end{aligned}
$$

- For $x \notin \mathsf{dom}\,(\Delta, \Gamma)$, we have $\rho\, x$ on both sides. ■

2.2.1 Discussions of modifications

My main Theorem 1 and the generalisation in Theorem 2 differ from Launchbury's corresponding Theorem 2. The additional requirement that the judgements are closed has already been discussed in Section 2.1.3.

Furthermore, the second part of Theorem 2 is phrased differently. Launchbury states $\{\!\{\Gamma\}\!\}\rho \le \{\!\{\Delta\}\!\}\rho$ where $\rho \le \rho'$ is defined as

$$\forall x.\, \rho\, x \neq \bot \implies \rho\, x = \rho'\, x,$$

i.e. ρ' agrees with ρ on all variables that have a meaning in ρ. The issue with this definition is that there are two reasons why $\{\!\{\Gamma\}\!\}\rho\, x = \bot$ can hold: Either $x \notin \mathsf{dom}\,\Gamma$, or $x \in \mathsf{dom}\,\Gamma$, but bound to a diverging value. Only the first case is intended here, and actually $\le$ is used as if only that case can happen, e.g. in the treatment of VAR in the correctness proof. I therefore avoid the problematic $\le$ relation and explicitly show $\{\!\{\Gamma\}\!\}\rho =_{|\mathsf{dom}\,\Gamma} \{\!\{\Delta\}\!\}\rho$.

2.3 Adequacy

A correctness theorem for a natural semantics is not worth much on its own. Imagine a mistake in side condition of the LET rule that accidentally prevents any judgement to be derived for programs with a **let** – the correctness theorem would still hold.

It is therefore desirable to prove that all programs that have a meaning, in this case according to the denotational semantics, indeed have a derivation:

Theorem 3 (Adequacy)
For all expressions e, heap Γ and set of variables L, if $[\![e]\!]_{\{\!\{\Gamma\}\!\}} \neq \bot$, then there exists a heap Δ and a value v so that $\Gamma : e \Downarrow_L \Delta : v$. ◇

The proof uses a modified denotational semantics that keeps track of the number of steps required to determine the non-bottomness of e, which I introduce in the next subsection. I will then show that the natural semantics is adequate with regard to the modified denotational semantics, and make the connection by showing how the two denotational semantics relate.

2.3.1 The resourced denotational semantics

The domain used to count the resources is a solution to the equation $\mathsf{C} = \mathsf{C}_\bot$. The lifting is done by the injection function $C \colon \mathsf{C} \to \mathsf{C}$, so the elements are

$$\bot \sqsubset C\,\bot \sqsubset C\,(C\,\bot) \sqsubset \cdots \sqsubset C^n \sqsubset \cdots \sqsubset C^\infty$$

This is isomorphic to the extended naturals. I use r for variables ranging over C. The notation $f|_r$ restricts a function f with domain C to take at most r resources: $(f|_r)\ r' := f\ (r \sqcap r')$.

The resourced semantics $\mathcal{N}[\![e]\!]_\sigma$ of an expression e in environment σ is now a function which takes an additional argument r of type C to indicate the number of steps the semantics is still allowed to perform: Every recursive call in the definition of $\mathcal{N}[\![e]\!]_\sigma\ r$ peels one application of C off r until none are left.

$$\begin{aligned}
\mathcal{N}[\![e]\!]_\sigma\ \bot &:= \bot \\
\mathcal{N}[\![\lambda x.\, e]\!]_\sigma\ (C\ r) &:= \mathsf{CFn}\ (\lambda v. \mathcal{N}[\![e]\!]_{\sigma \sqcup [x \mapsto v]}|_r) \\
\mathcal{N}[\![e\ x]\!]_\sigma\ (C\ r) &:= ((\mathcal{N}[\![e]\!]_\sigma\ r) \downarrow_{\mathsf{CFn}}\ (\sigma\ x)|_r)\ r \\
\mathcal{N}[\![x]\!]_\sigma\ (C\ r) &:= \sigma\ x\ r \\
\mathcal{N}[\![\textbf{let}\ \Delta\ \textbf{in}\ e]\!]_\sigma\ (C\ r) &:= \mathcal{N}[\![e]\!]_{\{\!\{\Delta\}\!\}\sigma}\ r
\end{aligned}$$

Figure 8: The resourced denotational semantics

The type of the environment changes as well: It is now $\mathsf{Var} \to (\mathsf{C} \to \mathsf{CValue})$. I use σ for variables ranging over such *resourced environments*.

The intuition is that if we pass in an infinite number of resources, the two semantics coincide:

$$\forall x.\, \rho\ x = \sigma\ x\ C^\omega \implies [\![e]\!]_\rho = \mathcal{N}[\![e]\!]_\sigma\ C^\omega,$$

as Launchbury puts it. While this intuition is intuitively true, it cannot be stated that naively: Because the semantics of an expression is now a function taking a C, this needs to be reflected in the domain equation, which therefore constructs a different domain, as observed by Sánchez-Gil *et al.*:

$$\mathsf{CValue} = ((\mathsf{C} \to \mathsf{CValue}) \to (\mathsf{C} \to \mathsf{CValue}))_\bot$$

The lifting and the projection functions are hence

$$\begin{aligned}
\mathsf{CFn}\ (_) &: (\mathsf{C} \to \mathsf{CValue}) \to (\mathsf{C} \to \mathsf{CValue}) \to \mathsf{CValue} \\
_ \downarrow_{\mathsf{CFn}} _ &: \mathsf{CValue} \to (\mathsf{C} \to \mathsf{CValue}) \to (\mathsf{C} \to \mathsf{CValue}).
\end{aligned}$$

The definition of the resourced semantics, given in Fig. 8, resembles the definition of the standard semantics with some additional resource bookkeeping. The semantics of the heap is defined as before:

$$\mathcal{N}\{\!\{\Gamma\}\!\}\sigma := (\mu\sigma'.\, \sigma \mathbin{++}_{\mathsf{dom}\,\Gamma} \mathcal{N}[\![\Gamma]\!]_{\sigma'}).$$

Given the similarity between this semantics and the standard semantics, it is not surprising that Lemmas 4, 5, 6 and 7 hold as well. In fact, in the formal development, they are stated and proved abstractly, using *locales* [Bal14] as a modularisation tool, and then simply instantiated for both variants of the semantics. I describe this approach in Section 2.6.3.

The correctness lemma needs some adjustments, as a more evaluated expression requires fewer resources. It therefore only provides an inequality:

Lemma 8 (Correctness, resourced)
If $\Gamma : e \Downarrow_L \Delta : v$ holds and is closed, then for all resourced environments σ we have $\mathcal{N}[\![e]\!]_{\{\!\{\Gamma\}\!\}\sigma} \sqsubseteq \mathcal{N}[\![v]\!]_{\{\!\{\Delta\}\!\}\sigma}$ and $(\mathcal{N}\{\!\{\Gamma\}\!\}\sigma)|_{\mathsf{dom}\,\Gamma} \sqsubseteq (\mathcal{N}\{\!\{\Delta\}\!\}\sigma)|_{\mathsf{dom}\,\Gamma}$. ◇

Proof
Analogously to the proof of Theorem 2. ∎

2.3.2 Denotational black holes

The major difficulty in proving computational adequacy is the blackholing behaviour of the operational semantics: During the evaluation of a variable x the corresponding binding is removed from the heap. Operationally, this is desirable: If the variable is called again during its own evaluation, we would have an infinite loop anyways.

But obviously, the variable is still mentioned in the current configuration, and simply removing the binding will change the denotation of the configuration in unwanted ways: There is no hope of proving $\mathcal{N}[\![e]\!]_{\mathcal{N}\{\!\{x \mapsto e, \Gamma\}\!\}} = \mathcal{N}[\![e]\!]_{\mathcal{N}\{\!\{\Gamma\}\!\}}$.

But a weaker statement holds, which reflects the idea of "not using x during its own evaluation" more closely:

Lemma 9 (Denotational blackholing)

$$\mathcal{N}[\![e]\!]_{\mathcal{N}\{\!\{x \mapsto e, \Gamma\}\!\}}\, r \neq \bot \implies \mathcal{N}[\![e]\!]_{\mathcal{N}\{\!\{\Gamma\}\!\}}\, r \neq \bot$$ ◇

This is a consequence of the following lemma, which states that during the evaluation of an expression using finite resources, only fewer resources will be passed to the members of the environment (which are of type $\mathsf{C} \to \mathsf{CValue}$):

Lemma 10

$$\mathcal{N}[\![e]\!]_\sigma|_{C\ r} = \mathcal{N}[\![e]\!]_{(\sigma|_r)}|_{C\ r}$$

where $\sigma|_r$ is an abbreviation for $\lambda x.(\sigma\ x)|_r$. ◇

Proof
by induction on the expression e.

In order to show $\mathcal{N}[\![e]\!]_\sigma|_{C\ r} = \mathcal{N}[\![e]\!]_{(\sigma|_r)}|_{C\ r}$ it suffices to show that $\mathcal{N}[\![e]\!]_\sigma\ (C\ r') = \mathcal{N}[\![e]\!]_{(\sigma|_r)}\ (C\ r')$ for any $r' \sqsubseteq r$.

The critical case is the one for variables, where $e = x$. We have

$$\mathcal{N}[\![x]\!]_\sigma\ (C\ r') = \sigma\ x\ r' = (\sigma\ x|_r)\ r' = \mathcal{N}[\![x]\!]_{(\sigma|_r)}\ (C\ r')$$

as $r' \sqsubseteq r$.

In the other cases, the result follows from the fact that nested expressions are evaluated with r' resources or, in the case of lambda abstraction, wrapped inside a $|_{r'}$ restriction operator.

For the case of **let**, a related lemma for heaps needs to be proven by parallel fixed-point induction, namely $\forall r.\ (\mathcal{N}\{\!\{\Gamma\}\!\}\sigma)|_r = (\mathcal{N}\{\!\{\Gamma\}\!\}(\sigma|_r))|_r$. ■

Equipped with this lemma, we can begin the

Proof (of Lemma 9)
Let r' be the least resource such that $\mathcal{N}[\![e]\!]_{\mathcal{N}\{\!\{x\mapsto e,\Gamma\}\!\}}(C\ r') \neq \bot$. Such an r' exists by the assumption, and $C\ r' \sqsubseteq r$, and by the continuity of the semantics $r' \neq C^\infty$. In particular, $\mathcal{N}[\![e]\!]_{\mathcal{N}\{\!\{x\mapsto e,\Gamma\}\!\}}\,r' = \bot$.

We first show

$$\mathcal{N}\{\!\{x \mapsto e, \Gamma\}\!\}|_{r'} \sqsubseteq \mathcal{N}\{\!\{\Gamma\}\!\} \tag{$*$}$$

by bounded fixed-point induction. So given an arbitrary environment $\sigma \sqsubseteq \mathcal{N}\{\!\{x \mapsto e, \Gamma\}\!\}$, we may assume $\sigma|_{r'} \sqsubseteq \mathcal{N}\{\!\{\Gamma\}\!\}$ and have to prove $\mathcal{N}[\![x \mapsto e, \Gamma]\!]_\sigma|_{r'} \sqsubseteq \mathcal{N}\{\!\{\Gamma\}\!\}$, which we do point-wise:

For $y \mapsto e' \in \Gamma$, this follows from

$$\begin{aligned}
\mathcal{N}[\![x \mapsto e, \Gamma]\!]_\sigma|_{r'}\ y &= \mathcal{N}[\![e']\!]_\sigma|_{r'} \\
&= \mathcal{N}[\![e']\!]_{\sigma|_{r'}}|_{r'} \qquad \{\text{ by Lemma 10 }\} \\
&\sqsubseteq \mathcal{N}[\![e']\!]_{\sigma|_{r'}}
\end{aligned}$$

$$
\begin{aligned}
&\sqsubseteq \mathcal{N}[\![e']\!]_{\mathcal{N}\{\!\{\Gamma\}\!\}} && \{\text{ by the induction hypothesis }\}\\
&= \mathcal{N}\{\!\{\Gamma\}\!\}\ y && \{\text{ by Lemma 4 }\}
\end{aligned}
$$

while for x, this follows from

$$
\begin{aligned}
\mathcal{N}[\![x \mapsto e, \Gamma]\!]_{\sigma}|_{r'}\ x &= \mathcal{N}[\![e]\!]_{\sigma}|_{r'}\\
&\sqsubseteq \mathcal{N}[\![e]\!]_{\mathcal{N}\{\!\{x\mapsto e,\Gamma\}\!\}}|_{r'} && \{\text{ using } \sigma \sqsubseteq \mathcal{N}\{\!\{x \mapsto e, \Gamma\}\!\}\ \}\\
&= \bot && \{\text{ by the choice of } r'\ \}\\
&= \mathcal{N}\{\!\{\Gamma\}\!\}\ x && \{\text{ as } x \notin \operatorname{dom}\Gamma.\ \}
\end{aligned}
$$

So we can conclude the proof with

$$
\begin{aligned}
\bot &\sqsubset \mathcal{N}[\![e]\!]_{\mathcal{N}\{\!\{x\mapsto e,\Gamma\}\!\}}(C\ r') && \{\text{ by the choice of } r'\ \}\\
&= \mathcal{N}[\![e]\!]_{\mathcal{N}\{\!\{x\mapsto e,\Gamma\}\!\}|_{r'}}(C\ r') && \{\text{ by Lemma 10 }\}\\
&\sqsubseteq \mathcal{N}[\![e]\!]_{\mathcal{N}\{\!\{\Gamma\}\!\}}(C\ r') && \{\text{ by } (*)\ \}\\
&\sqsubseteq \mathcal{N}[\![e]\!]_{\mathcal{N}\{\!\{\Gamma\}\!\}}r && \{\text{ as } C\ r' \sqsubseteq r\ \}
\end{aligned}
$$
■

2.3.3 Resourced adequacy

Now the necessary tools to handle blackholing are in place for the adequacy proof with regard to the resourced semantics.

Lemma 11 (Resourced semantics adequacy)
For all e, Γ and L, if $\mathcal{N}[\![e]\!]_{\mathcal{N}\{\!\{\Gamma\}\!\}}\ r \neq \bot$, then there exists Δ and v so that $\Gamma : e \Downarrow_L \Delta : v$. ◇

Proof
Because the semantics is continuous, it suffices to show this for $r = C^n\ \bot$, and perform induction on this n, with arbitrary e, Γ and L.

The case $r = C^0\ \bot = \bot$ is vacuously true, as $\mathcal{N}[\![e]\!]_{\mathcal{N}\{\!\{\Gamma\}\!\}}\ \bot = \bot$.

For the inductive case assume that the lemma holds for r, and that $\mathcal{N}[\![e]\!]_{\mathcal{N}\{\!\{\Gamma\}\!\}}\ (C\ r) \neq \bot$. We proceed by case analysis on the expression e.

Case: $e = x$.
From the assumption we know that $\Gamma = x \mapsto e', \Gamma'$ for some e' and Γ', as otherwise the denotation would be bottom, and furthermore that $\mathcal{N}[\![e']\!]_{\mathcal{N}\{\!\{x\mapsto e',\Gamma'\}\!\}}\ r \neq \bot$

With Lemma 9 this implies $\mathcal{N}[\![e']\!]_{\mathcal{N}\{\!\{\Gamma'\}\!\}}\ r \neq \bot$, so the induction hypothesis applies and provides Δ and v with $\Gamma' : e' \Downarrow_{L\cup\{x\}} \Delta : v$. This implies $x \mapsto e', \Gamma' : x \Downarrow_L \Delta : v$ by rule VAR, as desired.

Case: $e = e'\ x$.
Assume that $\mathsf{fv}(\Gamma, e') \subseteq L$. No generality is lost here: If a derivation in the natural semantics with a larger set of variables to avoid than required holds, then the same derivation is also valid with the required set L.

From the assumption we know $(\mathcal{N}[\![e']\!]_{\mathcal{N}\{\!\{\Gamma\}\!\}}\ r \downarrow_{\mathsf{CFn}} (\mathcal{N}\{\!\{\Gamma\}\!\}\ x)|_r)\ r \neq \bot$. In particular $(\mathcal{N}[\![e']\!]_{\mathcal{N}\{\!\{\Gamma\}\!\}}\ r) \neq \bot$, so by the induction hypothesis we have Δ, y and e'' with $\Gamma : e' \Downarrow_L \Delta : \lambda y.\, e''$, the first hypothesis of APP.

This judgement is closed by the extra assumption, so Lemma 8 ensures that $\mathcal{N}[\![e']\!]_{\mathcal{N}\{\!\{\Gamma\}\!\}} \sqsubseteq \mathcal{N}[\![\lambda y.\, e'']\!]_{\mathcal{N}\{\!\{\Delta\}\!\}}$ and $\mathcal{N}\{\!\{\Gamma\}\!\} \sqsubseteq \mathcal{N}\{\!\{\Delta\}\!\}$. We can insert that into the inequality above to calculate

$$
\begin{aligned}
\bot &\sqsubset (\mathcal{N}[\![e']\!]_{\mathcal{N}\{\!\{\Gamma\}\!\}}\ r \downarrow_{\mathsf{CFn}} (\mathcal{N}\{\!\{\Gamma\}\!\}\ x)|_r)\ r \\
&\sqsubseteq (\mathcal{N}[\![\lambda y.\, e'']\!]_{\mathcal{N}\{\!\{\Delta\}\!\}}\ r \downarrow_{\mathsf{CFn}} (\mathcal{N}\{\!\{\Delta\}\!\}\ x)|_r)\ r \\
&\sqsubseteq (\mathcal{N}[\![\lambda y.\, e'']\!]_{\mathcal{N}\{\!\{\Delta\}\!\}}\ r \downarrow_{\mathsf{CFn}} \mathcal{N}\{\!\{\Delta\}\!\}\ x)\ r \\
&= (\mathsf{CFn}\ (\lambda v.\, \mathcal{N}[\![e'']\!]_{\mathcal{N}\{\!\{\Delta\}\!\} \sqcup [y \mapsto v]}|_r) \downarrow_{\mathsf{CFn}} \mathcal{N}\{\!\{\Delta\}\!\}\ x)\ r \\
&\sqsubseteq (\mathsf{CFn}\ (\lambda v.\, \mathcal{N}[\![e'']\!]_{\mathcal{N}\{\!\{\Delta\}\!\} \sqcup [y \mapsto v]}) \downarrow_{\mathsf{CFn}} \mathcal{N}\{\!\{\Delta\}\!\}\ x)\ r \\
&= \mathcal{N}[\![e'']\!]_{\mathcal{N}\{\!\{\Delta\}\!\} \sqcup [y \mapsto (\mathcal{N}\{\!\{\Delta\}\!\}\ x)]}\ r \\
&= \mathcal{N}[\![e''[y := x]]\!]_{\mathcal{N}\{\!\{\Delta\}\!\}}\ r && \{\text{ by Lemma 5 }\}
\end{aligned}
$$

which, using the induction hypothesis again, provides us with Θ and v so that the second hypothesis of APP, $\Delta : e''[y := x] \Downarrow_L \Theta : v$, holds, concluding this case.

Case: $e = \lambda y.\, e'$
This case follows immediately from rule LAM with $\Delta = \Gamma$ and $v = \lambda y.\, e'$.

Case: $e = \textbf{let}\ \Delta\ \textbf{in}\ e'$
We have

$$
\begin{aligned}
\bot &\sqsubset \mathcal{N}[\![\textbf{let}\ \Delta\ \textbf{in}\ e']\!]_{\mathcal{N}\{\!\{\Gamma\}\!\}}\ r \\
&\sqsubseteq \mathcal{N}[\![e']\!]_{\mathcal{N}\{\!\{\Delta\}\!\}\mathcal{N}\{\!\{\Gamma\}\!\}} \\
&= \mathcal{N}[\![e']\!]_{\mathcal{N}\{\!\{\Delta, \Gamma\}\!\}} && \{\text{ by Lemma 7 }\}
\end{aligned}
$$

so we have Θ and v with $\Delta, \Gamma : e' \Downarrow_L \Theta : v$ and hence $\Gamma : \textbf{let } \Delta \textbf{ in } e' \Downarrow_L \Theta : v$ by rule LET, as desired. ■

2.3.4 Relating the denotational semantics

Lemma 11 is almost what we want, but it talks about the resourced denotational semantics. In order to obtain that result for the standard denotational semantics, we need to relate these two semantics. We cannot simply equate them, as they have different denotational domains Value and C → CValue. So we are looking for a relation $\triangleleft\triangleright$ between Value and CValue that expresses the intuition that they behave the same, if the latter is given infinite resources. In particular, it is specified by the two equations

$$\bot \triangleleft\triangleright \bot$$

and

$$(\forall x\, y.\, x \triangleleft\triangleright y\, C^\infty \implies f\, x \triangleleft\triangleright g\, y\, C^\infty) \iff \mathsf{Fn}(f) \triangleleft\triangleright \mathsf{CFn}\,(g).$$

Unfortunately, this is not admissible as an inductive definition, as it is self-referential in a non-monotone way, so the construction of this relation is non-trivial. This was observed and performed by Sánchez-Gil *et al.* [SHO11], and I have subsequently implemented this construction in Isabelle.

I lift this relation to environments $\rho \in \mathsf{Env}$ and resourced environments $\sigma \in \mathsf{Var} \to (\mathsf{C} \to \mathsf{Value})$ by

$$\rho \triangleleft\triangleright^* \sigma \iff \forall x.\, \rho\, x \triangleleft\triangleright \sigma\, x\, C^\infty.$$

This allows us to state precisely how the two denotational semantics are related:

Lemma 12 (The denotational semantics are related)
For all environments $\rho \in \mathsf{Env}$ and $\sigma \in \mathsf{Var} \to (\mathsf{C} \to \mathsf{Value})$ with $\rho \triangleleft\triangleright^* \sigma$, we have

$$[\![e]\!]_\rho \triangleleft\triangleright \mathcal{N}[\![e]\!]_\sigma\, C^\infty. \qquad \diamond$$

Proof
Intuitively, the proof is obvious: As we are only concerned with infinite resources, all the resource counting added to the denotational semantics becomes moot and the semantics are obviously related. A more rigorous proof can be found in [SHO11] and in my formal verification. ■

Corollary 13
For all heaps Γ, we have $\{\!\{\Gamma\}\!\} \mathrel{\triangleleft\triangleright^*} \mathcal{N}\{\!\{\Gamma\}\!\}$.

Proof
by parallel fixed-point induction and Lemma 12. ■

I describe my Isabelle formalisation of [SHO11] in Section 2.6.4, including the mistakes in the original work that I found and fixed.

2.3.5 Concluding the adequacy

With this in place, I can give the

Proof (of Theorem 3)
By Corollary 13 we have $\{\!\{\Gamma\}\!\} \mathrel{\triangleleft\triangleright^*} \mathcal{N}\{\!\{\Gamma\}\!\}$, and with Lemma 12 this implies $[\![e]\!]_{\{\!\{\Gamma\}\!\}} \mathrel{\triangleleft\triangleright} \mathcal{N}[\![e]\!]_{\mathcal{N}\{\!\{\Gamma\}\!\}}\ C^\infty$.

With the assumption $[\![e]\!]_{\{\!\{\Gamma\}\!\}} \neq \bot$ and the definition of $\triangleleft\triangleright$ this ensures that $\mathcal{N}[\![e]\!]_{\{\!\{\Gamma\}\!\}}\ C^\infty \neq \bot$, and we can apply Lemma 11, as desired. ■

2.3.6 Discussions of modifications

My adequacy proof diverges quite a bit from Launchbury's. As it is the first rigorous proof, I discuss the differences in greater detail.

Launchbury performs the adequacy proof by introducing an alternative natural semantics (ANS) that is closer to the denotational semantics than the original natural semantics (NS). He replaces the rules App and Var with the two rules given in Fig. 9. There are three differences to be spotted:

1. In the rule for applications, instead of substituting the argument x for the parameter y, the variable y is added to the heap, bound to x, adding an *indirection*.

$$\frac{\Gamma : e \Downarrow_L \Delta : \lambda y.\, e' \qquad y \mapsto x, \Delta : e' \Downarrow_L \Theta : v}{\Gamma : e\; x \Downarrow_L \Theta : v}\text{APP}'$$

$$\frac{x \mapsto e, \Gamma : e \Downarrow_L \Delta : v}{x \mapsto e, \Gamma : x \Downarrow_L \Delta : v}\text{VAR}'$$

Figure 9: Launchbury's alternative natural semantics

2. In the rule for variables, no update is performed: Even after x has been evaluated to the value v, the binding x on the heap is not modified at all.

3. Also in the rule for variables, no blackholing is performed: The binding for x stays on the heap during its evaluation.

Without much ado, Launchbury states that the original natural semantics and the alternative natural semantics are equivalent, which is intuitively convincing. Unfortunately, it turned out that a rigorous proof of this fact is highly non-trivial, as the actual structure of the heaps during evaluation differs a lot: The modification to the application rule causes many indirections, which need to be taken care of. Furthermore, the lack of updates in the variable rules causes possibly complex, allocating expressions to be evaluated many times, each time adding further copies of already existing expressions to the heap. On the other side, the updates in the original semantics further obscure the relationship between the heaps in the original and the alternative semantics. On top of all that add the technical difficulty that is due to naming issues: Variables that are fresh in one derivation might not be fresh in the other, and explicit renamings need to be carried along.

Sánchez-Gil *et al.* have attempted to perform this proof. They broke it down into two smaller steps, going from the original semantics to one with only the variable rule changes (called No-update natural semantics, NNS), and from there to the ANS. So far, they have performed the second step, the equivalence between NNS and ANS, in a pen-and-paper proof

[SHO15], while relation between NS and NNS has yet resisted a proper proof [SHO14].

Considering these difficulties, I went a different path, and bridged the differences not on the side of the natural semantics, but on the denotational side, which turned out to work well:

1. The denotational semantics for lambda expressions changes the environment ($[\![\lambda x.\, e]\!]_\rho := \mathsf{Fn}(\lambda v. [\![e]\!]_{\rho \sqcup [x \mapsto v]})$), while the natural semantics uses substitution into the expression: $e[y := x]$.

   This difference is easily bridged on the denotational side by the substitution Lemma 5, which we need anyways for the correctness proof. See the last line of the application case in the proof of Lemma 11 for this step.

2. The removal of updates had surprisingly no effect on the adequacy proof: The main chore of the adequacy proof is to produce evidence for the *assumptions* of the corresponding natural semantics inference rule, which is then, in the last step, applied to produce the desired judgement. The removal of updates only changes the *conclusion* of the rule, so the adequacy proof is unchanged.

   Of course updates are not completely irrelevant, and they do affect the adequacy proof indirectly. The adequacy proof uses the correctness theorem for the resourced natural semantics (Lemma 8), and there the removal of updates from the semantics would make a noticeable difference.

3. Finally, and most trickily, there is the issue of blackholing. I explain my solution in Section 2.3.2, which works due to a small modification to the resourced denotational semantics.

   My proof relies on the property that when we calculate the semantics of $\mathcal{N}[\![e]\!]_\sigma\, r$, we never pass more than r resources to the values bound in σ (Lemma 10). This concurs with the intuition about resources.

   In Launchbury's original definition of the resourced semantics, this lemma does not hold: The equation for lambda expression ignores the resources passed to it and returns a function involving the semantics of the body:

$$\mathcal{N}[\![\lambda x.\, e]\!]_\sigma\ (C\ r) := \mathsf{CFn}\ (\lambda v. \mathcal{N}[\![e]\!]_{\sigma \sqcup [x \mapsto v]})$$

With that definition, $\mathcal{N}[\![\lambda x.\, y]\!]_\sigma\ (C\ \bot) = \mathsf{CFn}\ (\lambda\_.\, \sigma\ y)$, which depends on $\sigma\ y\ r$ for all r, contradicting Lemma 10.

Therefore, I restrict the argument of $\mathsf{CFn}\ (\_)$ to cap any resources passed to it at r. Analogously I adjust the equation for applications to cap any resources passed to the value of the argument in the environment, $\sigma\ x$.

These modifications do not affect the proof relating the two denotational semantics (Lemma 12), as there we always pass infinite resources, and $|_{C^\infty}$ is the identity function.

2.4 Data type encodings and base values

Launchbury's semantics is a typical core calculus used for research: Minimalistic as far as possible. Lambda abstraction, application and variables are enough to have a full functional programming language, and **let** expressions are added to talk explicitly about sharing and recursion.

2.4.1 Data types via Church encoding

Many other features of a typical programming language are omitted, and that is fine, because they can often be modelled with these primitive building blocks. For example data constructors and case analysis are expressible using a suitable encoding, such as the Church encoding. Consider tuples:

The constructor of a product type can be implemented as

$$Pair = \lambda x\, y\, z.\, z\ x\ y$$

with the projection functions

$$fst = \lambda p.\, p\ (\lambda x\, y.\, x)$$
$$snd = \lambda p.\, p\ (\lambda x\, y.\, y).$$

For the purposes of analysing lazy evaluation, these encodings sufficiently capture the behaviour of constructors. In particular, the semantics is set up so that the arguments of such a constructor are evaluated at most once, matching the expected behaviour of "real" constructors in a lazy language.

Example
Consider the following code, which stores an unevaluated expression $f\ x$ in the *Pair* constructor, extracts it later and evaluates it twice.

$$\begin{aligned}&\textbf{let}\ f = \lambda x\, y.\, y\\ &\quad\ \ p = \mathit{Pair}\ (f\ x)\ (f\ y)\\ &\textbf{in}\ (\mathit{fst}\ p)\ (\mathit{fst}\ p)\ x\end{aligned}$$

We expect the redex $(f\ x)$ to be evaluated only once, and indeed, this is the case. But note that the example code does not actually follow my syntax, because we have non-trivial expressions as arguments. By the mentioned preprocessing, the code should actually be

$$\begin{aligned}&\textbf{let}\ f = \lambda x\, y.\, y\\ &\quad\ \ p = (\textbf{let}\ y_2 = f\ y\ \textbf{in let}\ y_1 = f\ x\ \textbf{in}\ \mathit{Pair}\ y_1\ y_2)\\ &\textbf{in let}\ y_3 = \mathit{fst}\ p\ \textbf{in}\ \mathit{fst}\ p\ y_3\ x\end{aligned}$$

If this expression is called e, then we have $[] : e \Downarrow_{\{\}} \Delta : v$ where

$$\begin{aligned}\Delta = f &\mapsto \lambda x\, y.\, y,\\ p &\mapsto \lambda z.\, z\ y_1\ y_2,\\ y_3 &\mapsto \lambda y.\, y,\\ y_2 &\mapsto f\ y,\\ y_1 &\mapsto \lambda y.\, y,\end{aligned}$$

and $v = x$, and the pair now stores its first argument in its evaluated form, while the second argument is still unevaluated. Tracing the complete derivation of this judgement (which is a too large to be reproduced here) we see that $(f\ x)$ is indeed evaluated only once. ◇

There is, however, a trait of "real" constructors and case analysis that is not easily modelled by the Church encoding: With the Haskell code

```
case b of True  → do this
          False → do that
```

it is obvious that either do this or do that is executed, but not both. The same cannot be said for the corresponding code in a Church encoding of Booleans:

$$\begin{aligned} \mathit{True} &= \lambda x\, y.\, x \\ \mathit{False} &= \lambda x\, y.\, y \\ \mathit{ifThenElse} &= \lambda p\, x\, y.\, p\ x\ y \end{aligned}$$

where the code *ifThenElse b* (*do this*) (*do that*) may well evaluate both branches – there is no guarantee that *b* is one of the well-behaving expressions *True* or *False*.

In the later chapters, I am modelling an analysis that makes use of exactly that: A case analysis evaluates at most one of its branches (and exactly one, unless the scrutinee diverges). To prove that analysis to be correct, I need the language at hand to include a built-in case analysis operator that exhibits that behaviour – the above Church encoding is not enough.

But as just that feature is needed, I add just what is required to model it, and not more: Two constructors without arguments, and an **if-then-else**-construct. I deliberately do not add more complex data types that can carry parameters: As just explained, that would not add anything of value to the semantics.

2.4.2 Adding Booleans

The extended language sports three additional syntactical constructs, two of which are also values:

$$\begin{aligned} e \in \mathsf{Exp} &::= \ldots \mid \mathbf{C_t} \mid \mathbf{C_f} \mid e \,\mathbf{?}\, e_{\mathbf{t}} \,\mathbf{:}\, e_{\mathbf{f}} \\ v \in \mathsf{Val} &::= \ldots \mid \mathbf{C_t} \mid \mathbf{C_f} \end{aligned}$$

The notation $e \,?\, e_{\mathbf{t}} : e_{\mathbf{f}}$, taken from the ternary operator in C-like languages, is a succinct way to write an **if-then-else** construct, and the use of **t** and **f** in variable indices avoids repeating rules for the two cases, if the meta variable b is used to represent either of these. This can be seen in the two additional rules for the natural semantics:

$$\frac{}{\Gamma : \mathbf{C}_b \Downarrow_L \Gamma : \mathbf{C}_b}\textsc{Con} \qquad \frac{\Gamma : e \Downarrow_L \Delta : \mathbf{C}_b \qquad \Delta : e_b \Downarrow_L \Theta : v}{\Gamma : e \,?\, e_{\mathbf{t}} : e_{\mathbf{f}} \Downarrow_L \Theta : v}\textsc{IfThenElse}$$

As the other rules of the semantics are unchanged, the proofs by induction performed in this chapter only need to be extended by the two additional cases.

The required changes to the denotational semantics are a bit more involved, as the semantic domain changes: Besides functions, the semantics can also return Booleans, and the equation becomes

$$\mathsf{Value} = ((\mathsf{Value} \to \mathsf{Value}) + 2)_\bot,$$

where $+$ is the disjoint sum and 2 the discrete two-element domain with the (conveniently named) elements $\{\mathbf{t}, \mathbf{f}\}$. In addition to the existing injection and deconstruction functions

$$\mathsf{Fn}(\_) \colon (\mathsf{Value} \to \mathsf{Value}) \to \mathsf{Value}$$
$$\_ \downarrow_{\mathsf{Fn}} \_ \colon \mathsf{Value} \to \mathsf{Value} \to \mathsf{Value}$$

there is the additional injection function

$$\mathsf{B}(\_) \colon 2 \to \mathsf{Value}$$

and the deconstruction function

$$\_ \downarrow_{\mathsf{B}} (\_,\_) \colon \mathsf{Value} \to \mathsf{Value} \to \mathsf{Value} \to \mathsf{Value}$$

where

$$v \downarrow_{\mathsf{B}} (v_1, v_2) = \begin{cases} v_1 & \text{if } v = \mathsf{B}(\mathbf{t}) \\ v_2 & \text{if } v = \mathsf{B}(\mathbf{f}) \\ \bot & \text{otherwise.} \end{cases}$$

The partial order $\sqsubseteq$ on Value relates neither values of the form $\mathsf{Fn}(f)$ with $\mathsf{B}(b)$ nor $\mathsf{B}(\mathbf{t})$ with $\mathsf{B}(\mathbf{f})$.

The denotation of the new syntactic constructs is given by

$$\begin{aligned} [\![\mathbf{C}_b]\!]_\rho &:= \mathsf{B}(b) \\ [\![e \mathbin{?} e_{\mathbf{t}} : e_{\mathbf{f}}]\!]_\rho &:= [\![e]\!]_\rho \downarrow_{\mathsf{B}} ([\![e_{\mathbf{t}}]\!]_\rho, [\![e_{\mathbf{f}}]\!]_\rho) \end{aligned}$$

The thus extended natural semantics is still correct with regard to the denotational semantics:

Proof (of Theorem 2)
Two additional cases need to be handled.

Case: CON
This case is trivial, just like case LAM.

Case: IFTHENELSE
The induction hypotheses are $[\![e]\!]_{\{\!\{\Gamma\}\!\}\rho} = [\![\mathbf{C}_b]\!]_{\{\!\{\Delta\}\!\}\rho}$ and $\{\!\{\Gamma\}\!\}\rho =|_{\mathsf{dom}\,\Gamma} \{\!\{\Delta\}\!\}\rho$ as well as $[\![e_b]\!]_{\{\!\{\Delta\}\!\}\rho} = [\![v]\!]_{\{\!\{\Theta\}\!\}\rho}$ and $\{\!\{\Delta\}\!\}\rho =|_{\mathsf{dom}\,\Delta} \{\!\{\Theta\}\!\}\rho$.

We have $[\![e_b]\!]_{\{\!\{\Gamma\}\!\}\rho} = [\![e_b]\!]_{\{\!\{\Delta\}\!\}\rho}$: Because the judgement is closed, i.e. $\mathsf{fv}(e_b) \subseteq \mathsf{dom}\,\Gamma \cup L$, it suffices to show $\{\!\{\Gamma\}\!\}\rho =|_{\mathsf{dom}\,\Gamma \cup L} \{\!\{\Delta\}\!\}\rho$. The induction hypothesis provides the equality on $\mathsf{dom}\,\Gamma$, and for $x \in L \setminus \mathsf{dom}\,\Gamma$ we also have $x \notin \mathsf{dom}\,\Delta$ by Lemma 2, so we have $\rho\, x$ on both sides.

Like in case APP, the second part follows from the corresponding induction hypotheses and $\mathsf{dom}\,\Gamma \subseteq \mathsf{dom}\,\Delta$. The first part can be calculated:

$$\begin{aligned} [\![e \mathbin{?} e_{\mathbf{t}} : e_{\mathbf{f}}]\!]_{\{\!\{\Gamma\}\!\}\rho} &= [\![e]\!]_{\{\!\{\Gamma\}\!\}\rho} \downarrow_{\mathsf{B}} ([\![e_{\mathbf{t}}]\!]_{\{\!\{\Gamma\}\!\}\rho}, [\![e_{\mathbf{f}}]\!]_{\{\!\{\Gamma\}\!\}\rho}) \\ &\quad \{ \text{ by the denotation of the !if-!then-!else construct } \} \\ &= [\![\mathbf{C}_b]\!]_{\{\!\{\Delta\}\!\}\rho} \downarrow_{\mathsf{B}} ([\![e_{\mathbf{t}}]\!]_{\{\!\{\Gamma\}\!\}\rho}, [\![e_{\mathbf{f}}]\!]_{\{\!\{\Gamma\}\!\}\rho}) \\ &\quad \{ \text{ by the induction hypothesis } \} \\ &= \mathsf{B}(b) \downarrow_{\mathsf{B}} ([\![e_{\mathbf{t}}]\!]_{\{\!\{\Gamma\}\!\}\rho}, [\![e_{\mathbf{f}}]\!]_{\{\!\{\Gamma\}\!\}\rho}) \\ &\quad \{ \text{ by the denotation of the constructor } \} \\ &= [\![e_b]\!]_{\{\!\{\Gamma\}\!\}\rho} \\ &= [\![e_b]\!]_{\{\!\{\Delta\}\!\}\rho} \\ &\quad \{ \text{ see above } \} \end{aligned}$$

$$= [\![v]\!]_{\{\!\{\Theta\}\!\}\rho}$$
{ by the induction hypothesis } ∎

The adequacy proof can also be recovered, after extending the resourced domain CValue to contain $\{\mathbf{t}, \mathbf{f}\}$, i.e.

$$\mathsf{CValue} = (((\mathsf{C} \to \mathsf{CValue}) \to (\mathsf{C} \to \mathsf{CValue})) + 2)_\perp$$

with the analogous injection function and deconstructor

$$\begin{aligned} \mathsf{CB}(\_) &: 2 \to \mathsf{CValue} \\ \_ \downarrow_{\mathsf{CB}} (\_, \_) &: \mathsf{CValue} \to \mathsf{CValue} \to \mathsf{CValue} \to \mathsf{CValue}. \end{aligned}$$

which allow the definition of the resourced denotational semantics to be extended by

$$\begin{aligned} \mathcal{N}[\![\mathbf{C}_b]\!]_\rho &:= \mathsf{CB}(b) \\ \mathcal{N}[\![e \mathbin{?} e_\mathbf{t} : e_\mathbf{f}]\!]_\rho &:= \mathcal{N}[\![e]\!]_\rho \downarrow_{\mathsf{CB}} (\mathcal{N}[\![e_\mathbf{t}]\!]_\rho, \mathcal{N}[\![e_\mathbf{f}]\!]_\rho). \end{aligned}$$

Proof (of Lemma 11)
We need to extend the case analysis on e:

Case: $e = \mathbf{C}_b$
follows immediately from the rule CON.

Case: $e = e' \mathbin{?} e_\mathbf{t} : e_\mathbf{f}$
The assumption $\mathcal{N}[\![e' \mathbin{?} e_\mathbf{t} : e_\mathbf{f}]\!]_{\mathcal{N}\{\!\{\Gamma\}\!\}} \neq \bot$ resolves to

$$\mathcal{N}[\![e']\!]_{\mathcal{N}\{\!\{\Gamma\}\!\}} \downarrow_{\mathsf{CB}} (\mathcal{N}[\![e_\mathbf{t}]\!]_{\mathcal{N}\{\!\{\Gamma\}\!\}}, \mathcal{N}[\![e_\mathbf{f}]\!]_{\mathcal{N}\{\!\{\Gamma\}\!\}}) \neq \bot.$$

From this, we can conclude that $\mathcal{N}[\![e']\!]_{\mathcal{N}\{\!\{\Gamma\}\!\}} = \mathsf{CB}(b)$ for a $b \in \{\mathbf{t}, \mathbf{f}\}$, and $\mathcal{N}[\![e_b]\!]_{\mathcal{N}\{\!\{\Gamma\}\!\}} \neq \bot$.

We can therefore apply the first induction hypothesis and obtain Δ and v so that $\Gamma : e' \Downarrow_{L'} \Delta : v$, where $L' = L \cup \mathsf{fv}(\Gamma, e')$ – the extended set of variables ensures that the judgement is closed. By the correctness of the resourced denotational semantics (Lemma 8, the proof of which can be extended analogously to Theorem 2), we have $\mathcal{N}[\![v]\!]_{\mathcal{N}\{\!\{\Delta\}\!\}} \sqsubseteq \mathcal{N}[\![e']\!]_{\mathcal{N}\{\!\{\Gamma\}\!\}} = \mathsf{CB}(b)$, so the value v necessarily is $v = \mathbf{C}_b$.

The correctness lemma also states $\mathcal{N}\{\!\{\Gamma\}\!\} \sqsubseteq \mathcal{N}\{\!\{\Delta\}\!\}$, so $\mathcal{N}[\![e_b]\!]_{\mathcal{N}\{\!\{\Delta\}\!\}} \neq \bot$ and the induction hypothesis provides Θ and v' with $\Delta : e_b \Downarrow_{L'} \Theta : v'$.

By rule IFTHENELSE, this shows $\Gamma : e' \mathbin{?} e_{\mathbf{t}} : e_{\mathbf{f}} \Downarrow_{L'} \Theta : v'$ and hence, as $L \subseteq L'$, we have $\Gamma : e' \mathbin{?} e_{\mathbf{t}} : e_{\mathbf{f}} \Downarrow_{L} \Theta : v'$ as desired. ∎

The three semantics and the corresponding proofs thus allowed for a modular extension by Booleans: I just added new cases to the syntax, the natural rules, the denotational domains and the various functions, but left the overall structure of the proofs and the other cases as they were. I had to be careful not to make use of the lemma "If $\Gamma : e \Downarrow_L \Delta : v$, then v is a lambda abstraction," which no longer holds in the extended version; this comes up in the proof of Lemma 11.

2.5 A small-step semantics

One important feature of Launchbury's natural big-step-semantic is that the stack is implicit: During the evaluation of an application, for example, the argument is not stored anywhere in the configuration, but lives only in the rules. This is elegant and convenient if during a proof the stack does not need to be taken into account, e.g. in the adequacy proof, but causes headaches when the stack *is* relevant to the discussion at hand, which will be the case in Chapter 4.

For such feats, a semantics with an explicit stack in the configuration is better suited. As explained in the beginning of the chapter, I need to refrain from just building my own semantics that happens to suit me[9] but rather build on existing, well-received definitions.

Sestoft has derived a small-step semantics with an explicit stack from Launchbury's semantics, called the *mark-1 abstract machine*, and proved it to be equivalent to Launchbury's semantics. I follow that path and pave it by formalising it in Isabelle. I include my addition of Booleans (Section 2.4.2) in the treatment, but it is a modular extension: Simply ignore the cases related to Booleans and you obtain the plain semantics.

9 I tried that, and it did not go well.

$$
\begin{array}{lrcll}
 & (\Gamma, e\,x, S) & \Rightarrow & (\Gamma, e, \$x \cdot S) & \text{APP}_1 \\
 & (\Gamma, \lambda y.\, e, \$x \cdot S) & \Rightarrow & (\Gamma, e[y := x], S) & \text{APP}_2 \\
(x \mapsto e) \in \Gamma \implies & (\Gamma, x, S) & \Rightarrow & (\Gamma \setminus x, e, \#x \cdot S) & \text{VAR}_1 \\
\mathsf{isVal}\, e \implies & (\Gamma, e, \#x \cdot S) & \Rightarrow & (\Gamma[x \mapsto e], e, S) & \text{VAR}_2 \\
 & (\Gamma, (e \mathbin{?} e_{\mathbf{t}} : e_{\mathbf{f}}), S) & \Rightarrow & (\Gamma, e, (e_{\mathbf{t}} : e_{\mathbf{f}}) \cdot S) & \text{IF}_1 \\
b \in \{\mathbf{t}, \mathbf{f}\} \implies & (\Gamma, \mathsf{C}_b, (e_{\mathbf{t}} : e_{\mathbf{f}}) \cdot S) & \Rightarrow & (\Gamma, e_b, S) & \text{IF}_2 \\
\mathsf{dom}\, \Delta \cap \mathsf{fv}(\Gamma, S) = \{\} \implies & & & & \\
 & (\Gamma, \textbf{let}\ \Delta\ \textbf{in}\ e, S) & \Rightarrow & ((\Delta, \Gamma), e, S) & \text{LET}_1
\end{array}
$$

Figure 10: The small-step semantics, due to Sestoft [Ses97]

2.5.1 Sestoft's mark-1 abstract machine

Sestoft's semantics operates on *configurations* (Γ, e, S) that consist of the heap Γ, the control e (i.e. the expression currently under evaluation) and the stack S.

The stack is constructed from

- the empty stack, $[]$,
- arguments, written $\$x \cdot S$ and put on the stack during the evaluation of an application,
- update markers, written $\#x \cdot S$ and put on the stack during the evaluation of a variable's right-hand-side, and
- alternatives, written $(e_{\mathbf{t}} : e_{\mathbf{f}}) \cdot S$ and put on the stack during the evaluation of the scrutinee of an **if-then-else**-construct.

Throughout this work we assume all configurations to be *good*, i.e. $\mathsf{dom}\,\Gamma$ and $\#S := \{x \mid \#x \in S\}$ are disjoint and the update markers on the stack are distinct.

The relation $\Rightarrow$, given in Fig. 10, defines the semantics of a one-step-reduction. As usual, $\Rightarrow^*$ denotes the reflexive transitive closure of this relation.

Note that the semantics takes good configurations to good configurations.

2.5.2 Relating Sestoft's and Launchbury's semantics

Sestoft's small-step and Launchbury's big-step semantics are closely related, this section explicates this relationship. I follow [Ses97] here, making minor adjustments to ease the implementation in Isabelle.

Lemma 14 (Small-step simulates big-step)
If $\Gamma : e \Downarrow_L \Delta : v$ and $\mathsf{fv}(\Gamma, e, S) \subseteq \mathsf{dom}\,\Gamma \cup L$, then $(\Gamma, e, S) \Rightarrow^* (\Delta, v, S)$.

Proof
By induction on the derivation of $\Gamma : e \Downarrow_L \Delta : v$, with S arbitrary.

Case: LAM and CON
are trivial, as $\Rightarrow^*$ is reflexive.

Case: APP
The side condition of the first induction hypothesis follows from the assumption by $\mathsf{fv}(\Gamma, e\ x, S) = \mathsf{fv}(\Gamma, e, \$x{\cdot}S)$.

From that follows the side condition of the second induction hypothesis, i.e. $\mathsf{fv}(\Delta, e'[y := x], S) \subseteq \mathsf{dom}\,\Delta \cup L$, using $\mathsf{dom}\,\Gamma \subseteq \mathsf{dom}\,\Delta$ (Lemma 1) and using that the natural semantics preserves closedness.

It remains to do a simple calculation:

$$\begin{aligned}
(\Gamma, e\ x, S) &\Rightarrow (\Gamma, x, \$x{\cdot}S) && \{\text{ by } \textsc{App}_1 \}\\
&\Rightarrow^* (\Delta, \lambda y.\, e', \$x{\cdot}S) && \{\text{ first induction hypothesis }\}\\
&\Rightarrow (\Delta, e'[y := x], S) && \{\text{ by } \textsc{App}_2 \}\\
&\Rightarrow^* (\Theta, v, S) && \{\text{ second induction hypothesis }\}
\end{aligned}$$

Case: VAR
follows from this calculation:

$$\begin{aligned}
((x \mapsto e, \Gamma), x, S) &\Rightarrow (\Gamma, e, \#x{\cdot}S) && \{\text{ by } \textsc{Var}_1 \}\\
&\Rightarrow^* (\Delta, v, \#x{\cdot}S) && \{\text{ induction hypothesis }\}\\
&\Rightarrow ((x \mapsto e, \Delta), e, S) && \{\text{ by } \textsc{Var}_2 \}
\end{aligned}$$

The side condition of the induction hypothesis, i.e. the inequality $\mathsf{fv}((\Gamma, e, \#x{\cdot}S)) \subseteq \mathsf{dom}\,\Gamma \cup (L \cup \{x\})$, follows directly from the given assumption $\mathsf{fv}((x \mapsto e, \Gamma), x, S) \subseteq \mathsf{dom}\,(x \mapsto e, \Gamma) \cup L$.

Case: LET
The calculation is short:

$$\begin{aligned}(\Gamma, \textbf{let}\ \Delta\ \textbf{in}\ e, S) &\Rightarrow ((\Delta,\Gamma), e, S) && \{\text{ by } \textsc{Let}_1 \}\\ &\Rightarrow^* (\Theta, v, S) && \{\text{ by induction hypothesis }\}\end{aligned}$$

where the side-condition of $\textsc{Let}_1$ follows from the side-condition of LET.

Case: IFTHENELSE
resembles the case for APP, with a similar proof for the side conditions, and the calculation

$$\begin{aligned}(\Gamma, e\,\mathbf{?}\,e_{\mathbf{t}} : e_{\mathbf{f}}, S) &\Rightarrow (\Gamma, e, (e_{\mathbf{t}} : e_{\mathbf{f}})\cdot S) && \{\text{ by } \textsc{If}_1 \}\\ &\Rightarrow^* (\Delta, \mathsf{C}_b, (e_{\mathbf{t}} : e_{\mathbf{f}})\cdot S) && \{\text{ induction hypothesis }\}\\ &\Rightarrow (\Delta, e_b, S) && \{\text{ by } \textsc{If}_2 \}\\ &\Rightarrow^* (\Theta, v, S) && \{\text{ induction hypothesis }\} \quad \blacksquare\end{aligned}$$

The proof of the other direction, i.e. that an evaluation in the small-step semantics has a corresponding derivation in the big-step-semantics, is a bit more involved, as we need to recover the tree-structure of the big-step-semantics from the flat sequence of configurations in the small step semantics.

To that end, we use the notion of a *balanced execution*: An execution $c_1 \Rightarrow \cdots \Rightarrow c_n$, $n \geq 1$, is balanced if the stack of each intermediate configuration c_i, $i \in \{1, \ldots, n-1\}$ is an extension of the stack of c_1, and the stack of c_n equals the stack of c_1. We write $c_1 \Rightarrow_b^* c_2$ for such a balanced execution.

As every rule of the semantics only pushes or pops at most one element off the stack, balanced executions can be broken into smaller parts, which are still balanced, as shown by the following "intermediate value theorem":

Lemma 15
Given a balanced execution $c_1 \Rightarrow c_2 \Rightarrow \cdots \Rightarrow c_5$ where the stack of c_2 is the stack of c_1 with one element pushed, then there are intermediate states c_3 and c_4 so that

$$c_1 \Rightarrow c_2 \Rightarrow_b^* c_3 \Rightarrow c_4 \Rightarrow_b^* c_5. \qquad \diamond$$

Proof
Because the execution is balanced, c_5 and c_1 have the same stack. In particular, the stack of c_5 does *not* extend the stack of c_2. Let c_4 be the first configuration in that sequence whose stack does not extend the stack of c_2, and c_3 be the configuration preceding c_4. I claim that $c_2 \Rightarrow^* c_3$ and $c_4 \Rightarrow^* c_5$ are indeed balanced.

Every stack in $c_2 \Rightarrow^* c_3$ extends the stack of c_2 by construction. Furthermore, the stack of c_3 is equal to the stack of c_2: If it was not, then the stack of the configuration following c_3, namely c_4, would still be an extension of c_2's stack, contradicting the choice of c_4.

The stack of c_4 is equal to the stack of c_5: As it follows an extension of c_2's stack, but itself is not an extension of that, it must be c_2 with the top element popped. By assumption, that is c_1's stack. So c_4 and c_5 have the same stack, and all intermediate states have a stack that is an extension of that. ■

Example
This execution is balanced and fulfils the assumptions of Lemma 15, as the second stack equals the first with one element pushed:

$$\begin{aligned}(\Gamma, x\ y, S) &\Rightarrow (\Gamma, x, \$x \cdot S)\\ &\Rightarrow ([], (\lambda y.\,(\lambda z.\,z)), \#x \cdot \$x \cdot S)\\ &\Rightarrow (\Gamma, (\lambda y.\,(\lambda z.\,z)), \$x \cdot S)\\ &\Rightarrow (\Gamma, (\lambda z.\,z), S)\end{aligned}$$

where $\Gamma = x \mapsto (\lambda y.\,(\lambda z.\,z))$.

Lemma 15 decomposes this sequences into the two balanced executions

$$(\Gamma, x, \$x \cdot S) \Rightarrow_b^* (\Gamma, (\lambda y.\,(\lambda z.\,z)), \$x \cdot S)$$

and

$$(\Gamma, (\lambda z.\,z), S) \Rightarrow_b^* (\Gamma, (\lambda z.\,z), S).$$

where the second balanced execution does not actually do any steps. ◇

Lemma 16 (Big-step simulates small-step)
Let $(\Gamma, e, S) \Rightarrow_b^* (\Delta, v, S)$ with $\mathsf{isVal}\, v$. Then $\Gamma : e \Downarrow_{\#S} \Delta : v$.

Proof
by complete induction on the number of steps in $(\Gamma, e, S) \Rightarrow_b^* (\Delta, v, S)$.

If there are no intermediate steps, then $\Gamma = \Delta$, $e = v$ and we have $\Gamma : v \Downarrow_{\#S} \Gamma : v$ either by LAM or CON.

Otherwise, we proceed by case analysis on the first rule applied in the execution. This rule cannot be APP_2, VAR_2 or IF_2, as these pop an element off the stack, in contradiction to the execution being balanced.

Case: APP_1
We have $e = e'\ x$ and using Lemma 15, we can decompose the execution as follows:

$$(\Gamma, e'x, S) \Rightarrow (\Gamma, e', \$x{\cdot}S) \Rightarrow_b^* (\Delta', e_3, \$x{\cdot}S) \Rightarrow (\Delta'', e_4, S) \Rightarrow_b^* (\Delta, v, S).$$

As only rule APP_2 pops argument marker $\$x$ off the stack, we obtain

$$\begin{aligned}(\Gamma, e'x, S) \Rightarrow (\Gamma, e', \$x{\cdot}S) &\Rightarrow_b^* (\Delta', \lambda y.\, e'', \$x{\cdot}S) \\ &\Rightarrow (\Delta', e''[y{:=}x], S) \Rightarrow_b^* (\Delta, v, S).\end{aligned}$$

By induction, the first balanced execution yields $\Gamma : e' \Downarrow_{\#S} \Delta' : \lambda y.\, e''$, while the second yields $\Delta' : e''[y{:=}x] \Downarrow_{\#S} \Delta : v$, which, by APP, concludes this case.

Case: VAR_1
By an analogous decomposition using Lemma 15 we find $e = x$ and

$$\begin{aligned}(\Gamma, x, S) \Rightarrow (\Gamma \setminus \{x\}, e', \#x{\cdot}S) &\Rightarrow_b^* (\Delta', z, \#x{\cdot}S) \\ &\Rightarrow ((x \mapsto z, \Delta'), z, S) \Rightarrow_b^* (\Delta, v, S)\end{aligned}$$

with $(x \mapsto e') \in \Gamma$ and $\mathsf{isVal}\, z$.

The balanced execution $(x \mapsto z, \Delta', z, S) \Rightarrow_b^* (\Delta, v, S)$ is actually empty: With a value as the current execution, only rules APP_2, VAR_2 and IF_2 can apply. But these pop an element off the stack, so they cannot begin a balanced execution. Therefore, $\Delta = x \mapsto z, \Delta'$ and $z = v$.

Using the induction hypothesis on the other balanced sub-execution, we obtain $\Gamma \setminus \{x\} : e' \Downarrow_{\#S \cup \{x\}} \Delta' : v$ which, by VAR, concludes this case.

Case: IF$_1$
Starting as before, we find $e = e' \mathbin{?} e_{\mathbf{t}} : e_{\mathbf{f}}$ and

$$(\Gamma, e' \mathbin{?} e_{\mathbf{t}} : e_{\mathbf{f}}, S) \Rightarrow (\Gamma, e', (e_{\mathbf{t}} : e_{\mathbf{f}}) \cdot S) \Rightarrow_b^* (\Delta', \mathbf{C}_b, (e_{\mathbf{t}} : e_{\mathbf{f}}) \cdot S)$$
$$\Rightarrow (\Delta', e_b, S) \Rightarrow_b^* (\Delta, v, S).$$

Using the induction hypothesis on the two balanced sub-execution, we obtain $\Gamma : e' \Downarrow_{\#S} \Delta' : \mathbf{C}_b$ and $\Delta' : e_b \Downarrow_S \Delta : v$ which, by IFTHENELSE, conclude this case.

Case: LET$_1$
As this rule does not modify the stack, we have

$$(\Gamma, \textbf{let } \Delta' \textbf{ in } e', S) \Rightarrow ((\Delta', \Gamma), e', S) \Rightarrow_b^* (\Delta, v, S).$$

Using the induction hypothesis on the balanced sub-execution, we obtain $(\Delta', \Gamma) : e' \Downarrow_{\#S} \Delta : v$ which, by LET, concludes this case. ∎

2.5.3 Discussions of modifications

Sestoft's paper [Ses97] is already on the rigorous side and quite suitable to be brought into a machine-checkable form. One difference is, of course, due to my choice of nominal logic to implement name binding: While Sestoft's rule for **let** expressions renames the let-bound variables to fresh ones, as they enter the the heap, my rule LET$_1$ simply assumes them to already be fresh. Intuitively, this is equivalent, but the practical benefit of not having to push the renaming into the expressions by substitution is great.

Constructors

This section already includes the addition of Booleans and the **if-then-else**-construct to the language. Sestoft, following Launchbury, initially only has variables, application, lambda abstraction and mutually recursive **let**-bindings. As before, my addition is modular: One can simply ignore the extra case and obtain a formalisation of Sestoft's machine.

He introduces constructors and **case** expressions in a separate chapter of his paper. His constructors support parameters, but the design is equivalent to mine.

Fusing a proof

The definition of a balanced execution is the same as Sestoft's, and the proof of Lemma 16 follows his idea, but is structured differently. Sestoft first notices, by use of Lemma 15 and rule inversion on the small step rules, that every balanced execution is of one of these forms:

- It is empty.
- It is a sequence of rule APP_1 followed by a balanced execution, followed by APP_2, followed by another balanced execution.
- It is a sequence of rule VAR_1 followed by a balanced execution, followed by VAR_2.
- It is a sequence of rule IF_1 followed by a balanced execution, followed by IF_2, followed by another balanced execution.
- It is a sequence of rule LET_1 followed by a balanced execution.

This describes a (context-free) grammar of balanced executions, and his proof of Lemma 16 proceeds by induction on the productions of that grammar.

I could have followed this path by defining another predicate for balanced executions, as an inductively defined predicate following these rules, then proving that all balanced executions are contained in that grammar and finally performing the proof of Lemma 16 by induction on that predicate. But that would be considerably more work for little gain, as long as this grammar of balanced executions is not used again, so I chose to fuse[10] these two steps of the proof into one, by using the complete induction on the length of the execution and recovering the tree structure "on the fly" using Lemma 15.

[10] It is interesting to see that the ideas behind list fusion, i.e. fusing generators and consumers of inductive data types, carry over to transforming proofs so well. The Curry-Howard correspondence at its best.

2.6 The Isabelle formalisation

A distinguishing feature of this dissertation's treatment of Launchbury's and Sestoft's semantics is that I have implemented the definitions, theorems and proofs in the interactive theorem prover Isabelle [NPW02]. Nevertheless, I chose to write most of this thesis mostly in the classical style of hand-written mathematics, addressing the reader who is interested in my constructions, results and proofs and who, although happy to know that everything is machine-checked, is not interested in the Isabelle formalisation itself.

In contrast, the following section addresses the reader who also wonders how I implemented this in Isabelle, what techniques I used, and why. The section also serves as a map to find your way around the Isabelle theories, and draws the connection between the artefacts in the thesis and the Isabelle development.

2.6.1 Employing nominal logic

In Section 2.1, I introduce the syntax of the lambda calculus and state that I consider these to be equal up to alpha-conversion. In the Isabelle formalisation, I use the nominal package (cf. Section 1.6) to create a data type for expressions in my syntax:

Terms.thy

```
nominal_datatype exp =
  Var var
| App exp var
| LetA as::assn body::exp binds bn as in body as
| Lam x::var body::exp binds x in body  (Lam [_]. _ [100, 100] 100)
| Bool bool
| IfThenElse exp exp exp  (((_)/ ? (_)/ : (_)) [0, 0, 10] 10)
and assn =
  ANil | ACons var exp assn
binder
  bn :: assn ⇒ atom list
where bn ANil = [] | bn (ACons x t as) = (atom x) # (bn as)
```

The annotation **binds** indicates where in the syntax tree binders are, and what their scope is. The command **nominal_datatype** then takes care of constructing the data type with the desired equalities.

The command does not support nested recursion, so it is not possible to simply write

| *Let* Γ::((*var* × *exp*) *list*) *body*::*exp* **binds** *domA* Γ **in** *body* Γ

Instead, I have to effectively re-define the list type along with the expression type and simultaneously define the function that collects all the binders. Luckily, the resulting type *assn* is indeed isomorphic to (*var* × *exp*) *list*, so subsequently I define conversion functions between these two types and define the function *Let* with the desired type.

A definitory command such as **nominal_datatype** produces a number of definitions and lemmas, such as distinctness of constructors, size lemmas and induction rules. I re-state all of these in terms of *Let* instead of *LetA*, which is slightly tedious, but from then on I can use *Let* exclusively, including in function definitions and inductive proofs, just as if **nominal_datatype** supported nested recursion directly.

2.6.2 The type of environments

The type for environments used here is *var* ⇒ *Value*, as one would expect. But it was non-trivial to actually implement it this way, and an earlier version went a different route that, although eventually abandoned, is worth describing.

The defining equation for the semantics of lambda abstractions is

$$\llbracket\ \lambda x.\ e\ \rrbracket_{\varrho} = Fn\cdot(\Lambda\ v.\ \llbracket\ e\ \rrbracket_{\varrho(x\ :=\ v)}).$$

Note that the argument on the left hand side is the representative of an equivalence class (defined using the Nominal package), so this definition is only allowed if the right hand side is indeed independent of the actual choice of x. The **nominal_function** command requires the user to discharge that proof obligation before the function is actually defined.

This is shown most commonly and easily if x is fresh in all the other arguments ($x \notin fv\ \varrho$), and indeed the Nominal package allows me to specify this as a side condition to the defining equation, which is what I did in the first version of [Bre13].

But this convenience comes as a price: Such side-conditions are only allowed if the argument has finite support (otherwise there might be no variable fulfilling $x \notin fv\ \varrho$). More precisely: The type of the argument must be a member of the *fs* typeclass provided by the Nominal package (cf. Section 1.7.2). The type *var* $\Rightarrow$ *Value* cannot be made a member of this class, as there obviously are elements that have infinite support.

My fix – inspired by HOLCF's handling of continuity using a dedicated type – was to introduce a new type constructor, *fmap*, for partial functions with *finite* domain. This is fine: Only functions with finite domain matter in my formalisation.

The introduction of *fmap* had further consequences. The main type class of the HOLCF package, which we use to define domains and continuous functions on them, is the class *cpo* of chain-complete partial orders. With the usual ordering on partial functions, *(var, Value) fmap* cannot be a member of this class: As there is an infinite supply of variables, there exists a chain of partial functions of ever increasing domain, and the limit of that chain would necessarily have an infinite domain, and hence no longer is in *fmap*.

The fix here is to use a different ordering on *fmap* and only let elements be comparable that have the same domain. In my formalisation, the domain is always known (e.g. all variables bound on some heap), so this seemed to work out.

But not without causing yet another issue: With this ordering, *(var, Value) fmap* is a *cpo*, but lacks a bottom element, i.e. it is no longer an *pcpo*, and HOLCF's built-in operator $\mu\, x.\, f\, x$ for expressing least fixed points, as they occur in the semantics of heaps, is not available. Furthermore, $\sqcup$ is not a total function, as it is only defined if the arguments have the same domain. In the end, I had to define a rather convoluted set of theories that formalise functions that are continuous on a specific set, fixed points on such sets etc.

Eventually, I finished all proofs using that approach, but it amounted to an unreasonable amount of extra work and awkward proofs infested with statements about the domains of environments.

In a later refinement, I found a way to solve this problem much more elegantly. Using a small trick I defined the semantics functions so that

$$[\![\, \lambda x.\, e \,]\!]_{\varrho} = Fn\cdot(\Lambda\, v.\, [\![\, e \,]\!]_{\varrho(x := v)})$$

holds unconditionally. Technically, the definition is

$$[\![\, \lambda x.\, e \,]\!]_{\varrho} = Fn\cdot(\Lambda\, v.\, [\![\, e \,]\!]_{\varrho|_{fv\,(\lambda x.\, e)}(x := v)})$$

where the right-hand-side can be shown to be independent of the choice of x, as $x \notin fv\ (\lambda x.\ e)$. This definition can more easily be shown to be well-formed, and once the function is defined, $[\![\, e \,]\!]_{\varrho} = [\![\, e \,]\!]_{\varrho|_{fv\, e}}$ can be proved by induction. By using that lemma, I can prove the desired equation for $[\![\, \lambda x.\, e \,]\!]_{\varrho}$ as a lemma. The same trick is applied to the equation for let bindings.

This allows me to use the type $var \Rightarrow Value$ for the semantic environments and considerably simplifies the formalisation compared to the initial version of [Bre13].

2.6.3 Abstracting over the denotational semantics

I have defined two denotational semantics in this chapter: The standard semantics ($[\![e]\!]_{\rho}$, see Fig. 7) and the resourced denotational semantics ($\mathcal{N}[\![e]\!]_{\sigma}$, see Fig. 8). The definitions are quite similar, and a number of lemmas hold for both of them. Moreover, both definitions are mutually recursive with the definition of the respective heap semantics ($\{\!\{\Gamma\}\!\}\rho$ resp. $\mathcal{N}\{\!\{\Gamma\}\!\}\sigma$), which is defined identically in both cases. In the Isabelle theories, I therefore abstracted over the differences in order to define a generic semantics function once and instantiate it twice. Given the rather large and annoying proofs required for a function definition over nominal terms, this pays off.

I define the heap semantics within a locale that abstractly assumes the presence of some denotation function for some type of expressions:

```
locale has_ESem =                                                   HasESem.thy
  fixes ESem :: 'exp::pt ⇒ ('var::at_base ⇒ 'value) → 'value::{pure,pcpo}
```

At this point, the concrete type of expressions, variables and semantics values is left open (the initial apostrophe in *'value* denotes a type variable). No further assumptions about *ESem* are required to define the heap semantics, besides those encoded in the type of *ESem*:

- The expressions contain variables (*pt*, provided by the Nominal package, as explained in Section 1.7.2).
- The type of variables is a base value in terms of the Nominal package (*at_base*). In our setting, *var* is the only such type.
- The semantics is continuous in the environment (use of $\rightarrow$ instead of $\Rightarrow$, provided by the HOLCF package).
- The type of the semantic values is oblivious to names (type class *pure*, provided by the Nominal package) and it forms a pointed chain-complete partial order (type class *pcpo*, provided by the HOLCF package).

The former restriction on *'value* makes it easier to prove the functions to be equivariant, while the latter is a natural requirement for the fixed point based definition for the heap semantics, which is

definition HeapSemantics.thy
$HSem :: ('var \times 'exp)\ list \Rightarrow ('var \Rightarrow 'value) \rightarrow ('var \Rightarrow 'value)$
where $HSem\ \Gamma = (\Lambda\ \varrho\ .\ (\mu\ \varrho'.\ \varrho\ {+}{+}_{domA\ \Gamma}\ [\![\Gamma]\!]_{\varrho'}))$

The Isabelle command **definition** allows to define regular functions (type constructor $\Rightarrow$) by giving the parameters on the left, but it does not know anything about HOLCF's type of continuous functions (type constructor $\rightarrow$). Therefore, the second argument is consumed by a lambda-abstraction using HOLCF's continuous lambda operator Λ.

The two denotational semantics differ in the concrete domain (Value vs. (C $\rightarrow$ CValue)), and therefore the injection and deconstruction functions are different. Furthermore the resourced denotational semantics needs to keep track of the consumed resources. In order to abstractly define the semantics of expressions, I define a locale that provides these components:

locale *semantic_domain* = AbstractDenotational.thy
  fixes $Fn :: ('Value \to 'Value) \to ('Value::\{pcpo\_pt,pure\})$
  fixes $Fn\_project :: 'Value \to ('Value \to 'Value)$
  fixes $B :: bool\ discr \to 'Value$
  fixes $B\_project :: 'Value \to 'Value \to 'Value \to 'Value$
  fixes $tick :: 'Value \to 'Value$

The locale parameter *tick* is used to count the resources as they are consumed.

The type class *pcpo_pt* combines the classes *pcpo* (for pointed chain-complete partial orders) with *pt* (for types that may contain names), additionally ensuring that the permutation of names is continuous.

Within this locale, I define the abstract denotational semantics:

nominal_function
  $ESem :: exp \Rightarrow (var \Rightarrow 'Value) \to 'Value$
where
 $ESem\ (Lam\ [x].\ e) = (\Lambda\ \varrho.\ tick\cdot(Fn\cdot(\Lambda\ v.\ ESem\ e\cdot((\varrho\ f|`\ fv\ (Lam\ [x].\ e))(x := v)))))$
$|\ ESem\ (App\ e\ x) = (\Lambda\ \varrho.\ tick\cdot(Fn\_project\cdot(ESem\ e\cdot\varrho)\cdot(\varrho\ x)))$
$|\ ESem\ (Var\ x) = (\Lambda\ \varrho.\ tick\cdot(\varrho\ x))$
$|\ ESem\ (Let\ as\ body) = (\Lambda\ \varrho.\ tick\cdot(ESem\ body\cdot(has\_ESem.HSem\ ESem\ as\cdot(\varrho\ f|`\ fv\ (Let\ as\ body)))))$
$|\ ESem\ (Bool\ b) = (\Lambda\ \varrho.\ tick\cdot(B\cdot(Discr\ b)))$
$|\ ESem\ (scrut\ ?\ e1 : e2) = (\Lambda\ \varrho.\ tick\cdot((B\_project\cdot(ESem\ scrut\cdot\varrho))\cdot(ESem\ e1\cdot\varrho)\cdot(ESem\ e2\cdot\varrho)))$

Note that this definition has a non-trivial recursion pattern: It uses nested recursion via the heap semantics defined in the *has_ESem* locale, to which I therefore have to pass the expression semantics *ESem* – the very thing that I am defining here – as an argument.

From the abstract denotational semantics I can produce the concrete ones by *interpretation*, where the parameters of the locale are specified. For the standard denotational semantics, no resource accounting takes place, so the last parameter is the (continuous) identity:

Denotational.thy
interpretation *semantic_domain Fn Fn_project B B_project* $(\Lambda\ x.\ x)$.

The arguments to pass for the resourced denotational semantics are not simply the injection and deconstruction function themselves, as the resource argument needs to be passed along:

interpretation *semantic_domain* ResourcedDenotational.thy
$\Lambda f\ .\ \Lambda r.\ CFn\cdot(\Lambda v.\ (f\cdot(v))|_r)$
$\Lambda x\ y.\ (\Lambda r.\ (x\cdot r \downarrow CFn\ y|_r)\cdot r)$
$\Lambda b\ r.\ CB\cdot b$
$\Lambda\ scrut\ v1\ v2\ r.\ CB\_project\cdot(scrut\cdot r)\cdot(v1\cdot r)\cdot(v2\cdot r)$
C_case.

The case analysis function on C, which was produced by the HOLCF package when I defined the domain C, happens to have the right type *(C → 'a) → C → 'a* to serve as the *tick* argument to the locale.

In order to convince myself that despite all this abstraction and definitional detours, I have defined the semantics that I claim I have defined, I stated the equations as a lemma and proved them. For the standard denotational semantics, this reads:

lemma *ESem_simps*: Denotational.thy
$[\![\ Lam\ [x].\ e\ ]\!]_\varrho = Fn\cdot(\Lambda v.\ [\![\ e\ ]\!]_{\varrho(x := v)})$
$[\![\ App\ e\ x\ ]\!]_\varrho = [\![\ e\ ]\!]_\varrho \downarrow Fn\ \varrho\ x$
$[\![\ Var\ x\ ]\!]_\varrho = \varrho\ x$
$[\![\ Bool\ b\ ]\!]_\varrho = B\cdot(Discr\ b)$
$[\![\ (scrut\ ?\ e_1 : e_2)\ ]\!]_\varrho = B\_project\cdot([\![\ scrut\ ]\!]_\varrho)\cdot([\![\ e_1\ ]\!]_\varrho)\cdot([\![\ e_2\ ]\!]_\varrho)$
$[\![\ Let\ \Gamma\ body\ ]\!]_\varrho = [\![body]\!]_{\{\!|\Gamma|\!\}\varrho}$
by *simp_all*

2.6.4 Relating the domains Value and CValue

In order to relate the two denotational semantics, I defined the relation ⊲⊳ in Section 2.3.4, closely following the work of Sánchez-Gil *et al.* in [SHO11]. Their domain D corresponds to my Value, their domain E is my type C → CValue and A is CValue.

While Sánchez-Gil *et al.* construct their domain "by hand", by a series of domain approximations D_n resp. E_n, I can use Isabelle's HOLCF package to construct the domain directly from its domain equation (which already includes Booleans; as mentioned in Section 2.4.2 this addition is modular and can be ignored to obtain a formalisation closer to the work of Sánchez-Gil *et al.*).

domain *Value* = *Fn* (**lazy** *Value* → *Value*) | *B* (**lazy** *bool discr*) Value.thy

domain *CValue* CValue.thy
  = *CFn* (**lazy** (*C* → *CValue*) → (*C* → *CValue*))
  | *CB* (**lazy** *bool discr*)

In my formalisation, the approximations are just subsets of the full domain, and the *n-injection* $\phi_n^E\colon E_n \to E$ is the identity here.

The projections in [SHO11] correspond to the *take-functions* generated by the HOLCF package, which produce finite approximations of their arguments. For example, $\psi_n^D\colon E \to E_n$ becomes *Value_take* with type *nat* ⇒ *Value* → *Value*. The Isabelle theories introduce the former notation as abbreviations for the latter to better match the presentation in [SHO11].

Section 2.3 of [SHO11] contains the following two equations without proof:

$$\psi_n^E((e \downarrow_{\mathsf{CFn}} a)\, c) = (\psi_{n+1}^E(e) \downarrow_{\mathsf{CFn}} \psi_n^A(a))\, c \tag{2}$$

$$\psi_n^D(d \downarrow_{\mathsf{Fn}} d') = \psi_{n+1}^D(d) \downarrow_{\mathsf{Fn}} \psi_n^D(d') \tag{3}$$

Unfortunately, these equations do not hold in general. A counter-example to (3) can be given by

$$\begin{aligned} d &= \mathsf{Fn}(\lambda e.(e \downarrow_{\mathsf{Fn}} \bot)), \\ d' &= \mathsf{Fn}(\lambda\_.\mathsf{Fn}(\lambda\_.\bot)) \text{ and} \\ n &= 1. \end{aligned}$$

In this case, the left-hand-side of the equation simplifies to $\mathsf{Fn}(\lambda\_.\bot)$, while the right-hand-side is simply $\bot$. A counter-example to (2) can be constructed analogously.

The critical property of d' is that it is "two levels deep". On the left hand side, $d \downarrow_{\mathsf{Fn}} d'$ passes one argument to d' and hence returns a result that is one level deep, which goes through ψ_1^D unaltered, while on the right hand side, $\psi_1^D(d')$ cuts off the structure of d' after one level and returns $\mathsf{Fn}(\lambda\_.\bot)$.

Therefore, in order for the equation to hold, the argument to d on the left-hand needs to be at most one level deep. An extra invocation of ψ_n^D on the left hand side can ensure this:

$$\psi_n^D(d \downarrow_{\mathsf{Fn}} \psi_n^D(d')) = \psi_{n+1}^D(d) \downarrow_{\mathsf{Fn}} \psi_n^D(d')$$

This lemma can already be found in [AO93], equation 4.3.5 (1).

The problematic equations are used in the proof of the only-if direction of Proposition 9 in [SHO11]. I fixed this by applying take-induction, which inserts the extra call to ψ_n^D in the right spot and allows me to proceed using the fixed lemma.

2.7 Related work

A large number of developments on formal semantics of functional programming languages in the last two decades build on Launchbury's work; here is a short selection: Van Eekelen & de Mol [EM04] add strictness annotations to the syntax and semantics of Launchbury's work. Nakata & Hasegawa [NH09] define a small-step semantics for call-by-need and relate it to a Launchbury-derived big-step semantics. Nakata [Nak10] modifies the denotational semantics to distinguish direct cycles from looping recursion. Sánchez-Gil *et al.* [SHO10] extend Launchbury's semantics with distributed evaluation. Baker-Finch *et al.* [BKT00] create a semantics for parallel call-by-need based on Launchbury's.

While many of them implicitly or explicitly rely on the correctness and adequacy proof as spelled out by Launchbury, some stick with the original definition of the heap semantics using $\sqcup$, for which the proofs do not got through [EM04; NH09; SHO10; BKHT99], while others use right-sided updates, without further explanation [Nak10; BKT00]. The work by Baker-Finch *et al.* is particularly interesting, as they switched from the original to the fixed definition between the earlier tech report and the later ICFP publication, unfortunately without motivating that change.

Such disagreement about the precise definition of the semantics is annoying, as it creates avoidable incompatibilities between these publications. I hope that my fully rigorous treatment will resolve this confusion and allows future work to standardise on the "right" definition.

Furthermore, none of these works discuss the holes in Launchbury's adequacy proof, even those that explicitly state the adequacy of their extended semantics. My adequacy proof is better suited for such extensions, as it is rigorous and furthermore avoids the intermediate natural semantics.

This list is just a small collection of many more Launchbury-like semantics. Often the relation to a denotational semantics is not stated, but nevertheless they are standing on the foundations laid by Launchbury. Therefore, it is not surprising that others have worked on formally fortifying these foundations as well:

In particular Sánchez-Gil *et al.* worked towards rigorously proving Launchbury's semantics correct and adequate. They noted that the relation between the standard and the resourced denotational semantics is not as trivial as it seemed at first, and worked out a detailed pen-and-paper proof [SHO11]. I have formalised this, fixing mistakes in the proof, and build on their result here (Lemma 12).

They also bridged half the gap between Launchbury's natural and alternative natural semantics [SHO15], and plan to bridge the other half. I avoided these very tedious proofs by bridging the difference on the denotational side (Section 2.3.6).

As a step towards a mechanisation of their work in Coq, they address the naming issues and suggest a mixed representation, using de Bruijn indices for locally bound variables and names for free variables [SHO12]. This approach corresponds to my treatment of names in the formal development, using the Nominal logic machinery [UK12] locally but not for names bound in heaps, and can be found in other formalisation works as well [PB10].

The aim of this development is to be able to formally prove properties of the language or the compiler, but not so much to prove individual functional programs to be correct; there are better ways to do that. In the context of using Isabelle to prove properties of Haskell programs, noteworthy approaches include Haskabelle [RH15], which transforms Haskell code into Isabelle code, but punts on issues of laziness; Isabelle's code generation facilities [Haf09], which go the other way; and HOLCF-Prelude [BHMS13], which models Haskell's lazy semantics, albeit without observable sharing, using HOLCF function definitions in Isabelle.

The problem with Haskell is that it's a language built on lazy evaluation and nobody's actually called for it.

Randall Munroe, xkcd #1312

CHAPTER 3

Call Arity

After more than two decades of development of Haskell compilers, one has become slightly spoiled by the quality and power of optimisations performed by the compiler. For example, list fusion allows us to write concise and easy to understand code using combinators and list comprehensions and still get the efficiency of a tight loop that avoids allocating the intermediate lists.

Unfortunately, not all list-processing functions used to take part in list fusion. In particular, before my work, left folds like foldl, foldl', length and derived functions like sum were not fusing, and an expression like sum (filter f [42..2016]) still allocated and traversed one list.

The issue is that in order to take part in list fusion, these need to be expressed as right folds, which requires higher-order parameters as in

$$\mathsf{foldl}\ k\ z\ xs = \mathsf{foldr}\ (\lambda v\ fn\ z \rightarrow fn\ (k\ z\ v))\ id\ xs\ z.$$

The resulting fused code would be allocating and calling function closures on the heap, causing the final program to run too slowly (see Section 1.4.3).

Already Andrew Gill noted that eta-expansion based on an arity analysis would help here [Gil96]. Previous arity analyses, however, are not precise enough to allow for a fusing foldl.

```
let tA = if f a then ... else ...
in let goA x = if f (tB + x) then goA (x+1) else x
       tB    = let goB y = if f y then goB (goA y) else tA
               in goB 0 1
  in goA (goA 1)
```

Figure 11: Is it safe to eta-expand tA?

Why is this so hard? Consider the slightly contrived example in Fig. 11: Our goal is to eta-expand the definition of tA. For that, we need to ensure that it is always called with one argument, which is not obvious: Syntactically, the only use of tA is in goB, and there it occurs without an argument. But we see that goB is initially called with two arguments, and under that assumption calls itself with two arguments as well, and it therefore always calls tA with one argument – done.

But tA is a thunk – i.e. not in head normal form – and even if there are many calls to tA, the call to f a is only evaluated once. If we were to eta-expand tA we would be duplicating that possibly expensive work! So we are only allowed to eta-expand tA if we know that it is called at most once. This is tricky: tA is called from a recursive function goB, which itself is called from the mutual recursion consisting of goA and tB, and that recursion is started multiple times!

Nevertheless we know that tA is evaluated at most once: tB is a thunk, so although it will be called multiple times by the outer recursion, its right-hand side is only evaluated once. Furthermore, the recursion involving goB is started once and stops when the call to tA happens. Together, this implies that we are allowed to eta-expand tA without losing any work.

I have developed an analysis, dubbed *Call Arity*, that is capable of this reasoning and correctly detects that tA can be eta-expanded. It is a combination of a standard forward call arity analysis ([Gil96], [XP05]) with a novel cardinality analysis, dubbed *co-call analysis*. The latter determines for an expression and two variables whether one evaluation of the expression can possibly call both variables and – as a special case

– which variables it calls at most once. I found that this is just the right amount of information to handle tricky cases as those in Fig. 11.

In this chapter, which is based on the work that I presented at the Trends in Functional Programming conference in 2014 [Bre15a], I approach the analysis from the practical, empirical side. Section 3.1 motivates the need for and the design of the Call Arity analysis. The following two sections describe the co-call graph data structure that is central to the analysis (Section 3.2) and the analysis itself (Section 3.3). Section 3.4 describes a few aspects of the implementation (which is reproduced in its entirety in Appendix B.2). Finally, Section 3.5 discusses the analysis and quantifies the performance improvements. Notes on related and future work follow.

3.1 The need for co-call analysis

The main contribution of this chapter is the description of the co-call cardinality analysis and its importance for arity analysis. I want to motivate the analysis based on a sequence of ever more complicated arity analysis puzzles.

3.1.1 A syntactical analysis

The simplest such puzzle is the following code, where a function is defined as taking one argument, but always called with two arguments:

let f x = . . .
in f 1 2 + f 3 4.

Are we allowed to eta-expand f by another argument? Yes! How would we find out about it? We would analyse each expression of the syntax tree and ask

> "For each free variable, what is a lower bound on the number of arguments passed to it?"

This will tell us that f is always called with two arguments, so we eta-expand it.

3.1.2 Incoming arity

Here is a slightly more difficult puzzle:

```
let f x = ...
    g y = f (y+1)
in g 1 2 + g 3 4.
```

Are we still allowed to eta-expand f? The previous syntactic approach fails, as the right-hand side of g mentions f with only one argument. However, g itself can be eta-expanded, and once that is done we would see that g's right hand side is called with one argument more. We could run the previous analysis, simplify the code, and run the analysis once more, but we can do better by asking, for every expression:

> "If this expression is called with n arguments, for each free variable, what is a lower bound on the number of arguments passed to it?"

The body of the **let** will report to call g with two arguments. The pattern on the left-hand side of the definition of g consumes one of them, so we can analyse the right-hand side with an *incoming arity* of 1, and thus find out that f is always called with two arguments.

For recursive functions this is more powerful than just running the simpler variant multiple times. Consider

```
let f x = . . .
    g y = if y > 10 then f y else g (y + 1)
in g 1 2 + g 3 4.
```

A purely syntactical approach will never be able to eta-expand g or f. But by assuming an incoming arity we can handle the recursive case: The body of the **let** reports that g is called with two arguments. We initially assume that to be true for all calls to g. Next we analyse the right-hand side of g and will learn – under our assumption – that it calls g with two arguments, too, so our assumption was justified and we can proceed.

Of course, it may well be that the assumption is refuted by analysing the definition of the recursive function:

```
let f x = ...
    g y = if y > 10 then f y else foo (g (y+1))
in g 1 2 + g 3 4.
```

The body still reports that it calls g with two arguments, but – even under that assumption – the right-hand side of g calls g with only one argument. So we have to re-analyse g with one argument, which in turn calls f with one argument and no eta-expansion is possible here.

This corresponds to the analysis outlined in [Gil96].

3.1.3 Called-once information

So far we have only eta-expanded functions; for these the final analysis in the previous section is sufficient. But there is also the case of *thunks*: If the expression bound to a variable x is not in head-normal form, i.e. the outermost syntactic construct is a function call, case expression or let-binding, but not a lambda abstraction or constructor, then that expression is evaluated upon its first call, and the result is shared with further calls to x.

If we were to eta-expand the expression, though, the expensive operation is hidden under a lambda and will be evaluated for every call to x. Therefore, it is crucial that thunks are only eta-expanded if they are going to be called at most once. So we need to distinguish the situation

```
let t = foo x
in if x then t 1 else t 2.
```

where t is called at most once and eta-expansion is allowed, from

```
let t = foo x
in t 1 + t 2.
```

where t is called multiple times and must not be eta-expanded.

An analysis that could help us here would be answering this question:

> "If this expression is called once with n arguments, for each free variable, what is a lower bound on the number of arguments passed to it, and are we calling it at most once?"

In the first example, both branches of the **if** would report to call t only once (with one argument), so the whole body of the **let** calls t only once and we can eta-expand t. In the second example the two subexpressions t 1 and t 2 are both going to be evaluated. Combined they call t twice and we cannot eta-expand t.

3.1.4 Mutually exclusive calls

What can we say in the case of a thunk that is called from within a recursion, like in the following code?

```
let t = foo x
in let g y = if y > 10 then t else g (y+1)
   in g 1 2
```

Clearly t is called at most once, but the current state of the analysis does not see that: The right-hand side of g reports to call t and g at most once. But

```
let t = foo x
in let g y = if y > 10 then id else g (t y)
   in g 1 2
```

would yield the same result, although t is called many times!

How can we extend our analysis to distinguish these two cases? The crucial difference is that in the first code, g calls *either* t *or* g, while the second one calls both of them together. So we would like to know, for each expression:

> "If this expression is called once with n arguments, for each free variable, what is a lower bound on the number of arguments passed to it? Additionally, what set of variables is called mutually exclusively and at most once?"

In the first example, the right-hand side would report to call $\{t, g\}$ mutually exclusively and this allows us to see that the call to t does not lie on the recursive path, so there will be at most one call to t in every run of the recursion. We also need the information that the body of the **let** (which reports $\{g\}$) and the right-hand side of g both call g at most once; if the recursion were started multiple times, or were not linear, then we would get many calls to t as well.

3.1.5 Co-call analysis

The final puzzle in this sequence is the code

```
let t1 = foo x
in let g x = if x > 10
             then t1
             else let t2 = bar x
                  in let h y = if y > 10
                               then g (t2 y)
                               else h (y+1)
                     in h 1 x
   in g 1 2
```

which shows the shortcomings of the previous iteration and the strength of the actual co-call analysis.

Note that both recursions are well-behaved: They are entered once and each recursive function calls either itself once or calls the thunk t1 resp. t2 once. So we would like to see both t1 and t2 eta-expanded. Unfortunately, with the analysis above, we can only get one of them.

The problematic subexpression is g (t2 y): We need to know that g is called at most once *and* that t2 is called at most once. But we cannot return $\{g, t2\}$ as that is a lie – they are not mutually exclusive – and the best we can do is to arbitrarily return either $\{g\}$ or $\{t2\}$.

To avoid this dilemma we extend the analysis one last time, in order to preserve all valuable information.

We now ask, for each expression:

> "If this expression is called once with n arguments, for each free variable, what is a lower bound on the number of arguments passed to it, and for each pair of free variables, can both be called during the same execution of the expression?"

The latter tells us, as a special case, whether one variable may be called multiple times.

For the problematic expression g (t2 y) we would find that g might be called together with t2, but neither of them is called twice. For the right-hand side of h the analysis would tell us that either h is called at most once and on its own, or g and t2 are called together, but each at most once. The whole inner **let** therefore calls t2 and g at most once, so we get to eta-expand t2 and learn that the outer recursion is well-behaved.

3.2 The type of co-call graphs

This information – i.e. which pairs of variables can both be called during the same execution – can be represented by a graph on the set of variables. These graphs are undirected, non-transitive and can have loops. I denote the set of such graphs with Graph, and the intuition is that

- only the nodes of G (denoted by $\operatorname{dom} G$) are called, and that
- an edge x—$y \in G$ indicates that x and y can be called together, while the absence of an edge guarantees that calls to x resp. y are mutually exclusive.

In particular, the absence of a loop, i.e. x—$x \in G$, implies that x is called at most once.

Example
Consider the three graphs

$$\begin{aligned} G_1 &= x \text{—} y, \\ G_2 &= x \text{—} y \circlearrowright, \text{ and} \\ G_3 &= x \quad y \circlearrowright. \end{aligned}$$

The first graph allows at most one call to y and at most one call to x, both of which can occur together. In contrast, the graph G_2 allows any number of calls to y, together with at most one call to x, while G_3 describes that any execution performs *either* at most one call to x *or* any number of calls to y. ◇

I often identify the graphs with their set of edges, e.g. in the definition of the Cartesian product of two sets of variables, which is

$$V \times V' := \{x—y \mid x \in V \wedge y \in V' \vee y \in V \wedge x \in V'\},$$

and specify its set of nodes separately – which in this case is given by $\mathsf{dom}\,(V \times V') := \mathsf{dom}\,V \cup \mathsf{dom}\,V'$.

I write $V^2 := V \times V$ for the complete graph on the variables in the set V.

The set of neighbours of a variable is $N_x(G) := \{y \mid x—y \in G\}$. The graph $G \setminus V$ is G with nodes in V removed, while $G|_V$ is G with only nodes in V retained.

The graphs are obviously partially ordered by inclusion, i.e.

$$G \sqsubseteq G' \iff \mathsf{dom}\,G \subseteq \mathsf{dom}\,G' \wedge G \subseteq G',$$

with the empty graph $\{\}$ being the least element.

3.3 The Call Arity analysis

Thus having motivated the need for a co-call-based analysis in order to get a precise arity analysis, I devote this section to a formal description of it. I build on the syntax introduced in Section 2.1, allowing expressions as arguments in function calls.

3.3.1 The specification

The goal of the analysis is to determine the *call arity* of every variable x. As defined in Section 1.5, this is a natural number α_x indicating that the compiler can replace a binding **let** $x = e$ with **let** $x = \lambda z_1 \ldots z_\alpha . e\ z_1 \ldots z_\alpha$ without losing any sharing.

The bottom-up analysis considers each expression e under the assumption of an *incoming arity* α – which is the number of arguments the expression is currently being applied to – and determines with at least how many arguments e calls its free variables, and which free variables can be called together.

Separating these two aspects into two functions, we have

$$\mathcal{A}_\alpha \colon \mathsf{Exp} \to (\mathsf{Var} \rightharpoonup \mathbb{N}) \qquad \text{arity analysis}$$
$$\mathcal{G}_\alpha \colon \mathsf{Exp} \to \mathsf{Graph} \qquad \text{co-call analysis}$$

where $\rightharpoonup$ denotes a partial map and Graph is the type of undirected graphs (with self-edges) over the set of variables.

The informal specifications for $\mathcal{A}_\alpha$ and $\mathcal{G}_\alpha$ are

- If $\mathcal{A}_\alpha(e)\,x = m$, then every call from e (applied to α arguments) to x passes at least m arguments.
- If x_1 and x_2 are not adjacent in $\mathcal{G}_\alpha(e)$, then no execution of e (applied to α arguments) will call both x_1 and x_2. In particular, if x—$x \notin \mathcal{G}_\alpha(e)$, then x will be called at most once.

We can define a partial order on the results that expresses the notion of precision: If x is correct and $x \sqsubseteq y$, then y is also correct, but possibly less precise.

In particular for $A, A' \colon (\mathsf{Var} \rightharpoonup \mathbb{N})$ we have

$$A \sqsubseteq A' \iff \forall x \in \mathsf{dom}\,(A).\, A\,x \geq A'\,x$$

(note the contravariance), because it is always safe to assume that x is called with fewer arguments.

The partial order on Graph introduced in Section 3.2 is also compatible with this notion of precision: If we have $G \sqsubseteq G'$, then every behaviour that is allowed by G is also allowed by G', as it is always safe to pessimistically assume that any two variables are called together, or to assume that one variable is called multiple times.

Thus the always correct and least useful analysis result maps every variable to 0 (making no statements about the number of arguments passed to them), and returns the complete graph on all variables as the co-call graph (allowing everything to be called with everything else).

The bottom of the lattice, i.e. the best information, is the empty map and the empty graph. This is the analysis result we expect for closed values such as $(\lambda y.\, y)$ or $\mathbf{C_t}$.

$$
\begin{aligned}
\mathcal{A}_\alpha(x) &= [x \mapsto \alpha] \\
\mathcal{G}_\alpha(x) &= x \\
\mathcal{A}_\alpha(e_1\ e_2) &= \mathcal{A}_{\alpha+1}(e_1) \sqcup \mathcal{A}_0(e_2) \\
\mathcal{G}_\alpha(e_1\ e_2) &= \begin{cases} \mathcal{G}_{\alpha+1}(e_1) \sqcup \{x\}^2 \sqcup \mathsf{fv}(e_1) \times \{x\} & \text{if } e_2 = x \\ \mathcal{G}_{\alpha+1}(e_1) \sqcup \mathcal{G}_0(e_2) \sqcup \mathsf{fv}(e_1) \times \mathsf{fv}(e_2) & \text{otherwise} \end{cases} \\
\mathcal{A}_0(\lambda x.\, e) &= \mathcal{A}_0(e) \\
\mathcal{A}_{\alpha+1}(\lambda x.\, e) &= \mathcal{A}_\alpha(e) \\
\mathcal{G}_0(\lambda x.\, e) &= (\mathsf{fv}\, e)^2 \\
\mathcal{G}_{\alpha+1}(\lambda x.\, e) &= \mathcal{G}_\alpha(e) \\
\mathcal{A}_\alpha(e\,\mathbf{?}\,e_1 : e_2) &= \mathcal{A}_0(e) \sqcup \mathcal{A}_\alpha(e_1) \sqcup \mathcal{A}_\alpha(e_2) \\
\mathcal{G}_\alpha(e\,\mathbf{?}\,e_1 : e_2) &= \mathcal{G}_0(e) \sqcup \mathcal{G}_\alpha(e_1) \sqcup \mathcal{G}_\alpha(e_2) \sqcup \mathsf{fv}\, e \times (\mathsf{fv}(e_1) \cup \mathsf{fv}(e_2))
\end{aligned}
$$

Figure 12: The Call Arity analysis equations

3.3.2 The equations

From the specification we can derive equations for every syntactical construct, given in Figs. 12, 13 and 14.

Note that from the above definition of $\sqsubseteq$, the least upper bound of two arity analysis results $A, A' \in (\mathsf{Var} \rightharpoonup \mathbb{N})$ is the pointwise minimum.

Case 1: Variables

Evaluating a variable with an incoming arity of α yields a call to that variable with α arguments, so the arity analysis returns a singleton map. Because we are interested in the effect of *one* evaluation, we return x as called at-most once, i.e. the graph has the node x, but no edges.

Case 2: Application

In this case, the incoming arity is adjusted: If $e_1\ e_2$ is being called with α arguments, then e_1 is called with $\alpha + 1$ arguments. On the other hand we do not know how many arguments e_2 is called with – this analysis is not higher order (see Section 3.6.2) – so we analyse it with an incoming arity of 0.

The co-call analysis reports all possible co-calls from both e_1 and e_2. Additionally, it reports that everything that may be called by e_1 can be called together with everything called by e_2.

In the evaluation of a Core program, an argument to a function is shared and thus evaluated only once. Therefore, the co-call information in $\mathcal{G}_0(e_2)$ can be used as is. There is, however, an exception: If the argument is trivial, i.e. a variable x, the Core-to-STG transformation does not introduce an explicit binding for the argument, and no sharing happens at this point. So if e_1 uses its argument more than once, x will itself be called multiple times. Hence the analysis pessimistically includes $\{x\}^2$ in the result. This corner case was not handled in an earlier version of Call Arity, see Section 4.5.2 for a discussion of this bug.

Case 3: Lambda abstraction

For lambda abstractions, we have to distinguish two cases. The good case is if the incoming arity is nonzero, i.e. we want to know the behaviour of the expression when applied once to some arguments. In that case, we know that the body is evaluated once, applied to one argument less, and the co-call information from the body can be used directly.

If the incoming arity is zero we have to assume that the lambda abstraction is used as-is, for example as a parameter to a higher-order function, or stored in a data type. In particular, it is possible that it is going to be called multiple times. So while the incoming arity on the body of the lambda stays zero (which is always correct), we cannot obtain any useful co-call results and have to assume that every variable mentioned in e is called with every other.

Naturally, there is no point in passing arity or co-call information about the abstracted variable out of its scope. In the interest of a concise presentation, this is not explicated in Fig. 12. Section 4.3.4 contains a more pedantic formal presentation.

Example
The expression $e = \lambda x.\,(x_0\,\textbf{?}\,x_1 : x_2)$ will, when analysed with an incoming arity of 1 resp. 0 yield

$\mathcal{G}_1(e) =$ 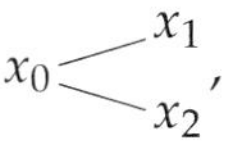 , resp. $\mathcal{G}_0(e) =$ 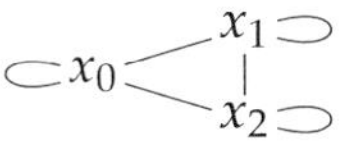 . ◇

Case 4: Case analysis

The arity analysis of a case expression is straightforward: The incoming arity is fed into each of the alternatives, while the scrutinee is analysed with an incoming arity of zero; the results are combined using $\sqcup$.

The co-call analysis proceeds likewise. Furthermore, extra co-call edges are added, connecting everything that may be called by the scrutinee with everything that may be called in the alternatives – analogous to analysing applications.

This may be an over-approximation: The analysis will yield

$\mathcal{G}_0((z\,\textbf{?}\,x_1 : x_2)(z\,\textbf{?}\,x_3 : x_4)) =$ 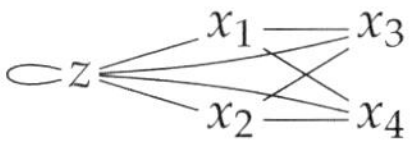

which contains the edge x_1—x_4, although x_1 cannot be called together with x_4 (and analogously for x_2—x_3), as the conditionals will choose the same branch in both cases.

Case 5: Non-recursive let

This case is slightly more complicated than the previous, so we describe it in multiple equations in Fig. 13.

We analyse the body of the let-expression first, using the incoming arity of the whole expression. Based on that we determine our main analysis result, the call arity of the variable. There are two cases:

1. If the right-hand side expression e_1 is a thunk and the body of the **let** may possibly call it twice, i.e. there is a self-loop in the co-call graph, then there is a risk of losing work when eta-expanding e_1, so we do not do that.

$$\alpha_x = \begin{cases} 0 & \text{if } x\text{—}x \in \mathcal{G}_\alpha(e_2) \text{ and } \neg\mathsf{isVal}(e_1) \\ \mathcal{A}_\alpha(e_2)\,x & \text{otherwise} \end{cases}$$

$$G_{\text{rhs}} = \begin{cases} \mathcal{G}_{\alpha_x}(e_1) & \text{if } x\text{—}x \notin \mathcal{G}_\alpha(e_2) \text{ or } \alpha_x = 0 \\ \mathsf{fv}(e_1)^2 & \text{otherwise} \end{cases}$$

$$E = \mathsf{fv}(e_1) \times N_x(\mathcal{G}_\alpha(e_2))$$

$$A = \mathcal{A}_{\alpha_x}(e_1) \sqcup \mathcal{A}_\alpha(e_2)$$

$$G = G_{\text{rhs}} \sqcup \mathcal{G}_\alpha(e_2) \sqcup E$$

$$\mathcal{A}_\alpha(\textbf{let } x = e_1 \textbf{ in } e_2) = A \qquad \mathcal{G}_\alpha(\textbf{let } x = e_1 \textbf{ in } e_2) = G$$

Figure 13: Equations for a non-recursive **let** $x = e_1$ **in** e_2

2. Otherwise, the call arity is the minimum number of arguments passed to x by the code in e_2, as reported by $\mathcal{A}_\alpha(e_2)$.

Depending on this result we need to adjust the co-call information obtained from e_1. Again, there are two cases:

1. We can use the co-call graph from e_1 if e_1 is evaluated at most once. This is obviously the case if x is called at most once in the first place. It is also the case if e_1 is (and stays!) a thunk, because its result will be shared and further calls to x can be ignored here.

2. If e_1 may be evaluated multiple times we cannot get useful co-call information and therefore return the complete graph on everything that is possibly called by e_1.

Finally we combine the results from the body and the right-hand side, and add the appropriate extra co-call edges. We can be more precise than in the application case because we can exclude variables that are not called together with x from the complete bipartite graph.

Note again that we do not clutter the presentation here with removing the local variable from the final analysis results. The implementation removes x from A and G before returning them.

Example
Consider the expression

$$e = \textbf{let } z = (x \,?(\lambda y.\, x_2) : x_3) \textbf{ in } \lambda\_.\,(x_1 \,?\, x_2 : z\ y)$$

with an incoming arity of 1. The co-call graph of the body is

$$\mathcal{G}_1(\lambda\_.\,(x_1 \,?\, x_2 : z\ y)) =$$ 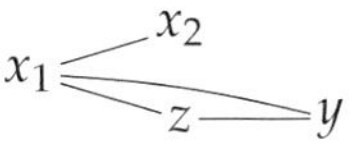

and $\mathcal{A}_1(\lambda\_.\,(x_1 \,?\, x_2 : z\ y))\,z = 1$. The right-hand side of z's definition is a thunk, so we must be careful when eta-expanding it. But there is no self-loop at z in the graph, so z is called at most once. The call-arity of z is thus $\alpha_z = 1$ and we analyse its right-hand side with an incoming arity of 1 to obtain

$$\mathcal{G}_1(x \,?(\lambda y.\, x_2) : x_3) =$$ 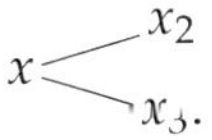

The additional edges E connect all free variables of the right-hand side ($\{x, x_2, x_3\}$) with everything called together with z from the body ($\{x_1, y\}$) and the overall result (skipping the now out-of-scope z) is

$$\mathcal{G}_1(e) =$$ 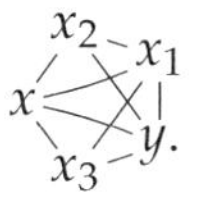

Note that although x_2 occurs in both the body and the right-hand side, there is no self-loop at x_2: The analysis has detected that x_2 is called at most once.

The results are very different if we analyse e with an incoming arity of 0. The body is a lambda abstraction, so it may be called many times, and we have

$$\mathcal{G}_0(\lambda\_.\,(x_1 \,?\, x_2 : z\ y)) =$$ 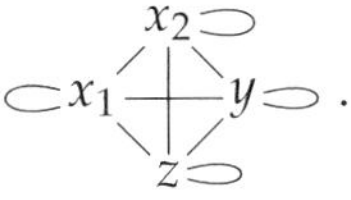

This time there is a self-loop at z, and we need to set $\alpha_z = 0$ to be on the safe side. This also means that z stays a thunk and we still get some useful information from the right-hand side:

$$\mathcal{G}_0(x\,?(\lambda\_.\,x_2):x_3) =$$ 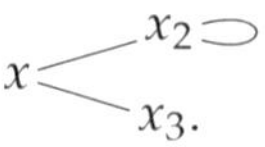

Due to the lower incoming arity we can no longer rule out that x_2 is called multiple times, as it is hidden inside a lambda abstraction. The final graph now becomes quite large, because everything in the body is potentially called together with z:

$$\mathcal{G}_0(e) =$$ 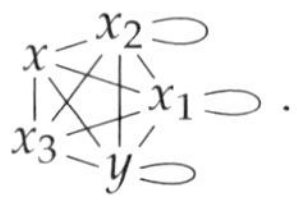

This is almost the complete graph, but it is still possible to derive that x and x_3 are called at most once. ◇

Case 6: Recursive let

The final case, described in Fig. 14, is the most complicated. It is also the reason why the figures are labelled "Equations" and not "Definitions": They are also mutually recursive and it is the task of the implementation to find a suitable solution strategy (see Section 3.4.2).

The complication arises from the fact that the result of the analysis affects its parameters: If the right-hand side of a variable calls itself with a lower arity than the body, we need to use the lower arity as the call arity. Therefore, the final result (A and G in the equations) is also used to determine the basis for the call-arity and co-call information of the variables.

Thunks aside, we can think of one recursive binding **let** $x = e_1$ **in** e_2 as an arbitrarily large number of nested non-recursive bindings

let $x = e_1$
in let $x = e_1$
  in let $x = e_1$
    in
      ⋱ **let** $x = e_1$
        in e_2.

The co-call information G can be thought of the co-call information of this expression, and this is how x_i—$x_i \notin G$ has to interpreted: Not that there is at most one call to x_i in the whole recursion (there probably are many, why else would there be a recursive **let**), but rather that when doing such an unrolling of the recursion, there is at most one call to x_i leaving the scope of the outermost non-recursive **let**.

This analogy is flawed for thunks, where multiple nested non-recursive bindings would have a different sharing behaviour. Therefore, I set $\alpha_{x_i} = 0$ for all thunks in a recursive **let**; this preserves sharing.

The formulas for the additional co-calls E^i are a bit more complicated than in the non-recursive case, and differ for thunks and non-thunks. Consider one execution that reaches a call to x_i. What other variables might have been called on the way? If the call came directly from the body e, then we need to consider everything that is adjacent to x_i in $\mathcal{G}_\alpha(e)$. But it is also possible that the body has called some other x_j, $j \neq i$ and e_j then has called x_i – in that case, we need to take those variables adjacent to x_j in $\mathcal{G}_\alpha(e)$ and those adjacent to x_i in G^j.

$$A = \mathcal{A}_\alpha(e) \sqcup \bigsqcup_i \mathcal{A}_{\alpha_{x_i}}(e_1)$$

$$G = \mathcal{G}_\alpha(e) \sqcup \bigsqcup_i G^i \sqcup \bigsqcup_i E^i$$

$$\alpha_{x_i} = \begin{cases} 0 & \text{if } \neg\mathsf{isVal}(e_i) \\ A\, x_i & \text{otherwise} \end{cases}$$

$$G^i = \begin{cases} \mathcal{G}_{\alpha_{x_i}}(e_i) & \text{if } x_i \text{—} x_i \notin G \text{ or } \alpha_{x_i} = 0 \\ \mathsf{fv}(e_i)^2 & \text{otherwise} \end{cases}$$

$$E^i = \begin{cases} \mathsf{fv}(e_i) \times N(\mathcal{G}_\alpha(e) \sqcup \bigsqcup_j G^j) & \text{if } \alpha_{x_i} \neq 0 \\ \mathsf{fv}(e_i) \times N(\mathcal{G}_\alpha(e) \sqcup \bigsqcup_{j \neq i} G^j) & \text{if } \alpha_{x_i} = 0 \end{cases}$$

$$N(G) = \{z \mid z\text{—}x_i \in G, i = 1\ldots\}$$

$$\mathcal{A}_\alpha(\textbf{let}\ \overline{x_i = e_i}\ \textbf{in}\ e) = A \qquad \mathcal{G}_\alpha(\textbf{let}\ \overline{x_i = e_i}\ \textbf{in}\ e) = G$$

Figure 14: Equations for a recursive **let** $\overline{x_i = e_i}$ **in** e

In general, every call that can occur together with any recursive call in any of the expressions can occur together with whatever x_i does.

For a thunk we can get slightly better information: A non-thunk e_i can be evaluated multiple times during the recursion, so its free variables can be called together with variables on e_i's own recursive path. A thunk, however, is evaluated at most once, even in a recursive group, so for the calculation of additional co-call edges it is sufficient to consider only the *other* right-hand sides (and the body of the **let**, of course).

Example
Consider the expression

$$\begin{aligned} \textbf{let}\ x_1 &= \lambda y.\,(y_1\ \textbf{?}\ x_2\ y : z_1) \\ x_2 &= \lambda y.\,(y_2\ \textbf{?}\ x_1\ y : z_2) \\ \textbf{in}\ \lambda y.\,& x_1\ y\ y \end{aligned}$$

with an incoming arity of 1. It is an example for a nice tail-call recursion as it is commonly produced by list fusion: The body has one call into the recursive group, and each function in the group also calls at most one of them.

The minimal solution to the equations in Fig. 14 in this example is

$$\begin{aligned} \mathcal{G}_1(e) &= \{\} \\ \alpha_{x_1} = \alpha_{x_2} &= 2 \\ G^1 = \mathcal{G}_2(e_1) &= \{y_1\} \times \{x_2, z_1\} \\ G^2 = \mathcal{G}_2(e_2) &= \{y_2\} \times \{x_1, z_2\} \\ E^1 &= \{y_1, x_2, z_1\} \times \{y_1, y_2\} \\ E^2 &= \{y_2, x_1, z_2\} \times \{y_1, y_2\} \end{aligned}$$

and the final result is

$G =$ 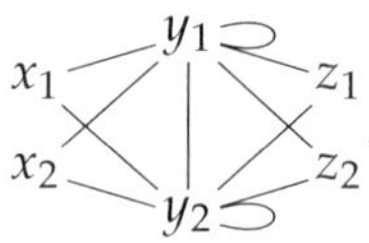 , where we see that at most one of z_1 and z_2 is called by the recursive group, and neither of them twice.

In contrast consider this recursion which forks in x_2:

$$\begin{aligned}\textbf{let } x_1 &= \lambda y.\, (y_1 \mathbin{?} x_2\, y : z_1)\\ x_2 &= \lambda y.\, (y_2 \mathbin{?} x_1\, (x_1\, y\, y) : z_2)\\ \textbf{in } &\lambda y.\, x_1\, y\, y.\end{aligned}$$

We see that now z_1 and z_2 are possibly called together and multiple times. Indeed x_1—$x_1 \in \mathcal{G}_2(e_2)$ causes $x_1 \in N(\ldots)$ in the equation for E^i, so especially x_1—$x_1 \in E^2 \subseteq G$. Therefore, $G^1 = \mathsf{fv}(e_1)^2$ and we also have x_2—$x_2 \in G$ and $G^2 = \mathsf{fv}(e_2)^2$. Eventually, we find that the result is the complete graph on all variables, i.e. $E = \{x_1, x_2, y_1, y_2, z_1, z_2\}^2$, and in particular z_1—$z_2 \in E$, as expected. ◇

3.4 The implementation

This section is of primary interest to those readers who want to understand the implementation of Call Arity in GHC. I explain some of the design choices and how the the code relates to the definitions in this thesis.

The Call Arity analysis is implemented in GHC as a separate Core-to-Core pass, where Core is GHC's typed intermediate language based on System F_C (cf. Section 1.4.1). See Appendix B.2 for the code of the analysis.

This pass does not actually do the eta-expansion; it merely annotates let-bound variables with their call arity. A subsequent pass of GHC's simplifier then performs the expansion, using the same code as for the regular, definition-based arity analysis, and immediately applies optimisations made possible by the eta-expansion. This separation of concerns keeps the Call Arity implementation concise and close to the formalisation presented here.

GHC Core obviously has more syntactical constructs than our toy lambda calculus, including literals, coercion values, casts, profiling annotations ("ticks"), type lambdas and type applications, but these are irrelevant for our purposes: For literals and coercion values Call Arity returns the bottom of the lattice; the others are transparent to the analysis. In particular type arguments are not counted towards the arity here, which coincides with the meaning of arity as returned by GHC's regular arity analysis.

I want the analysis to make one pass over the syntax tree (up to the iterative calculation of fixed points for recursive bindings, Section 3.4.2). So instead of having two functions – one for the arity analysis and one for the co-call analysis – I defined one function callArityAnal which returns a tuple (UnVarGraph, VarEnv Arity), where the UnVarGraph is a data structure for undirected graphs on variable names (see Section 3.4.4) and VarEnv Arity is a partial map from variable names to Arity, which is a type synonym for Int.

The equations refer to fv e, the set of free variables of an expression. In the implementation, I do not use GHC's corresponding function exprFreeIds, as this would require another traversal of the expression. Instead I use dom $(\mathcal{A}_\alpha(e))$, which by construction happens to be the set of free variables of e, independent of α, as at this stage in the compiler pipeline, "obviously" dead code has been removed.

In the sequence of Core-to-Core passes, I inserted Call Arity and its eta-expanding simplifier pass after the simplifier's phase 0, as that is when all the rewrite rules have been active [PTH01], and before the strictness analyser. This way, the latter has a chance to unbox any new function parameters introduced by Call Arity, such as the accumulator in a call to sum.

3.4.1 Interesting variables

The analysis as presented in the previous section would be too expensive if implemented as is. This can be observed when compiling GHC's DynFlags module, which defines a record type with 157 elements. The Core code for a setter of one of the fields is

```
setX42 x  (DynFlags x1 ... x41 _ x43 ... x157)
        = (DynFlags x1 ... x41 x x43 ... x157).
```

For the body of the function, the analysis would report that 157 variables are called with (at least) 0 arguments, and that all of them are co-called with every other, a graph with 12246 edges. And none of this information is useful: The variables come from function parameters or pattern matches and there is no definition that we can possibly eta-expand!

Therefore, the code keeps track of the set of *interesting variables*, and only returns information about them. Currently, interesting variables are all let-bound variables of function type, while function parameters and pattern match variables are not interesting.

Generally, considering fewer variables as interesting will trade precision for performance, but preserves soundness: It would be perfectly sound, for example, to consider the variables of a very large recursive group to be uninteresting.

The complete type signature of the analysis is therefore

```
callArityAnal :: Arity → VarSet → CoreExpr →
                 ((UnVarGraph, VarEnv Arity), CoreExpr)
```

where the arguments are

- the incoming arity,
- the set of interesting variables and
- the expression to analyse

and the return values are the co-call graph and arity information (both restricted to the set of interesting variables) and the expression with the Call Arity result annotation added.

3.4.2 Finding the fixed points

The equations in the previous section specify the analysis, but do not provide an algorithm: In the case of a recursive **let** (Fig. 14), the equations are mutually recursive and the implementation has to employ a suitable strategy to find a solution.

The implementation finds the solution by iteratively approaching the fixpoint, using memorisation of intermediate results.

- Initially, it sets $A = \mathcal{A}_\alpha(e)$ and $G = \mathcal{G}_\alpha(e)$.

- For every variable $x_i \in \operatorname{dom} A$ that has not been analysed before, or has been analysed before with different values for α_{x_i} or x_i—$x_i \in G$, it (re-)analyses it, remembering the parameters and memorising the result $\mathcal{A}_{\alpha_{x_i}}(e_1)$ and G^i.
- If any variable has been (re)analysed in this iteration, it recalculates A and G and repeats from step 2.

This process will terminate, as shown by a simple standard argument: The variant that proves this consists of α_{x_i} and whether x_i—$x_i \in G$. The former starts at some natural number and decreases, the latter may start as not true, but once it is true, it stays true. Therefore, these parameters can change only a finite number of times, and the loop terminates once all of them are unchanged during one iteration. The monotonicity of the parameters follows from the monotonicity of the equations for $\mathcal{A}_\alpha$ and $\mathcal{G}_\alpha$: We have that $\alpha \geq \alpha'$ implies $\mathcal{A}_\alpha(e) \sqsubseteq \mathcal{A}_{\alpha'}(e)$ and $\mathcal{G}_\alpha(e) \sqsubseteq \mathcal{G}_{\alpha'}(e)$.

3.4.3 Top-level values

GHC supports modular compilation. Therefore, for exported functions, the compiler does not have the call sites available to analyse. Nevertheless I do want it to be able to analyse and eta-expand at least non-exported top-level functions.

To solve this elegantly I treat a module

module Foo(foo) **where**
bar = ...
foo = ...

as if it were a sequence of let-bindings

let bar = ... **in**
let foo = ... **in**
e

where e represents the external code for which I assume the worst: It calls all exported variables (foo here) with 0 arguments and the co-call graph is the complete graph. This prevents unwanted expansion of foo, but still allows us to eta-expand bar based on how it is called by foo.

Unfortunately, it also means that adding a top-level function to the export list of the module can prevent Call Arity from eta-expanding it and other functions in the module. If, for example, I export all difference-list producing functions in the code mentioned in Section 3.5.3, then I lose the benefits from Call Arity. In this sense, Call Arity can be considered a whole program analysis that happens to be useful in a setting with separate compilation as well.

3.4.4 The graph data structure

The analysis often builds complete bipartite graphs and complete graphs between sets of variables. A usual graph representation like adjacency lists would be quadratic in size and too inefficient for this use.

Hence, the data type UnVarGraph used in the implementation is specifically crafted for this purpose, see Appendix B.1 for the code. It represents graphs symbolically, as multisets ("bags" in the lingua of GHC code) of complete bipartite and complete graphs:

```
data Gen  =  CBPG VarSet VarSet
          |  CG VarSet
type UnVarGraph = Bag Gen
```

This allows for very quick, $O(1)$, creation and combination of graphs. The important query operation, calculating the set of neighbours of a node, is done by traversing the generating subgraphs.

One disadvantage of this data structure is that it does not normalise the representation. In particular, the union of a graph with itself is twice as large. I had to take that into account when I implemented the calculation of fixed points: It would be very inefficient to update G by merging it with the new results in each iteration. Instead, G is always reassembled from $\mathcal{G}_\alpha(e)$ and the – new or memorised – results from the bound expressions.

I experimented with simplifying the graph representation using identities like $S_1 \times S_2 \cup S_1^2 \cup S_2^2 = (S_1 \cup S_2)^2$, but it did not pay off, especially as deciding set equality can be expensive.

3.5 Discussion

3.5.1 Call Arity and list fusion

As hinted at in the introduction, I devised Call Arity mainly to allow for a fusing foldl, i.e. a definition of foldl in terms of foldr that takes part in list fusion while still producing good code. How exactly does Call Arity help here?

Consider the code sum (filter f [42..2016]). Previously, only filter would fuse with the list comprehension, eliminating one intermediate list, but the call to sum, being a left-fold, would remain: Compiled with previous versions of GHC, this produces code roughly equivalent to

```
let go = λx → let r = if x == 2016
                       then []
                       else  go (x + 1)
              in if f x then x : r else r
in foldl (+) 0 (go 42).
```

If we changed the definition of foldl to use foldr, as in

```
foldl k z xs = foldr (λv fn z → fn (k z v)) id xs z.
```

all lists are completely fused and we obtain the code

```
let go = λx → let r = if x == 2016
                       then id
                       else go (x + 1)
              in if f x
                 then λa → r (a + x)
                 else r
in go 42 0.
```

Without Call Arity, this was the final code, and as such quite inefficient: The recursive loop go has become a function that takes one argument, then allocates a function closure for r on the heap, and finally returns another heap-allocated function closure which will pop the next argument from the stack – not the fastest way to evaluate this simple program.

With Call Arity the compiler detects that go and r can both safely be eta-expanded with another argument, yielding the code

```
let go = λ x a → let r = λa → if x == 2016
                               then a
                               else go (x + 1) a
                 in if f x
                    then r (a + x)
                    else r a
in go 42 0
```

where the number of arguments passed matches the number of lambdas that are manifest on the outer level. This avoids allocations of function closures and allows the runtime to do fast calls [MP06], or even tail-recursive jumps.

3.5.2 Limitations

A particularly tricky case is list fusion with generators with multiple (or non-linear) recursion. This arises when flattening a tree to a list. Consider the code

```
data Tree = Tip Int | Bin Tree Tree

toList :: Tree → [Int]
toList tree = build (toListFB tree)

toListFB root cons nil = go root nil
  where
    go (Tip x)   rest = cons x rest
    go (Bin l r) rest = go l (go r rest)
```

which is a good producer; for example filter f (toList t) is compiled to

```
let go = λt rest → case t of
      Tip x   → if f x then x : rest else rest
      Bin l r → go l (go r rest)
in go t [].
```

If we add a left-fold to the pipeline, i.e. foldl (+) 0 (filter f (toList t)), where the foldl is implemented via foldr, the resulting code (before Call Arity) is

```
let go = λt fn → case t of
        Tip x   → if f x then (λa → fn (x + a)) else fn
        Bin l r → go l (go r fn)
in go t id 0.
```

Although go is always being called with three arguments, my analysis does not see this. For that it would have to detect that go calls its second parameter with one argument; as it is a forward analysis (in the nomenclature of [XP05]) it cannot do that.

And even if GHC could eta-expand it (in fact it can, due to the one-shot annotation discussed in Section 3.6.3), the result would not be much better: For the recursion, the runtime still needs to create a function closure for the unsaturated call go r fn, which is then called slowly by go, as explained in Section 1.4.3.

Things look better if we adjust the definition of toList so that the worker is tail-recursive. This requires an explicit stack, keeping track of the branches of the tree that are yet to be visited:

```
toListFB root cons nil = go root nil []
  where
    go (Tip x)   s = cons x (goS s)
    go (Bin l r) s = go l (r:s)
    goS []       = nil
    goS (x:xs) = go x xs
```

Now the resulting code is a nice tail-recursive loop, and it even allows GHC to unbox the accumulator, which usually provides a large performance benefit.

But the code that we would really want to see, and which we would write by hand, is

```
let go = λt a → case t of
        Tip x   → if f x then a + x else a
        Bin l r → go l (go r a)
in go t 0
```

with no continuations or explicit stack whatsoever and just the accumulator (unboxed by GHC) is being passed through the recursion. Such a transformation would require much more involved changes to the code than just eta-expansion followed by simplification, and is out of scope for Call Arity.

We (the GHC developers) still decided to let foldl take part in list fusion based on the benchmark results, presented in the next section. They indicate that the real-world benefits in the common case of linear recursion are larger than the penalty in the non-linear recursion, and if necessary, the producer can be adjusted to be linearly recursive.

3.5.3 Measurements

No work on compiler optimisations without some benchmark results! I compare four variants, all based on the GHC 7.10.3 codebase (revision 97e7c29):

(A) For the baseline, I removed the Call Arity analysis code and undid the changes to the library code, i.e. reverted foldl to its naive, non-fusing definition.

(B) To measure the effect of Call Arity analysis alone I enable it again, but left foldl with the naive definition.

(C) The current, unmodified state of the compiler, with Call Arity enabled and foldl implemented via foldr, is the most relevant variant; in the table this column is highlighted.

(D) To assess the importance of Call Arity for allowing foldl to take part in list fusion, I also measure GHC without Call Arity, but with foldl implemented via foldr.

Setup

The ubiquitous benchmark suite for Haskell is nofib [Par93], a set of 100 example Haskell programs, ranging from small micro-benchmarks to "real" applications. Most benchmarks support different modes to make them run longer. My numbers all result from the "slow" mode.

The measurements are taken on an 8-core Intel i7-3770 machine with 16 GB of RAM running Ubuntu 14.04 on Linux 3.13.0.

Initially, I attempted to use the actual run time measurements, but it turned out to be a mostly pointless endeavour. For example the `knights` benchmark would become 9% *slower* when enabling Call Arity (i.e. when comparing (A) to (B)), a completely unexpected result, given that the changes to the GHC Core code were reasonable. Further investigation using performance data obtained from the CPU indicated that with the changed code, the CPU's instruction decoder was idling for more cycles, hinting at cache effects and/or bad program layout.

Indeed: When I compiled the code with the compiler flag -g, which includes debugging information in the resulting binary, but should otherwise not affect the relative performance characteristics much, the unexpected difference vanished. I conclude that non-local changes to the Haskell or Core code will change the layout of the generated program code in unpredictable ways and render such run time measurements mostly meaningless.

This conclusion has been drawn before [MDHS09], and recently, tools to mitigate this effect, e.g. by randomising the code layout [CB13], were created. Unfortunately, these currently target specific C compilers, so I could not use them here.

In the following measurements, I avoid this problem by not measuring program execution time, but simply by counting the number of instructions performed. This way, the variability in execution time due to code layout does not affect the results. To obtain the instruction counts I employ valgrind [NS07], which runs the benchmarks on a virtual CPU and thus produces more reliable and reproducible measurements.

Results

My results are shown in Table 1. The three columns correspond to the variants (B), (C) and (D) described above, and the given percentages are changes relative to (A). Negative numbers indicate improvement. I list those benchmarks where there a difference of 1% or more is observed.

Table 1: Nofib results, relative to (A)

	Bytes allocated			Instructions executed		
	(B)	**(C)**	(D)	(B)	**(C)**	(D)
Arity Analysis	✓	✓		✓	✓	
Co-call Analysis	✓	✓		✓	✓	
foldl via foldr		✓	✓		✓	✓
`anna`	-1.5%	**-1.7%**	+0.1%	-0.5%	**-0.4%**	+0.7%
`bernouilli`	-0.0%	**-4.2%**	+4.5%	+0.0%	**-3.5%**	+22.5%
`binary-trees`	-0.0%	**-0.0%**	0.0%	-7.3%	**-7.3%**	-0.0%
`fem`	0.0%	**-2.6%**	-1.6%	-0.0%	**-4.4%**	-1.4%
`fft2`	-0.0%	**-48.2%**	-48.1%	+0.0%	**-18.6%**	-14.3%
`fibheaps`	-4.5%	**-4.5%**	0.0%	-12.0%	**-12.0%**	-0.0%
`fish`	-5.1%	**-5.1%**	0.0%	-3.9%	**-3.9%**	+0.0%
`fluid`	0.3%	**-8.4%**	-7.7%	+0.7%	**-3.6%**	-4.5%
`fulsom`	-0.4%	**-0.4%**	0.0%	-1.5%	**-1.5%**	+0.0%
`gen_regexps`	0.0%	**-53.9%**	+33.8%	-0.0%	**-7.8%**	+205.8%
`gg`	0.0%	**0.0%**	0.0%	+0.0%	**+0.0%**	-1.1%
`hidden`	-0.2%	**-6.0%**	+1.2%	-0.3%	**-4.6%**	+1.2%
`hpg`	-0.1%	**-1.3%**	-1.2%	-0.0%	**-1.8%**	-0.8%
`integrate`	-0.0%	**-60.9%**	-60.9%	+0.0%	**-47.2%**	-47.2%
`lcss`	-0.0%	**-0.0%**	0.0%	-2.5%	**-2.5%**	-0.0%
`life`	-0.0%	**-0.0%**	+0.0%	-0.3%	**-0.3%**	+2.1%
`maillist`	0.0%	**0.0%**	0.0%	-0.1%	**-0.6%**	+1.0%
`minimax`	0.0%	**-15.5%**	+4.0%	-0.0%	**-13.6%**	+4.7%
`scs`	-1.7%	**-2.5%**	+0.4%	-1.5%	**-1.9%**	-0.2%
`simple`	0.0%	**-9.4%**	+8.2%	-0.0%	**-1.9%**	+17.6%
`x2n1`	-0.0%	**-77.4%**	+84.0%	-0.0%	**-8.3%**	+245.7%
...and 78 more						
Min	-5.1%	**-77.4%**	-60.9%	-12.0%	**-47.2%**	-47.2%
Max	0.0%	**+0.0%**	+84.0%	+0.7%	**+0.8%**	+245.7%
Geometric Mean	-0.2%	**-4.5%**	-0.6%	-0.3%	**-1.7%**	+2.0%

As expected, enabling Call Arity does not increase the number of dynamic allocations; if it did, something would be wrong – see Chapter 4 for a formal proof of that statement.

On its own, the analysis rarely has an effect: Programmers tend to give their functions the right arities in the first place, and this includes the code in nofib.

Some of the improvements, e.g. in `fibheaps`, can be attributed to the use of take: Even before the introduction of Call Arity, it was set up to be a good consumer, producing similar higher-order code as foldl would. Call Arity can successfully optimise that.

But the real strength of Call Arity can only be seen in combination with making foldl a good consumer: Allocation improves considerably and without the analysis, this change to foldl would actually degrade the run time performance.

The last column (D) shows that without Call Arity, making foldl a good consumer is a bad idea, and that in some cases, the number of allocations and instructions go through the roof.

Difference lists

Another setting, besides list fusion, where non-expanded function definitions may emerge is when function types are hidden behind a type abstraction, and combined using abstract combinators. A good example for this is the type of *difference lists*, which represent lists as functions of type [a] $\rightarrow$ [a]. Module DList in Fig. 15 contains a standard implementation of difference lists. Note that all combinators are eta-reduced: The argument providing the tail of the list is omitted.

As a micro-benchmark, the code in module Bench in Fig. 15 converts a list of non-negative integers into their decimal representation, space separated.

Table 2 lists the execution time of applying doIt to a list of 1,000,000 integers, measured using `criterion` [OSu15]. We can see that without the help of Call Arity, the code is actually 16% slower than the equivalent

```
module DList where
  newtype DList a = DL ([a] → [a])

  fromDList :: DList a → [a]
  fromDList (DL f) = f []

  singleton :: a → DList a
  singleton c = DL (c:)

  empty :: DList a
  empty = DL id

  (<>) :: DList a → DList a → DList a
  DL f <> DL g = DL (f . g)

module Bench (doIt) where
  import DList
  import Data.Char (intToDigit)

  showInt :: Int → DList Char
  showInt n | n < 10    = singleton (intToDigit n)
            | otherwise = showInt (n `div` 10) <> showInt (n `mod` 10)

  go :: [Int] -> DList Char
  go []     = empty
  go (x:xs) = showInt x <> singleton ' ' <> go xs

  doIt :: [Int] → String
  doIt xs = fromDList (go xs)
```

Figure 15: Difference lists

code using String and string concatenation naively. With Call Arity enabled, the difference list code runs twice as fast, beating the String code by 35%.

The benefits of Call Arity are less pronounced if some of the involved functions are exported. In that case, the compiler has to make conservative assumptions about how often the function is called and Call Arity cannot eta-expand it. If showInt or go is added to the export list of module Bench the performance advantage compared to the String version disappears in the noise.

Table 2: Difference list speedup

	Running time			
Call Arity		✓	✓	✓
showInt exported			✓	✓
go exported				✓
String	129ms	128ms	128ms	136ms
DList	151ms	84ms	131ms	130ms

3.5.4 Compiler performance

Call Arity could affect the compile times in two ways: It increases them, because the compiler does more work. But it also reduces them, as the compiler itself has been optimised more. Table 3 shows the change in allocations done and time spent by the compiler while compiling the nofib test suite, as well as while compiling GHC itself.

In the nofib row we can see that the latter is indeed happening – enabling Call Arity reduces the number of allocations performed by the compiler, despite it doing more work – but this does not incur a significant change in compiler run time. The change to foldl alone increases compile times slightly.

In the second row, there is a third factor: The code base itself increases, due to the addition of the Call Arity code itself, which is reflected by the benchmark results.

Note that the benchmark suite is *not* designed to produce stable measurements of compile time, e.g. the compiler is run only once, so the significance of these numbers should not be taken too serious.

Ağacan measured the contribution of individual compiler passes to the overall compilation time, by compiling selected, widely used Haskell libraries and their dependencies. He reported his findings on the GHC developer's mailing list[11], and found that Call Arity is responsible for 1.1% of the compilation time.

Table 3: Compiling nofib and GHC, relative to (A)

	Bytes allocated			Compile time		
	(B)	**(C)**	(D)	(B)	**(C)**	(D)
Arity Analysis	✓	✓		✓	✓	
Co-call Analysis	✓	✓		✓	✓	
foldl via foldr		✓	✓		✓	✓
nofib	-0.1%	**-0.1%**	+0.1%	-0.1%	**-1.4%**	+0.3%
ghc	+3.8%	**+3.8%**	-0.0%	+5.7%	**+6.0%**	-0.2%

3.6 Related work

Gill mentions in his thesis on list fusion [Gil96] that eta-expansion is required to make foldl a good consumer that produces good code, and outlines a simple arity analysis. It does not discuss thunks at all and is equivalent to the second refinement in Section 3.1.

3.6.1 GHC's arity analyses

The compiler already comes with an arity analysis, which works complementary to Call Arity: It ignores how functions are being used and takes their definition into account. It traverses the syntax tree and for each expression returns its arity, i.e. the number of arguments the expression

[11] March 29, 2016; https://mail.haskell.org/pipermail/ghc-devs/2016-March/011651.html

can be applied to before doing any real work. This allows the transformation to turn $x\,?(\lambda y.\, e_1):(\lambda y.\, e_2)$ into $\lambda y.\,(x\,?\,e_1 : e_2)$ on the grounds that the check whether x is true or false is a negligible amount of work, and it is therefore better to eta-expand the expression, even if this means that the check is done repeatedly. But this is just a heuristics, and can lead to unwanted performance losses, e.g. if the scrutinee does a deep pattern match.[12] Therefore, Call Arity would refrain from doing this unless it knows for sure that the expression is going to be called at most once.

This arity analyser can make use of one-shot annotations on lambda binders. Such an annotation indicates that the lambda will be called at most once, which allows the analysis to derive greater arities and expand thunks: If the lambdas in $(f\ x)\,?(\lambda y.\, e_1):(\lambda y.\, e_2)$ are annotated as one-shot, this would be expanded to $\lambda y.\,((f\ x)\,?\,e_1 : e_2)$.

The working notes in [XP05] describe this analysis as the *forward arity analysis*. Like Call Arity, it can only determine arities of let-bound expressions and will not make any use of arity information on parameters.

Consider, for example,

```
let g   = ...
    s f = f 3
in ... (s g) ...
```

where we would have a chance to find out that g is always called with at least one argument.

A *backward arity analysis* capable of doing this is also described in [XP05]. This analysis calculates the *arity transformer* of a function f: A mapping from the number of arguments f is called with to the number of arguments passed to f's parameters. It is not implemented in GHC as such, but subsumed by the combined strictness/demand/cardinality analyser.

This analyser would assign to function s a strictness signature of `<C(S),1*C1(U)>`. The strictness information on the left indicates that s is strict in its first argument, and also in the value returned by calling its first argument as a function; the usage information on the right indicates that evaluating s f will evaluate f at most once, call it at most once, and

12 See for example http://ghc.haskell.org/trac/ghc/ticket/11029.

the result of that call will be used. The latest description of this analyser can be found in [SVP14].

Neither of these two analyses is capable of transforming the bad code from Fig. 11 into the desired form: The former has to give up as the expression f a might be expensive; the latter looks at the definition of goB before analysing the body and is therefore unable to make use of the fact that goB is always called with two arguments.

3.6.2 Higher order sharing analyses

The role of the co-call analysis in this setting is to provide a simple form of sharing analysis (using the nomenclature of [HHM07]), which is required to safely eta-expand thunks. Such analyses have been under investigation for a long time, e.g. to avoid the updating of thunks that are used at most once, or to enforce uniqueness constraints. These systems often support a higher-order analysis in some way, e.g. using detailed usage types [SVP14], possibly with polyvariance [HHM07].

It would be desirable to have such expressive usage types available in our analysis, and I do not foresee a problem in using them. It will, however, be hard to obtain them: The co-call analysis does not just analyse the code as it is, but rather anticipates its shape after eta-expansion based on the Call Arity result. So in order to determine a precise higher-order demand type for a function f, we need to know its Call Arity. For that we need to analyse the scope of f for how it is used, which is where we want to make use of the higher-order information on f. Going this route would require a fixed-point iteration for every binding, which is prohibitively expensive.

This is also why integrating Call Arity directly into GHC's existing demand analyser [SVP14], which analyses function bodies before their uses, would be difficult.

Another noteworthy difference to the cited analyses is that these either skip the discussion of recursive bindings, or treat them too imprecisely to handle code resulting from list fusion. It would be interesting to see if the concept of a co-call graph could be used in a stand-alone backward sharing analysis to improve precision in the presence of recursion.

3.6.3 Explicit one-shot annotation

While I was pondering the issue of a well-fusing foldl, I was pursuing also another way of solving the problem, besides Call Arity:

For that I created a magic, built-in function

```
oneShot :: (a → b) → a → b.
```

It is semantically the identity, but the compiler may assume that the function oneShot f is called at most once. I can use this function when implementing foldl in terms of foldr:

```
foldl k z xs = foldr (λ v fn → oneShot (λz → fn (k z v))) id xs z
```

This solves our problem with the bad code generated for sum (filter f [42..2016]) from Section 3.5.1: The compiler sees

```
let go = λx → let r = if x == 2016 then id else go (x + 1)
              in if f x then oneShot (λa → r (a + x)) else r
in go 42 0
```

and, because the λa is marked as oneShot, the existing arity analysis will happily eta-expand go.

Note that oneShot is unchecked: The programmer or library author has the full responsibility to ensure that the function is really applied only once. This is given in the case of foldl, as we know the definition of foldr and that it applies its argument at most once for each element of the list.

The GHC developers initially decided to go the Call Arity route because it turned out to be no less powerful than the explicit annotation, has the potential to optimise existing user code as well, and ensures the correctness of the transformation.

Later, the developers decided that it does not hurt to simply employ both approaches in GHC. The nofib benchmark suite does not exhibit such a case, but it is quite possible that there are instances out there, maybe similar to the tree example in Section 3.5.2, where Call Arity fails and the oneShot annotation might save the day.

Table 4 compares the performance of

- using only oneShot,
- using only Call Arity and
- using both, as it is the case in the released version of GHC

against the baseline of GHC 7.10.3 without oneShot and Call Arity, but with foldl implemented as foldr (i.e. variant (D) in Section 3.5.3). It shows that in most cases, oneShot and Call Arity yield the same performance gains, and only a few benchmarks (e.g. `fibheaps`, `scs`) show that Call Arity is a bit more powerful.

Table 4: Measuring the effect of one-shot annotations

	Bytes allocated			Instructions executed		
Call Arity		✓	✓		✓	✓
oneShot	✓		✓	✓		✓
`anna`	-0.2%	-1.7%	**-1.8%**	-0.6%	-1.1%	**-1.1%**
`bernouilli`	-8.3%	-8.3%	**-8.3%**	-21.3%	-21.2%	**-21.3%**
`binary-trees`	0.0%	-0.0%	**-0.0%**	-0.0%	-7.3%	**-7.3%**
`cacheprof`	-1.2%	-0.6%	**-0.0%**	-1.6%	-2.7%	**+0.9%**
`fem`	-1.0%	-1.0%	**-1.0%**	-3.1%	-3.1%	**-3.1%**
`fft2`	-0.2%	-0.2%	**-0.2%**	-5.2%	-5.1%	**-5.1%**
`fibheaps`	0.0%	-4.5%	**-4.5%**	+0.0%	-12.0%	**-12.0%**
`fish`	0.0%	-5.1%	**-5.1%**	-0.0%	-3.9%	**-3.9%**
`fulsom`	0.0%	-0.4%	**-0.4%**	-0.0%	-1.5%	**-1.5%**
`gen_regexps`	-65.6%	-65.6%	**-65.6%**	-69.9%	-69.9%	**-69.9%**
`gg`	0.0%	0.0%	**0.0%**	+1.2%	+1.2%	**+1.1%**
`hidden`	-6.9%	-7.0%	**-7.0%**	-5.5%	-5.7%	**-5.7%**
`hpg`	0.0%	-0.1%	**-0.1%**	+0.0%	-1.0%	**-1.0%**
`lcss`	0.0%	-0.0%	**-0.0%**	+0.0%	-2.5%	**-2.5%**
`life`	-0.0%	-0.0%	**-0.0%**	-2.7%	-0.2%	**-2.4%**
`maillist`	+0.0%	+0.0%	**0.0%**	-1.5%	-0.2%	**-1.6%**
`minimax`	-18.8%	-18.8%	**-18.8%**	-17.5%	-17.5%	**-17.5%**
`scs`	-1.2%	-2.9%	**-2.9%**	-0.4%	-2.1%	**-1.7%**
`simple`	-16.3%	-16.3%	**-16.3%**	-16.6%	-16.6%	**-16.6%**
`x2n1`	-87.7%	-87.7%	**-87.7%**	-73.5%	-73.5%	**-73.5%**
... and 80 more						
Min	-87.7%	-87.7%	**-87.7%**	-73.5%	-73.5%	**-73.5%**
Max	+0.0%	+0.0%	**0.0%**	+1.2%	+1.2%	**+1.1%**
Geometric Mean	-3.7%	-3.8%	**-3.8%**	-3.3%	-3.6%	**-3.6%**

3.6.4 unfoldr/destroy and stream fusion

There are various contenders to foldr/build-based list fusion, such as unfoldr/destroy [Sve02] and stream fusion [CLS07]. They have no problem fusing foldl, but have their own shortcomings, such as difficulties fusing unzip, filter and/or concatMap; a thorough comparison is contained in [Cou10]. After two decades, this is still an area of active research [FHG14].

These systems are in practical use in array libraries like `bytestring` and `vector`. For the typical uses of lists they were inferior to foldr/build-based fusion, and hence the latter is used for the standard Haskell list type. Given the recent advances on both fronts, a reevaluation of this choice is due.

3.6.5 Worker-wrapper list fusion

On the GHC mailing list, Takano suggested an extension to foldr/build-based list fusion that will generate good code for left folds directly [Tak14]. The idea is that the consumer not only specifies what the generator should use instead of the list constructors (:) and [], but also a pair of worker-wrapper functions.

Slightly simplified, he extends foldr to foldrW. This function takes two additional arguments, here called wrap and unwrap, which can be used by the consumer to specify the actual type of the recursion.

```
foldrW :: (forall e. f e → (e → b → b))
       → (forall e. (e → b → b) → f e)
       → (a → b → b) → b → [a] → b
foldrW wrap unwrap f z0 list0 = wrap go list0 z0
  where
    go = unwrap $ λ list z' → case list of []     → z'
                                           x:xs → f x (wrap go xs z')
```

Conversely, he extends build to buildW: Besides passing the list constructors, this also passes a wrapper that does not actually change the type:

```
newtype Simple b e = Simple { runSimple :: e → b → b }

buildW  :: (forall b f . (forall e. f e → (e → b → b))
                       → (forall e. (e → b → b) → f e)
                       → (a → b → b) → b → b)
        → [a]
buildW g = g runSimple Simple (:) []
```

This way, he can specify a fusion rule similar to the foldr/build rule:

```
{-# RULES
  "foldrW/buildW" forall wrap unwrap f z g.
    foldrW wrap unwrap f z (buildW g) = g wrap unwrap f z
  #-}
```

Now every list consuming function that wants to benefit from this system needs to specify a custom pair of wrapper and unwrapper functions. For example, his definition of foldl in terms of the extended foldrW becomes

```
foldl :: forall a b. (b → a → b) → b → [a] → b
foldl f z = λxs → foldrW wrap unwrap g id xs z
  where
    wrap :: forall e. Simple b e → (e → (b → b) → (b → b))
    wrap s e k a = k (s e a)
    unwrap :: forall e. (e → (b → b) → (b → b)) → Simple b e
    unwrap u = λe a → u e id a
    g x next acc = next (f acc x).
```

Conversely, list producing functions should be defined in terms of buildW, and making sure that the wrappers are used to shape the recursion:

```
[from..to] = buildW (eftFB from to)
eftFB from to wrap unwrap c n = wrap go from n
  where
    go = unwrap $ λi rest → if i <= to
                            then c i (wrap go (i + 1) rest)
                            else rest.
```

This proposal initially looked promising: It handles the case of fusing foldl well, and appears to be more powerful in tricky cases like fusing foldl with a list produced by treeToList (see Section 3.5.2).

Nevertheless, a thorough evaluation[13] by David Feuer and Dan Doel revealed that the system is rather unsafe: The above fusion rule is not universally correct, and with certain combinations of producers and consumers, this can yield wrong results. A way forward would be to identify sufficient conditions about the arguments to foldrW resp. buildW that guarantee that fusion is safe, but so far, such conditions have not been found. Given these problems, the GHC developers decided to not pursue this approach any further for now.

3.6.6 Control flow based analyses

The Call Arity analysis uses domain theory to describe its result, and iteratively finds a fixed point in the case of recursive bindings. This suggests connections to the field of data flow analysis, where analysis results are commonly calculated on a control-flow graph representation of the program. It is not obvious how to represent a Core program as such a graph, and although there are approaches to control-flow analysis of functional programs (see [Mid12] for a recent survey), they are not used in the Haskell compiler.

GHC does employ data flow analysis based transformations, but at a much later phase and lower level, namely in the code generator [RDP10]. We do not want Call Arity to happen that late in the pipeline, as some Core-to-Core transformations benefit from the effect of Call Arity, e.g. by unboxing the accumulator of sum specialised to Int.

3.7 Future work

As usual, there is always room for improvement, both in the analysis itself and in how it is used.

[13] https://ghc.haskell.org/trac/ghc/ticket/9545

3.7.1 Improvements to the analysis

Call Arity does not fully exploit the behaviour of thunks in mutual recursion. Consider this example:

```
let go x = if x > 10 then x                 else go (t1 x)
    t1   = if f (t2 a) then (λy → go (y+1)) else (λy → go (y+2))
    t2   = if f b      then (λy → go (y+1)) else (λy → go (y+2))
in go 1 2
```

Currently, Call Arity will refrain from eta-expanding t1 and t2, as they are part of a recursive binding. But t2 is in fact called at most once! All calls to t2 are done by t1, and t1's result will be shared.

It remains to be seen if such situations occur in the wild and whether the benefits justify the implementation overhead.

3.7.2 Tighter integration into GHC

As explained in Section 3.6.2, Call Arity cannot be directly merged into GHC's existing demand analyser [SVP14], as they need to process let-bindings in a different order.

There is, however, a potential for better cooperation of Call Arity with the existing analyses and transformations in both directions:

Call Arity could make some use of the strictness and demand annotation that happen to be already present in the code, e.g. on imported identifiers. If, for example, the function f in the expression f (λx. g x) happens to be annotated with the information that it calls its first argument at most once with one argument, then we could improve the analysis result and report that g is called at most once.

I am, however, reluctant to add this functionality: It would imply that some programs might be optimised *better* by splitting them into more modules, which is a harsh violation of the principle of least surprise.

Similarly, the other passes could use the information that was found out by the Call Arity pass: Thunks that are determined by Call Arity to be called at most once can be marked as one-shot, even if no eta-expansion is possible, which would allow the code generator to omit the code that implements the updating.

If we were willing to pay the price to include function parameters in the set of interesting variables (Section 3.4.1), then although Call Arity cannot make use of the thus found information to eta-expand anything, it could create a preliminary demand signature for the function that might help the subsequent pass of the demand analyser to get more precise results, or at least to converge earlier.

Finally, the information that a let-bound function or thunk is called at most once from within a recursive function allows more aggressive inlining.

For example, currently GHC does not transform

```
let a = f x0
    b = g x0
in let go 0 = a
       go 1 = b
       go i = go (h i)
   in go n
```

into

```
let go 0 = f x0
    go 1 = g x0
    go i = go (h i)
in go n
```

as in general, inlining into a recursive group can duplicate work [PM02]. In this case, it would be safe, as a and b are called at most once, and Call Arity is able to determine that. In principle, extending GHC to do this is not a problem; practically, the so-called float-out pass will simply undo this change, because – again in general – floating things out of a recursive group is a good idea, as it can increase sharing. In this case, no sharing can be gained, as the expression f x0 is evaluated only once, but this fact is not visible to GHC after a and b have been inlined.[14]

[14] https://ghc.haskell.org/trac/ghc/ticket/10918

I started with $P \wedge \neg P$ and derived your Mom's phone number.

Randall Munroe, xkcd #704

CHAPTER 4

The safety of Call Arity

The previous chapter introduced a new analysis and transformation for an optimising compiler, and analyses it in the usual detail: A somewhat formal description of the transformation is accompanied by empirical evidence of its usefulness based on benchmark results.

That none of the benchmarks exhibited reduced performance, at least when measured by the number of allocations, suggests that the transformation is indeed a *safe* optimisation, i.e. does not make matters worse. Nevertheless, I found this unsatisfying: The benchmark suite only contains a small number of example programs – how can I be sure that my transformation really never makes matters worse?

To that end, I want to actually prove that my transformation is safe, and I want to do it in a machine-verified way, in order to attain the highest level of assurance that the proof is correct.

Therefore, I set out to go all the way: I took the Call Arity analysis, formalised it in the interactive theorem prover Isabelle and created a machine-checked proof not only of functional correctness, but also that the performance of the transformed program is not worse than that of the original program. This chapter, parts of which I have presented at the Haskell Symposium 2015 [Bre15b], describes this endeavour.

Recall that it is only safe to eta-expand a thunk if the thunk is called at most once. So an arity analysis requires a cardinality analysis, which determines how often a function or a thunk is called, in order to be able to eta-expand a thunk. If the cardinality analysis were wrong and we would eta-expand a thunk that is called multiple times, we would lose the benefits of sharing and suddenly repeat work.

A correctness proof with regard to a standard denotational semantics would not rule that out! A more detailed semantics is required instead. I use the abstract machine introduced in Chapter 2, where the explicit heap allows me to prove that the number of heap allocations does not increase by transforming the program. This is a suitable criterion for safety in this context, as explained shortly.

4.1 Proof outline

In my introduction of the Call Arity analysis in Chapter 3, I explain and motivate the various details of the definition. These might be convincing points that Call Arity might indeed be safe, but are far from a general, rigorous proof. How can I go about producing such a proof?

First, I need to find a suitable semantics. The elegant standard denotational semantics for functional programs, such as the one in Section 2.1.2, are unfortunately too abstract and admit no observation of program performance. Therefore, I use a standard small-step operational semantics similar to Sestoft's mark 1 abstract machine, introduced in Section 2.5.

With that semantics, I could have followed Sands [MS99] and measured performance by counting evaluation steps. But that turns out to be too finegrained: The eta-expansion transformation causes additional beta-reductions to be performed during evaluation, and without subsequent simplification – which does happen in a real compiler, but which I do not want to include in the proof – these increase the number of steps in my semantics.

Therefore, I measure the performance by counting the number of allocations performed during the evaluation. This is sufficient to detect accidental duplication of work, as shown by this gedankenexperiment: Consider a program e_1, which is transformed to e_2, and a subexpression e of e_1 that also occurs in e_2. By replacing e with **let** x1 = x1,..., xn = xn **in** e, where the variables are fresh, we can force each evaluation of e to perform at least n allocations, for an arbitrary large choice of n. So if e_2 happens to evaluate e more often than e_1, we can choose n large enough to make e_2 allocate more than e_1. Conversely, if our criterion holds, we can conclude that the transformation does not duplicate work.

This measure is also realistic: When working on GHC, the number of bytes allocated by a benchmark or a test case is the prime measure that developers observe to detect improvements and regressions, as in practice, it correlates very well with execution time and memory usage, while being more stable across differing environments.

A transformation is *safe* in this sense if the transformed program performs no more allocations than the original program.

The arity transformation eta-expands expressions, so in order to prove it safe, I identify conditions when eta-expansion itself is safe, and ensure that these conditions are always met.

A sufficient condition for the safety of an n-fold eta-expansion of an expression e is that whenever e is evaluated, the top n elements on the stack are arguments, and neither continuations of a case expression, as eta-expansion would introduce a type error, nor update markers for thunks, as eta-expansion would prevent the sharing. This is stated as Lemma 17.

The safety proof for the arity analysis (Lemma 18) keeps track of some invariants during the evaluation which ensure that we can apply Lemma 17 whenever an eta-expanded expression is about to be evaluated.

I perform the proof first for a naive arity analysis without a cardinality analysis, i.e. one that needs to be conservative in this case. This corresponds to previous work on arity analysis, and furthermore, this is sufficient to prove that the transformation is semantics preserving (Theorem 4).

I then formally introduce the concept of a cardinality analysis in Section 4.3. I do not simply prove safety of the co-call graph based analysis directly, but split it up into a series of increasingly concrete proofs, each building on the result of the previous, for two reasons:

- It is nice to separate various aspects of the proof (i.e. the interaction of the arity analysis with the cardinality analysis; the gap between the steps of the semantics and the structurally recursive nature of the analysis; different treatments of recursive and non-recursive bindings) into individual steps, but more importantly
- while the co-call graph data structure is sufficiently expressive to implement the analysis, it is an unsuitable abstraction for the safety proof. There, we need to describe the possibly complex recursion patterns of the heap as a whole with sufficient detail to identify and make use that some expressions call each other in a nice and linear fashion.

In the first refinement, the cardinality analysis is completely abstract: Its input is the whole configuration and its result is simply which variables on the heap are going to be called more than once. We give conditions (Definition 11) when an arity analysis using such a cardinality analysis is safe (Lemma 23).

The next refinement assumes a cardinality analysis that now looks just at expressions, not whole configurations, and returns a much richer analysis result: A *trace tree* which is a (possibly) infinite tree where each path corresponds to one possible execution and the edges are labelled by the variables called during that evaluation.

Given such a trace tree analysis, an abstract analysis as described in the first refinement can be implemented: The trees describing the expressions in a configuration (on the heap, as the control or in the stack) can be combined to a tree describing the behaviour of the whole configuration. This calculation, named s in Section 4.3.2, is quite natural for trace trees, but would be hard to define on co-call graphs only. From that tree I can determine the cardinalities of the individual variables. I specify conditions on the trace tree analysis (Definition 14) and in Lemma 26 show them to be sufficient to fulfil the specification of the first refinement.

The third and final refinement assumes an analysis that returns a co-call graph for each expression. Co-call graphs can be seen as compact approximations of trace trees, with edges between variables that can occur on the same path in the tree. The specification in Definition 15 is shown in Lemma 27 to be sufficient to fulfil the specification of the second refinement.

Eventually, I give the definition of the real Call Arity analysis in Section 4.3.4, and as it fulfils the specification of the final refinement, the desired safety theorem (Theorem 5) follows.

4.2 Arity analyses

In general, an arity analysis is a function that, given a binding (Γ, e), consisting of variable names bound to right-hand-sides in Γ and the body e, determines the arity of each of the bound expressions. It depends on the number α of arguments passed to e and may return $\bot$ for a name that is not called at all:

$$\mathcal{A}_\alpha(\Gamma, e) \colon \mathsf{Var} \to \mathbb{N}_\bot.$$

Given such an analysis, we can run it over a program and transform it accordingly. The transformation function traverses the syntax tree, keeping track of the number of arguments passed along the way:

$$\begin{aligned}
\mathsf{T}_\alpha(x) &= x \\
\mathsf{T}_\alpha(e\ x) &= \mathsf{T}_{\alpha+1}(e)\ x \\
\mathsf{T}_\alpha(\lambda x.\, e) &= (\lambda x.\, \mathsf{T}_{\alpha-1}(e)) \\
\mathsf{T}_\alpha(\mathbf{C}_b) &= \mathbf{C}_b \qquad \text{for } b \in \{\mathbf{t}, \mathbf{f}\} \\
\mathsf{T}_\alpha(e\ \mathbf{?}\ e_\mathbf{t} : e_\mathbf{f}) &= \mathsf{T}_0(e)\ \mathbf{?}\ \mathsf{T}_\alpha(e_\mathbf{t}) : \mathsf{T}_\alpha(e_\mathbf{f}) \\
\mathsf{T}_\alpha(\mathbf{let}\ \Gamma\ \mathbf{in}\ e) &= \mathbf{let}\ \overline{\mathsf{T}}_{\mathcal{A}_\alpha(\Gamma, e)}(\Gamma)\ \mathbf{in}\ \mathsf{T}_\alpha(e)
\end{aligned}$$

The actual transformation happens at a binding, where it eta-expands bound expressions according to the result of the arity analysis, using the n-fold eta expansion operator introduced in Section 1.5. If the analysis determines that a binding is never called, it simply leaves it alone:

$$\overline{\mathsf{T}}_{\bar\alpha}(\Gamma) = \left[x \mapsto \begin{cases} e & \text{if } \bar\alpha(x) = \bot \\ \mathcal{E}_\alpha(\mathsf{T}_\alpha(e)) & \text{if } \bar\alpha(x) = \alpha \end{cases} \middle| (x \mapsto e) \in \Gamma \right].$$

As motivated earlier, I consider an arity analysis $\mathcal{A}$ to be safe if the transformed program does not perform more allocations than the original program. A – technical – benefit of this measure is that the number of allocations always equals the size of the heap plus the number of update markers on the stack, as no garbage collector is modelled in the semantics:

Definition 5 (Safe transformation)
A program transformation T is *safe* if for every execution

$$([], e, []) \Rightarrow^* (\Gamma, v, [])$$

with isVal v, there is an execution

$$([], \mathsf{T}(e), []) \Rightarrow^* (\Gamma', v', [])$$

with $\mathsf{isVal}(v')$ and $|\mathsf{dom}\,\Gamma'| \leq |\mathsf{dom}\,\Gamma|$.

An arity analysis $\mathcal{A}$ is safe if the transformation T is safe. $\diamond$

This formulation of safety works nicely as the semantics is deterministic up to the choice of variable names. For a genuinely non-deterministic semantics, a definition of safety would have to distinguish different executions and ensure that for each of them, a corresponding execution of the transformed expression exists and does not allocate more.

Note that this definition does not entail functional, i.e. semantic, correctness, which is discussed and proved in Section 4.2.2.

Specification

I begin by stating sufficient conditions for an arity analysis to be safe. In order to phrase the conditions, I also need to know the arities an expression e calls its free variables with, assuming it is itself called with α arguments:

$$\mathcal{A}_\alpha(e) \colon \mathsf{Var} \to \mathbb{N}_\perp$$

For notational simplicity, I define $\mathcal{A}_\perp(e) := \perp$.

The specification consists of a few naming hygiene conditions and an inequality for most syntactical constructs:

Definition 6 (Arity analysis specification)

$$\operatorname{dom} \mathcal{A}_\alpha(e) \subseteq \operatorname{fv} e \qquad \text{(A-dom)}$$

$$\operatorname{dom} \mathcal{A}_\alpha(\Gamma, e) \subseteq \operatorname{dom} \Gamma \qquad \text{(Ah-dom)}$$

$$z \notin \{x, y\} \implies \mathcal{A}_\alpha(e[x := y])\, z = \mathcal{A}_\alpha(e)\, z \qquad \text{(A-subst)}$$

$$x, y \notin \operatorname{dom} \Gamma \implies$$

$$\mathcal{A}_\alpha(\Gamma[x := y], e[x := y]) = \mathcal{A}_\alpha(\Gamma, e) \qquad \text{(Ah-subst)}$$

$$[x \mapsto \alpha] \sqsubseteq \mathcal{A}_\alpha(x) \qquad \text{(A-Var)}$$

$$\mathcal{A}_{\alpha+1}(e) \sqcup [x \mapsto 0] \sqsubseteq \mathcal{A}_\alpha(e\ x) \qquad \text{(A-App)}$$

$$\mathcal{A}_{\alpha-1}(e) \setminus \{x\} \sqsubseteq \mathcal{A}_\alpha(\lambda x.\, e) \qquad \text{(A-Lam)}$$

$$\mathcal{A}_0(e) \sqcup \mathcal{A}_\alpha(e_{\mathbf{t}}) \sqcup \mathcal{A}_\alpha(e_{\mathbf{f}}) \sqsubseteq \mathcal{A}_\alpha(e\,?\,e_{\mathbf{t}} : e_{\mathbf{f}}) \qquad \text{(A-If)}$$

$$\overline{\mathcal{A}}_{\mathcal{A}_\alpha(\Gamma,e)}(\Gamma) \sqcup \mathcal{A}_\alpha(e) \sqsubseteq \mathcal{A}_\alpha(\Gamma, e) \sqcup \mathcal{A}_\alpha(\textbf{let } \Gamma \textbf{ in } e) \qquad \text{(A-Let)}$$

where

$$\overline{\mathcal{A}}_{\bar{\alpha}}(\Gamma) := \bigsqcup \{\mathcal{A}_{(\bar{\alpha}\ x)}(e) \mid (x \mapsto e) \in \Gamma\}. \qquad \diamond$$

These conditions come quite naturally: An expression should not report calls to names that it does not know about. Replacing one variable by another should not affect the arity of other variables. A variable, evaluated with a certain arity, should report (at most) that arity.

In the rules for application and lambda abstraction we keep track of the number of arguments. As this models a forward analysis which looks at bodies before right-hand-sides, we get no useful information on how the argument x in an application $e\ x$ is called by e.

In rule (A-If), the scrutinee is evaluated without arguments, hence it is analysed with arity 0.

The rule (A-Let) is a concise way to capture a few requirements. Note that, by (A-dom) and (Ah-dom), the domains of $\mathcal{A}_\alpha(\Gamma, e)$ and $\mathcal{A}_\alpha(\textbf{let } \Gamma \textbf{ in } e)$ are disjoint, i.e. $\mathcal{A}_\alpha(\Gamma, e)$ contains the information on how the names of the current binding are called, while $\mathcal{A}_\alpha(\textbf{let } \Gamma \textbf{ in } e)$ informs us about the free variables. The left-hand side contains all possible calls, both from the body of the binding and from each bound expression. These are analysed with the arity reported by $\mathcal{A}_\alpha(\Gamma, e)$. The occurrence of $\mathcal{A}_\alpha(\Gamma, e)$ on both sides of the inequality anticipates the fixed-point iteration in the implementation of the analysis.

Definition 6 suffices to prove functional correctness (Section 4.2.2 contains a proof of that) but not safety, as the issue of thunks is not touched upon yet. The simplest way to handle thunks – and the only way without the aid of a cardinality analysis – is to simply give up when encountering a thunk:

Definition 7 (No-cardinality analysis specification)

$$x \in \mathsf{thunks}\,\Gamma \implies \mathcal{A}_\alpha(\Gamma, e)\ x = 0 \qquad \text{(Ah-thunk)}$$

◇

Safety

The safety of an eta-expanding transformation rests on the simple observation that, given enough arguments on the stack, an eta-expanded expression evaluates straight to the original expression:

Lemma 17 (Safety of eta-expansion)

$$(\Gamma, \mathcal{E}_\alpha(e), \$x_1 \cdots \$x_\alpha \cdot S) \Rightarrow^* (\Gamma, e, \$x_1 \cdots \$x_\alpha \cdot S)$$

◇

Proof

$$\begin{aligned}
&(\Gamma, \mathcal{E}_\alpha(e), \$x_1 \cdots \$x_\alpha \cdot S) \\
&= (\Gamma, (\lambda z_1 \ldots z_\alpha.\, e\ z_1 \ldots z_\alpha), \$x_1 \cdots \$x_\alpha \cdot S) \\
&\Rightarrow^* (\Gamma, e\ x_1 \ldots x_\alpha, S) && \{\text{ by } \mathrm{APP}_2 \} \\
&\Rightarrow^* (\Gamma, e, \$x_1 \cdots \$x_\alpha \cdot S) && \{\text{ by } \mathrm{APP}_1 \}
\end{aligned}$$

■

So the safety proof for the whole transformation now just has to make sure that whenever we evaluate an eta-expanded value, there are enough arguments on top of the stack. Let args S denote the number of arguments on top of the stack.

While tracking the evaluation of the original program in the proof, we need to construct the corresponding configurations in the evaluation of the transformed program. Therefore, we need to keep track of the arity argument to each of the expressions that occurs in a configuration: those on the heap, the control and those in alternatives on the stack. Together, these arguments form an *arity annotation* written $(\bar{\alpha}, \alpha, \dot{\alpha})$. Given such an annotation, we can transform a configuration:

$$\mathsf{T}_{(\bar{\alpha},\alpha,\dot{\alpha})}((\Gamma, e, S)) = (\overline{\mathsf{T}}_{\bar{\alpha}}(\Gamma), \mathsf{T}_{\alpha}(e), \dot{\mathsf{T}}_{\dot{\alpha}}(S))$$

where the stack is transformed by

$$\begin{aligned}
\dot{\mathsf{T}}_{\alpha\cdot\dot{\alpha}}((e_{\mathbf{t}} : e_{\mathbf{f}})\cdot S) &= (\mathsf{T}_{\alpha}(e_{\mathbf{t}}) : \mathsf{T}_{\alpha}(e_{\mathbf{f}}))\cdot\dot{\mathsf{T}}_{\dot{\alpha}}(S) \\
\dot{\mathsf{T}}_{\dot{\alpha}}(\$x\cdot S) &= \$x\cdot\dot{\mathsf{T}}_{\dot{\alpha}}(S) \\
\dot{\mathsf{T}}_{\dot{\alpha}}(\#x\cdot S) &= \#x\cdot\dot{\mathsf{T}}_{\dot{\alpha}}(S) \\
\dot{\mathsf{T}}_{\dot{\alpha}}([]) &= [].
\end{aligned}$$

While carrying the arity annotation through the evaluation of our programs, we need to ensure that it stays *consistent* with the current configuration.

Definition 8 (Arity annotation consistency)
An arity annotation is consistent with a configuration, written $(\bar{\alpha}, \alpha, \dot{\alpha}) \triangleright (\Gamma, e, S)$, if

- $\mathsf{dom}\,\bar{\alpha} \subseteq \mathsf{dom}\,\Gamma \cup \#S$,
- $\mathsf{args}\,S \sqsubseteq \alpha$,
- $(\overline{\mathcal{A}}_{\bar{\alpha}}(\Gamma) \sqcup \mathcal{A}_{\alpha}(e) \sqcup \dot{\mathcal{A}}_{\dot{\alpha}}(S))|_{\mathsf{dom}\,\Gamma\cup\#S} \sqsubseteq \bar{\alpha}$, where

$$\begin{aligned}
\dot{\mathcal{A}}_{[]}([]) &:= \bot \\
\dot{\mathcal{A}}_{\alpha\cdot\dot{\alpha}}((e_{\mathbf{t}} : e_{\mathbf{f}})\cdot S) &:= \mathcal{A}_{\alpha}(e_{\mathbf{t}}) \sqcup \mathcal{A}_{\alpha}(e_{\mathbf{f}}) \sqcup \dot{\mathcal{A}}_{\dot{\alpha}}(S) \\
\dot{\mathcal{A}}_{\dot{\alpha}}(\$x\cdot S) &:= [x \mapsto 0] \sqcup \dot{\mathcal{A}}_{\dot{\alpha}}(S) \\
\dot{\mathcal{A}}_{\dot{\alpha}}(\#x\cdot S) &:= [x \mapsto 0] \sqcup \dot{\mathcal{A}}_{\dot{\alpha}}(S), \text{ and}
\end{aligned}$$

- $\dot{\alpha} \triangleright S$, defined as

$$\begin{aligned}
&[] \triangleright [] \\
&\alpha\cdot\dot{\alpha} \triangleright (e_{\mathbf{t}} : e_{\mathbf{f}})\cdot S \iff \dot{\alpha} \triangleright S \wedge \mathsf{args}\,S \sqsubseteq \alpha \\
&\dot{\alpha} \triangleright \$x\cdot S \iff \dot{\alpha} \triangleright S \\
&\dot{\alpha} \triangleright \#x\cdot S \iff \dot{\alpha} \triangleright S.
\end{aligned}$$ ◇

As this definition does not consider the issue of thunks, I extend it by one additional requirement:

Definition 9 (No-cardinality arity annotation consistency)
An arity annotation is *no-cardinality consistent* with a configuration, written $(\bar{\alpha}, \alpha, \dot{\alpha}) \rhd_{\mathsf{N}} (\Gamma, e, S)$, iff $(\bar{\alpha}, \alpha, \dot{\alpha}) \rhd (\Gamma, e, S)$ and $\bar{\alpha}\ x = 0$ for all $x \in \mathsf{thunks}\,\Gamma$. ◇

I do not include this requirement in the definition of $\rhd$ as I will extend it differently when I add a cardinality analysis in Definition 13.

Clearly $(\bot, 0, [])$ is a consistent annotation for an initial configuration $([], e, [])$. The rules take consistently annotated configurations to consistently annotated configurations during the evaluation – with one exception which causes a minor technical overhead: Upon evaluation of a variable x, its binding $x \mapsto e$ is always taken off the heap first, even when it is already evaluated, i.e. $\mathsf{isVal}\,e$:

$$(\Gamma[x \mapsto e], x, S) \Rightarrow (\Gamma, e, \#x{\cdot}S) \Rightarrow (\Gamma[x \mapsto e], e, S)$$

I would not be able to prove consistency in the intermediate state. To work around this issue, assume that rule $\textsc{var}_1$ has an additional constraint $\neg\mathsf{isVal}\,e$ and that the rule

$$(x \mapsto e) \in \Gamma,\ \mathsf{isVal}\,e \implies (\Gamma, x, S) \Rightarrow (\Gamma, e, S) \qquad (\textsc{var}'_1)$$

is added. This modification makes the semantics skip over one step, which is fine (and closer to what happens in reality).

Lemma 18
Assume $\mathcal{A}$ fulfils Definitions 6 and 7.

If we have $(\Gamma, e, S) \Rightarrow^* (\Gamma', e', S')$ and $(\bar{\alpha}, \alpha, \dot{\alpha}) \rhd_{\mathsf{N}} (\Gamma, e, S)$, then there exists an arity annotation $(\bar{\alpha}', \alpha', \dot{\alpha}')$ with $(\bar{\alpha}', \alpha', \dot{\alpha}') \rhd_{\mathsf{N}} (\Gamma', e', S')$, and $\mathsf{T}_{(\bar{\alpha},\alpha,\dot{\alpha})}((\Gamma, e, S)) \Rightarrow^* \mathsf{T}_{(\bar{\alpha}',\alpha',\dot{\alpha}')}((\Gamma', e', S'))$. ◇

Proof
by the individual steps of $\Rightarrow^*$. For $\textsc{app}_1$ we have

$$\begin{aligned}\mathcal{A}_{\alpha+1}(e) \sqcup \dot{\mathcal{A}}_{\dot{\alpha}}(\$x{\cdot}S) &= \mathcal{A}_{\alpha+1}(e) \sqcup [x \mapsto 0] \sqcup \dot{\mathcal{A}}_{\dot{\alpha}}(S) \\ &\sqsubseteq \mathcal{A}_{\alpha}(e\ x) \sqcup \dot{\mathcal{A}}_{\dot{\alpha}}(S)\end{aligned}$$

using (A-App) and the definition of $\dot{\mathcal{A}}$. So with $(\bar{\alpha}, \alpha, \dot{\alpha}) \rhd_{\mathsf{N}} (\Gamma, e\ x, S)$ we have $(\bar{\alpha}, \alpha + 1, \dot{\alpha}) \rhd_{\mathsf{N}} (\Gamma, e, \$x \cdot S)$. Furthermore

$$\begin{aligned} \mathsf{T}_{(\bar{\alpha},\alpha,\dot{\alpha})}((\Gamma, e\ x, S)) &= (\overline{\mathsf{T}}_{\bar{\alpha}}(\Gamma), (\mathsf{T}_{\alpha+1}(e))\ x, \dot{\mathsf{T}}_{\dot{\alpha}}(S)) \\ &\Rightarrow (\overline{\mathsf{T}}_{\bar{\alpha}}(\Gamma), \mathsf{T}_{\alpha+1}(e), \$x \cdot \dot{\mathsf{T}}_{\dot{\alpha}}(S)) \\ &= \mathsf{T}_{(\bar{\alpha},\alpha+1,\dot{\alpha})}((\Gamma, e, \$x \cdot S)) \end{aligned}$$

by rule APP_1.

The other cases follow this pattern, where the inequalities in Definition 6 ensure the preservation of consistency.

In case VAR_1 the variable x is bound to a thunk. From consistency we obtain $\bar{\alpha}\ x = 0$, so we can use $\mathcal{E}_0(\mathsf{T}_0(e)) = \mathsf{T}_0(e)$. Similarly, $\alpha = \bar{\alpha}\ x = 0$ holds in case VAR_2.

The actual eta-expansion is handled in case VAR'_1: We have

$$\mathsf{args}(\dot{\mathsf{T}}_{\dot{\alpha}}(S)) = \mathsf{args}\, S \sqsubseteq \alpha \sqsubseteq \mathcal{A}_\alpha(x)\ x \sqsubseteq \bar{\alpha}\ x,$$

from consistency and (A-Var) and hence

$$\begin{aligned} \mathsf{T}_{(\bar{\alpha},\alpha,\dot{\alpha})}((\Gamma, x, S)) &\Rightarrow (\overline{\mathsf{T}}_{\bar{\alpha}}(\Gamma), \mathcal{E}_{\bar{\alpha}\ x}(\mathsf{T}_{\bar{\alpha}\ x}(e)), \dot{\mathsf{T}}_{\dot{\alpha}}(S)) && \{\ \text{VAR}'_1\ \} \\ &\Rightarrow^* (\overline{\mathsf{T}}_{\bar{\alpha}}(\Gamma), \mathsf{T}_{\bar{\alpha}\ x}(e), \dot{\mathsf{T}}_{\dot{\alpha}}(S)) && \{\ \text{by Lemma 17}\ \} \\ &= \mathsf{T}_{(\bar{\alpha},\bar{\alpha}\ x,\dot{\alpha})}((\Gamma, e, S)). \end{aligned}$$

Case: LET_1
The new variables in Δ are fresh with regard to Γ and S, hence also with regard to $\bar{\alpha}$ according to the naming hygiene conditions in $(\bar{\alpha}, \alpha, \dot{\alpha}) \rhd_{\mathsf{N}} (\Gamma, \textbf{let}\ \Delta\ \textbf{in}\ e, S)$. So in order to have $(\mathcal{A}_\alpha(\Delta, e) \sqcup \bar{\alpha}, \alpha, \dot{\alpha}) \rhd (\Delta \cdot \Gamma, e, S)$, it suffices to show

$$(\overline{\mathcal{A}}_{\mathcal{A}_\alpha(\Delta,e)}(\Delta) \sqcup \mathcal{A}_\alpha(e))|_{\mathsf{dom}\,\Delta \cup \mathsf{dom}\,\Gamma \cup \# S} \sqsubseteq \mathcal{A}_\alpha(\Delta, e) \sqcup \bar{\alpha},$$

which follows from (A-Let) and $\mathcal{A}_\alpha(\textbf{let}\ \Delta\ \textbf{in}\ e)|_{\mathsf{dom}\,\Gamma \cup \# S} \sqsubseteq \bar{\alpha}$. The requirement $\mathcal{A}_\alpha(\Delta, e)\ x = 0$ for $x \in \mathsf{thunks}\,\Delta$ holds by (Ah-thunk). ■

The main take-away of this lemma is the following corollary, which states that the transformed program performs the same number of allocations as the original program.

Corollary 19
The arity analysis is safe (in the sense of Definition 5): If $([], e, []) \Rightarrow^* (\Gamma, v, [])$, then there exists Γ' and v' such that $([], \mathsf{T}_0(e), []) \Rightarrow^* (\Gamma', v', [])$ where Γ and Γ' contain the same number of bindings. ◇

Proof
We have $(\bot, 0, []) \triangleright_{\mathsf{N}} ([], e, [])$. Lemma 18 gives us $\bar{\alpha}$, α and $\dot{\alpha}$ so that $\mathsf{T}_{(\bot,0,[])}(([], e, [])) \Rightarrow^* \mathsf{T}_{(\bar{\alpha},\alpha,\dot{\alpha})}((\Gamma, v, []))$ and $\overline{\mathsf{T}}_{\bar{\alpha}}(\Gamma)$ binds the same names as Γ. ■

4.2.1 A concrete arity analysis

So far, we have a specification for an arity analysis and a proof that every analysis that fulfils the specification is safe.

One possible implementation is the trivial arity analysis which does not do anything useful and simply returns the most pessimistic result: $\mathcal{A}_\alpha(e) := [x \mapsto 0 \mid x \in \mathsf{fv}\, e]$ and $\mathcal{A}_\alpha(\Gamma, e) := [x \mapsto 0 \mid x \in \mathsf{dom}\, \Gamma]$.

A more realistic arity analysis is defined by

$$\begin{aligned}
\mathcal{A}_\alpha(x) &:= [x \mapsto \alpha] \\
\mathcal{A}_\alpha(e\ x) &:= \mathcal{A}_{\alpha+1}(e) \sqcup [x \mapsto 0] \\
\mathcal{A}_\alpha(\lambda x.\, e) &:= \mathcal{A}_{\alpha-1}(e) \setminus \{x\} \\
\mathcal{A}_\alpha(e\, \mathbf{?}\, e_{\mathbf{t}} : e_{\mathbf{f}}) &:= \mathcal{A}_0(e) \sqcup \mathcal{A}_\alpha(e_{\mathbf{t}}) \sqcup \mathcal{A}_\alpha(e_{\mathbf{f}}) \\
\mathcal{A}_\alpha(\mathbf{C}_b) &:= \bot \qquad \text{for } b \in \{\mathbf{t}, \mathbf{f}\} \\
\mathcal{A}_\alpha(\textbf{let}\ \Gamma\ \textbf{in}\ e) &:= (\mu\bar{\alpha}.\, \overline{\mathcal{A}}_{\bar{\alpha}}(\Gamma) \sqcup \mathcal{A}_\alpha(e) \sqcup [x \mapsto 0 \mid x \in \mathsf{thunks}\, \Gamma]) \setminus \mathsf{dom}\, \Gamma
\end{aligned}$$

and

$$\mathcal{A}_\alpha(\Gamma, e) := (\mu\bar{\alpha}.\, \overline{\mathcal{A}}_{\bar{\alpha}}(\Gamma) \sqcup \mathcal{A}_\alpha(e) \sqcup [x \mapsto 0 \mid x \in \mathsf{thunks}\, \Gamma])\big|_{\mathsf{dom}\, \Gamma}$$

where $(\mu\bar{\alpha}.\ldots)$ denotes the least fixed point, which exists as the involved operations are continuous and monotone in $\bar{\alpha}$. Moreover, the fixed point can be found in a finite number of steps by iterating from $\bot$, as the carrier of $\bar{\alpha}$ is bounded by the finite set $\mathsf{fv}\, \Gamma \cup \mathsf{fv}\, e$, and the pointwise partial order on arities has no infinite ascending chains. As this ignores the issue of thunks, it corresponds to the analysis described in [Gil96].

This implementation fulfils the specifications in Definition 6 and Definition 7, so by Corollary 19, it is safe.

4.2.2 Functional correctness

This section on the functional correctness of the transformation is a slight detour in this chapter, which is mainly about the safety of the transformation. I include it here not only because functional correctness, i.e. the preservation of semantics, is an important property, but also to demonstrate that it holds independent of the correctness of a cardinality analysis.

For this section, we expect the analysis to fulfil the specification in Definition 6, but do not require any specific behaviour with regard to thunks, i.e. Definition 7 does not need to hold.

Theorem 4 (Functional correctness of Call Arity)
For all expressions e, we have

$$[\![\mathsf{T}_0(e)]\!] = [\![e]\!]. \qquad \diamond$$

As usual, in order to prove this, I need to generalise the statement. In this case, the statement needs to hold for arbitrary incoming arities, instead of just 0, and furthermore for arbitrary environments instead of just $\bot$.

But in the general case, I would not be able to prove plain equality: Consider the expression $e = \textbf{let } x = x \textbf{ in } x$: When analysed with an incoming arity of 1, we have

$$\mathsf{T}_1(e) = \textbf{let } x = \lambda y.\, x\, y \textbf{ in } x$$

but

$$[\![e]\!]_\bot = \bot \neq \mathsf{Fn}(\lambda\_.\, \bot) = [\![\mathsf{T}_1(e)]\!]_\bot.$$

Therefore, I need to generalise the notion of equality as well, to a weaker notion that only demands equality when applied to enough arguments:

Definition 10 (Equality up to eta-expansion)
For every $\alpha \in \mathbb{N}$ and $v_1, v_2 \in \mathsf{Value}$ let $e_1 \approx_\alpha e_2$ denote that

$$v_1 \downarrow_{\mathsf{Fn}} z_1 \downarrow_{\mathsf{Fn}} \cdots \downarrow_{\mathsf{Fn}} z_\alpha = v_2 \downarrow_{\mathsf{Fn}} z_1 \downarrow_{\mathsf{Fn}} \cdots \downarrow_{\mathsf{Fn}} z_\alpha.$$

for all $z_1, \ldots, z_\alpha \in \mathsf{Value}$

Furthermore, for every arity environment $\bar\alpha \in \mathsf{Var} \to \mathbb{N}_\bot$ and environments $\rho_1, \rho_2 \in \mathsf{Var} \to \mathsf{Value}$, let

$$\rho_1 \approx_{\bar\alpha} \rho_2 := \forall x \in \mathsf{dom}\, \bar\alpha.\, (\rho_1\, x) \approx_{\bar\alpha\, x} (\rho_2\, x). \qquad \diamond$$

Note that $\approx_0$ coincides with plain equality. If we have $v_1 \approx_{\alpha+1} v_2$, then also $v_1 \downarrow_{\mathsf{Fn}} z \approx_\alpha v_2 \downarrow_{\mathsf{Fn}} z$ for all $z \in \mathsf{Value}$. Conversely, $v_1[v] \approx_{\alpha-1} v_2[v]$ for all $v \in \mathsf{Value}$ implies $\mathsf{Fn}(\lambda v.\, v_1[v]) \approx_\alpha \mathsf{Fn}(\lambda v.\, v_2[v])$.

The relation is monotone in the sense that for $\alpha \sqsubseteq \alpha'$, $\approx_{\alpha'}$ implies $\approx_\alpha$, and analogously for the relation on environments.

The main motivation for this definition is that it does not see eta-expansion:

Lemma 20
$[\![\mathcal{E}_\alpha(e)]\!]_\rho \approx_\alpha [\![e]\!]_\rho$

Proof
by induction of α. ∎

I proceed by proving soundness of the analysis and then the correctness of the transformation, in its general form.

Lemma 21
If $\rho_1 \approx_{\mathcal{A}_\alpha(e)} \rho_2$, then $[\![e]\!]_{\rho_1} \approx_\alpha [\![e]\!]_{\rho_2}$.

Proof
by induction over the expression e.

Case: $e = x$
By (A-Var), we have $\alpha \sqsubseteq \mathcal{A}_\alpha(e)$, so the assumption of the lemma implies $(\rho_1\, x) \approx_{\mathcal{A}_\alpha(e)\, x} (\rho_2\, x)$, which in turn provides $(\rho_1\, x) \approx_\alpha (\rho_2\, x)$ as required.

Case: $e = e'\ x$
By (A-App), the assumption of the lemma implies both $\rho_1 \approx_{\mathcal{A}_{\alpha+1}(e')} \rho_2$ as well as $(\rho_1\, x) \approx_0 (\rho_2, x)$. By induction, the former yields $[\![e']\!]_{\rho_1} \approx_{\alpha+1} [\![e']\!]_{\rho_2}$. Therefore

$$\begin{aligned}
[\![e'\ x]\!]_{\rho_1} &= [\![e']\!]_{\rho_1} \downarrow_{\mathsf{Fn}} \rho_1\, x \\
&= [\![e']\!]_{\rho_1} \downarrow_{\mathsf{Fn}} \rho_2\, x \\
&\approx_\alpha [\![e']\!]_{\rho_2} \downarrow_{\mathsf{Fn}} \rho_2\, x \\
&= [\![e'\ x]\!]_{\rho_2}.
\end{aligned}$$

Case: $e = \lambda x.\, e'$
By (A-Lam) and the assumption we have $\rho_1 \approx_{\mathcal{A}_{\alpha-1}(e')\setminus\{x\}} \rho_2$, which, for any $v \in \mathsf{Value}$, yields $(\rho_1 \sqcup [x \mapsto v]) \approx_{\mathcal{A}_{\alpha-1}(e')} (\rho_2 \sqcup [x \mapsto v])$. By the induction hypothesis, this implies $[\![e']\!]_{\rho_2 \sqcup [x \mapsto v]} \approx_{\alpha-1} [\![e']\!]_{\rho_2 \sqcup [x \mapsto v]}$, and thus

$$\begin{aligned}[\![\lambda x.\, e']\!]_{\rho_1} &= \mathsf{Fn}(\lambda v.\, [\![e']\!]_{\rho_1 \sqcup [x \mapsto v]}) \\ &\approx_\alpha \mathsf{Fn}(\lambda v.\, [\![e']\!]_{\rho_2 \sqcup [x \mapsto v]}) = [\![\lambda x.\, e']\!]_{\rho_2}.\end{aligned}$$

Case: $e = \textbf{let}\ \Gamma\ \textbf{in}\ e'$
This follows immediately from the denotation of let-expressions and the inductive hypothesis, once we have $(\{\!\{\Gamma\}\!\}\rho_1) \approx_{\mathcal{A}_\alpha(e)} (\{\!\{\Gamma\}\!\}\rho_2)$. By (A-Let), this can be generalised to $(\{\!\{\Gamma\}\!\}\rho_1) \approx_{\bar\alpha} (\{\!\{\Gamma\}\!\}\rho_2)$ where $\bar\alpha = \mathcal{A}_\alpha(\Gamma, e) \sqcup \mathcal{A}_\alpha(\textbf{let}\ \Gamma\ \textbf{in}\ e)$.

We prove this by parallel fixed-point induction. The base case is trivial, so we assume we have

$$\rho_1' \approx_{\bar\alpha} \rho_2'$$

for some ρ_1', ρ_2', and we need to show

$$(\rho_1 +\!\!+_{\mathsf{dom}\,\Gamma} [\![\Gamma]\!]_{\rho_1'}) \approx_{\bar\alpha} (\rho_2 +\!\!+_{\mathsf{dom}\,\Gamma} [\![\Gamma]\!]_{\rho_2'})$$

which we do point-wise. Let $\alpha' = \bar\alpha\, x$.

For $x \mapsto e'' \in \Gamma$, we need to show $([\![e'']\!]_{\rho_1'}) \approx_{\alpha'} ([\![e'']\!]_{\rho_1'})$. By the induction hypothesis, this requires $\rho_1' \approx_{\mathcal{A}_{\alpha'}(e'')} \rho_2'$, which in turn follows from $\rho_1' \approx_{\bar\alpha} \rho_2'$ and (A-Let).

For $x \notin \mathsf{dom}\,\Gamma$, we need to show $(\rho_1\, x) \approx_{\alpha'} (\rho_2\, x)$. This follows from $\bar\alpha\, x = \mathcal{A}_\alpha(\textbf{let}\ \Gamma\ \textbf{in}\ e)\, x$ and the assumption of the lemma, namely $\rho_1 \approx_{\mathcal{A}_\alpha(\textbf{let}\ \Gamma\ \textbf{in}\ e)} \rho_2$.

Case: $e = \mathsf{C}_b$
Trivial.

Case: $e = e'\ \textbf{?}\ e_{\mathbf{t}} : e_{\mathbf{f}}$
By the assumption, (A-If) and the monotonicity of $\approx_{\bar\alpha}$, we can invoke all three induction hypotheses and obtain $[\![e']\!]_{\rho_1} \approx_0 [\![e']\!]_{\rho_2}$, $[\![e_{\mathbf{t}}]\!]_{\rho_1} \approx_\alpha [\![e_{\mathbf{t}}]\!]_{\rho_2}$ and $[\![e_{\mathbf{f}}]\!]_{\rho_1} \approx_\alpha [\![e_{\mathbf{f}}]\!]_{\rho_2}$. From this, $[\![e'\ \textbf{?}\ e_{\mathbf{t}} : e_{\mathbf{f}}]\!]_{\rho_1} \approx_\alpha [\![e'\ \textbf{?}\ e_{\mathbf{t}} : e_{\mathbf{f}}]\!]_{\rho_2}$ follows by a case analysis on $[\![e']\!]_{\rho_1}$. ■

With this in place, we can prove that the transformation is semantics-preserving:

Lemma 22
$[\![\mathsf{T}_\alpha(e)]\!]_\rho \approx_\alpha [\![e]\!]_\rho$.

Proof
Again, by induction on e, for arbitrary α and ρ.

Case: $e = x$
Trivial.

Case: $e = e'\ x$
By the induction hypothesis, we have $[\![\mathsf{T}_{\alpha+1}(e')]\!]_\rho \approx_{\alpha+1} [\![e']\!]_\rho$, so

$$\begin{aligned}
[\![\mathsf{T}_\alpha(e'\ x)]\!]_\rho &= [\![\mathsf{T}_{\alpha+1}(e')\ x]\!]_\rho \\
&= [\![\mathsf{T}_{\alpha+1}(e')]\!]_\rho \downarrow_{\mathsf{Fn}} \rho\, x \\
&\approx_\alpha [\![e']\!]_\rho \downarrow_{\mathsf{Fn}} \rho\, x \\
&= [\![e'\ x]\!]_\rho.
\end{aligned}$$

Case: $e = \lambda x.\, e'$
By the induction hypothesis, we have $[\![\mathsf{T}_{\alpha-1}(e')]\!]'_\rho \approx_{\alpha-1} [\![e']\!]'_\rho$ for any ρ', so

$$\begin{aligned}
[\![\mathsf{T}_\alpha(\lambda x.\, e')]\!]_\rho &= [\![\lambda x.\, \mathsf{T}_{\alpha-1}(e')]\!]_\rho \\
&= \mathsf{Fn}(\lambda v.\, [\![\mathsf{T}_{\alpha+1}(e')]\!]_{\rho \sqcup [x \mapsto v]}) \\
&\approx_\alpha \mathsf{Fn}(\lambda v.\, [\![e']\!]_{\rho \sqcup [x \mapsto v]}) \\
&= [\![\lambda x.\, e']\!]_\rho.
\end{aligned}$$

Case: $e = \textbf{let}\ \Gamma\ \textbf{in}\ e'$
We first need to prove

$$\{\!\{\overline{\mathsf{T}}_{\mathcal{A}_\alpha(\Gamma,e)}(\Gamma)\}\!\}\rho \approx_{\mathcal{A}_\alpha(e)} \{\!\{\Gamma\}\!\}\rho. \qquad (*)$$

which, using (A-let), follows from

$$\{\!\{\overline{\mathsf{T}}_{\mathcal{A}_\alpha(\Gamma,e)}(\Gamma)\}\!\}\rho \approx_{\bar{\alpha}} \{\!\{\Gamma\}\!\}\rho$$

with $\bar{\alpha} = \mathcal{A}_\alpha(\Gamma, e) \sqcup \mathcal{A}_\alpha(\textbf{let}\ \Gamma\ \textbf{in}\ e)$.

Similar to above, we can prove this using parallel fixedpoint induction. Again, the base case is trivial, so let ρ_1, ρ_2 be environments for which

$$\rho_1 \approx_{\bar{\alpha}} \rho_2$$

holds. We need to show

$$[\![\overline{\mathsf{T}}_{\mathcal{A}_\alpha(\Gamma,e)}(\Gamma)]\!]_{\rho_1} \approx_{\bar{\alpha}} [\![\Gamma]\!]_{\rho_2}.$$

which we verify point-wise. Let $x \mapsto e'' \in \Gamma$ and $\alpha' = \mathcal{A}_\alpha(\Gamma, e)\, x = \bar{\alpha}\, x$. We have

$$\begin{aligned}
[\![\overline{\mathsf{T}}_{\mathcal{A}_\alpha(\Gamma,e)}(\Gamma)]\!]_{\rho_1}\, x &= [\![\mathcal{E}_{\alpha'}(\mathsf{T}_{\alpha'}(e''))]\!]_{\rho_1} \\
&\approx_{\alpha'} [\![\mathsf{T}_{\alpha'}(e'')]\!]_{\rho_1} && \{\text{ Lemma 20 }\} \\
&\approx_{\alpha'} [\![e'']\!]_{\rho_1} && \{\text{ ind. hypothesis }\} \\
&\approx_{\alpha'} [\![e'']\!]_{\rho_2} && \{\text{ Lemma 21 }\} \\
&= [\![\Gamma]\!]_{\rho_2}\, x
\end{aligned}$$

where in order to invoke Lemma 21, we need $\rho_1 \approx_{\mathcal{A}_{\alpha'}(e'')} \rho_2$, which follows from $\rho_1 \approx_{\bar{\alpha}} \rho_2$ and (A-Let).

Now we can calculate

$$\begin{aligned}
[\![\mathsf{T}_\alpha(\textbf{let } \Gamma \textbf{ in } e')]\!]_\rho &= [\![\textbf{let } \overline{\mathsf{T}}_{\mathcal{A}_\alpha(\Gamma,e')}(\Gamma) \textbf{ in } \mathsf{T}_\alpha(e')]\!]_\rho \\
&= [\![\mathsf{T}_\alpha(e')]\!]_{\{\!\{\overline{\mathsf{T}}_{\mathcal{A}_\alpha(\Gamma,e')}(\Gamma)\}\!\}\rho} \\
&\approx_\alpha [\![e']\!]_{\{\!\{\overline{\mathsf{T}}_{\mathcal{A}_\alpha(\Gamma,e')}(\Gamma)\}\!\}\rho} && \{\text{ ind. hypothesis }\} \\
&\approx_\alpha [\![e']\!]_{\{\!\{\Gamma\}\!\}\rho} && \{\text{ Lemma 21 and } (*)\ \} \\
&= [\![\textbf{let } \Gamma \textbf{ in } e']\!]_\rho.
\end{aligned}$$

Case: $e = \mathbf{C}_b$
Trivial.

Case: $e = e' \mathbin{\textbf{?}} e_{\mathbf{t}} \mathbin{\textbf{:}} e_{\mathbf{f}}$
By induction we have $[\![\mathsf{T}_0(e)]\!]_\rho \approx_0 [\![e]\!]_\rho$, so $[\![\mathsf{T}_0(e)]\!]_\rho = [\![e]\!]_\rho$, and by case analysis on this value, this follows from the induction hypotheses. ∎

Proof (of Theorem 4)
This follows from Lemma 22 with $\rho = \bot$, as $\approx_0$ coincides with regular equality. ∎

4.3 Cardinality analyses

The previous section proved the safety of a straight-forward arity analysis. But it was severely limited by not being able to eta-expand thunks, which is desirable in practice.

4.3.1 Abstract cardinality analysis

So the arity analysis needs an accompanying *cardinality analysis* which prognoses how often a bound variable is going to be evaluated: I model this as a function

$$\mathcal{C}_\alpha(\Gamma, e) \colon \mathsf{Var} \to \mathsf{Card}$$

where Card is the three element lattice

$$\bot \sqsubset 1 \sqsubset \infty,$$

corresponding to "not called", "called at most once" and "no information", respectively. We use γ for an element of Card and $\bar{\gamma}$ for a mapping $\mathsf{Var} \to \mathsf{Card}$.

The expression $\bar{\gamma} - x$, which subtracts one call from the prognosis, is defined as

$$(\bar{\gamma} - x)\, y = \begin{cases} \bot & \text{if } y = x \text{ and } \bar{\gamma}\, y = 1 \\ \bar{\gamma}\, y & \text{otherwise.} \end{cases}$$

Specification

I start with a very abstract specification for a safe cardinality analysis and prove that an arity transformation that makes use of it it is still safe. I stay oblivious in how the analysis works and defer that to the next refinement step in Section 4.3.2.

For the specification we not only need the local view on one binding, as provided by $\mathcal{C}_\alpha(\Gamma, e)$, but also a prognosis on how often each variable is going to be called in the further execution of a complete and arity-annotated configuration:

$$\mathcal{C}_{(\bar{\alpha}, \alpha, \dot{\alpha})}((\Gamma, e, S)) \colon \mathsf{Var} \to \mathsf{Card}$$

Definition 11 (Cardinality analysis specification)
The cardinality prognosis and cardinality analysis fulfil some obvious naming hygiene conditions:

$$\mathsf{dom}\, \mathcal{C}_\alpha(\Delta, e) = \mathsf{dom}\, \mathcal{A}_\alpha(\Delta, e) \tag{Ch-dom}$$

$$\mathsf{dom}\, \mathcal{C}_{(\bar\alpha,\alpha,\dot\alpha)}((\Gamma, e, S)) \subseteq \mathsf{fv}\,(\Gamma, e, S) \tag{C-dom}$$

$$\bar\alpha\big|_{\mathsf{dom}\,\Gamma} = \bar\alpha'\big|_{\mathsf{dom}\,\Gamma} \implies$$
$$\mathcal{C}_{(\bar\alpha,\alpha,\dot\alpha)}((\Gamma, e, S)) = \mathcal{C}_{(\bar\alpha',\alpha,\dot\alpha)}((\Gamma, e, S)) \tag{C-cong}$$

$$\bar\alpha\ x = \bot \implies \mathcal{C}_{(\bar\alpha,\alpha,\dot\alpha)}((\Gamma, e, S)) = \mathcal{C}_{(\bar\alpha,\alpha,\dot\alpha)}((\Gamma \setminus \{x\}, e, S)) \tag{C-not-called}$$

Furthermore, the cardinality analysis is likewise a forward analysis and has to be conservative about function arguments:

$$\$x \in S \implies [x \mapsto \infty] \sqsubseteq \mathcal{C}_{(\bar\alpha,\alpha,\dot\alpha)}((\Gamma, e, S)) \tag{C-args}$$

The prognosis may ignore update markers on the stack:

$$\mathcal{C}_{(\bar\alpha,\alpha,\dot\alpha)}((\Gamma, e, \#x \cdot S)) \sqsubseteq \mathcal{C}_{(\bar\alpha,\alpha,\dot\alpha)}((\Gamma, e, S)) \tag{C-upd}$$

An imminent call better be prognosed:

$$[x \mapsto 1] \sqsubseteq \mathcal{C}_{(\bar\alpha,\alpha,\dot\alpha)}((\Gamma, x, S)) \tag{C-call}$$

Evaluation improves the prognosis: Note that in (C-Var$_1$) and (C-Var$_1'$), we account for the call to x with the $-$ operator.

$$\mathcal{C}_{(\bar\alpha,\alpha+1,\dot\alpha)}((\Gamma, e, \$x \cdot S)) \sqsubseteq \mathcal{C}_{(\bar\alpha,\alpha,\dot\alpha)}((\Gamma, e\ x, S)) \tag{C-App}$$

$$\mathcal{C}_{(\bar\alpha,\alpha-1,\dot\alpha)}((\Gamma, e[y := x], S)) \sqsubseteq \mathcal{C}_{(\bar\alpha,\alpha,\dot\alpha)}((\Gamma, \lambda y.\, e, \$x \cdot S)) \tag{C-Lam}$$

$$(x \mapsto e) \in \Gamma,\ \neg\mathsf{isVal}\, e \implies$$
$$\mathcal{C}_{(\bar\alpha,\bar\alpha\ x,\dot\alpha)}((\Gamma \setminus \{x\}, e, \#x \cdot S)) \sqsubseteq \mathcal{C}_{(\bar\alpha,\alpha,\dot\alpha)}((\Gamma, x, S)) - x \tag{C-Var$_1$}$$

$$(x \mapsto e) \in \Gamma,\ \mathsf{isVal}\, e \implies$$
$$\mathcal{C}_{(\bar\alpha,\bar\alpha\ x,\dot\alpha)}((\Gamma, e, S)) \sqsubseteq \mathcal{C}_{(\bar\alpha,\alpha,\dot\alpha)}((\Gamma, x, S)) - x \tag{C-Var$_1'$}$$

$$\mathsf{isVal}\, e \implies$$
$$\mathcal{C}_{(\bar\alpha,0,\dot\alpha)}((\Gamma[x \mapsto e], e, S)) \sqsubseteq \mathcal{C}_{(\bar\alpha,0,\dot\alpha)}((\Gamma, e, \#x \cdot S)) \tag{C-Var$_2$}$$

$$\mathcal{C}_{(\bar\alpha,0,\alpha\cdot\dot\alpha)}((\Gamma, e, (e_{\mathbf{t}} : e_{\mathbf{f}}) \cdot S)) \sqsubseteq \mathcal{C}_{(\bar\alpha,\alpha,\dot\alpha)}((\Gamma, e\, \mathbf{?}\, e_{\mathbf{t}} : e_{\mathbf{f}}, S)) \tag{C-If$_1$}$$

$$b \in \{\mathbf{t}, \mathbf{f}\} \implies \mathcal{C}_{(\bar\alpha,\alpha,\dot\alpha)}((\Gamma, e_b, S)) \sqsubseteq \mathcal{C}_{(\bar\alpha,0,\alpha\cdot\dot\alpha)}((\Gamma, \mathbf{C}_b, (e_{\mathbf{t}} : e_{\mathbf{f}}) \cdot S)) \tag{C-If$_2$}$$

The specification for the **let**-bindings connects the arity analysis, the cardinality analysis and the cardinality prognosis:

$$\begin{aligned}&\mathsf{dom}\,\Delta \cap \mathsf{fv}\,(\Gamma, S) = \{\},\ \mathsf{dom}\,\bar{\alpha} \subseteq \mathsf{dom}\,\Gamma \cup \#S \implies\\ &\quad \mathcal{C}_{(\mathcal{A}_\alpha(\Delta,e)\sqcup\bar{\alpha},\alpha,\dot{\alpha})}((\Delta\cdot\Gamma, e, S)) \sqsubseteq \mathcal{C}_\alpha(\Delta, e) \sqcup \mathcal{C}_{(\bar{\alpha},\alpha,\dot{\alpha})}((\Gamma, \textbf{let}\ \Delta\ \textbf{in}\ e, S))\end{aligned} \tag{C-Let}$$

Finally, we need to ensure that the analysis returns the top element of the lattice for thunks that might be called more than once. In contrast to the corresponding Definition 7, this can now make use of the cardinality analysis:

$$x \in \mathsf{thunks}\,\Gamma,\ \mathcal{C}_\alpha(\Gamma, e)\ x = \infty \implies \mathcal{A}_\alpha(\Gamma, e)\ x = 0 \tag{Ah-∞-thunk}$$

◇

Safety

The safety proof proceeds similarly to the one for Lemma 18. But now we are allowed to eta-expand thunks that are called at most once. This has considerable technical implications for the proof:

- An eta-expanded expression is a value, so in the transformed program, VAR_2 occurs immediately after VAR_1. In the original program, however, an update marker stays on the stack until the expression is evaluated to a value, and then VAR_2 fires without a correspondence in the evaluation of the transformed program. In particular, the update marker can interfere with uses of Lemma 17.
- Because the eta-expanded expression is a value, it stays on the heap as it is, whereas in the original program, it is first evaluated. Evaluation can reduce the number of free variables of the expression, so subsequent choices of fresh variables in LET_1 in the original evaluation might not be suitable in the evaluation of the transformed program.

A more complicated variant of Lemma 17 and carrying a variable renaming around throughout the proof might solve these problems, but would complicate it too much. I therefore apply a small trick and simply allow unwanted update markers to disappear, by defining a variant of the semantics:

Definition 12 (Forgetful semantics)
The relation $\Rightarrow_{\#}$ is defined by

$$(\Gamma, e, S) \Rightarrow (\Gamma', e', S') \implies (\Gamma, e, S) \Rightarrow_{\#} (\Gamma', e', S')$$

and

$$(\Gamma, e, \#x \cdot S) \Rightarrow_{\#} (\Gamma, e, S). \qquad \text{DROPUPD}$$

◇

This way, a one-shot binding can disappear completely after it has been called, making it easier to relate the original program to the transformed program. Because $\Rightarrow_{\#}$ contains $\Rightarrow$, Lemma 17 holds here as well. Afterwards, and outside the scope of the safety proof, I will recover the original semantics from the forgetful semantics.

In the proof I keep track of the set of removed bindings (named r), and write $(\Gamma, e, S) - r := (\Gamma \setminus r, e, S - r)$ for the configuration with bindings from the set r removed. The stack $(S - r)$ is S without update markers $\#x$ where $x \in r$.

I also keep track of $\bar{\gamma}\colon \mathsf{Var} \to \mathsf{Card}$, the current cardinalities of the variables on the heap:

Definition 13 (Cardinality arity annotation consistency)
I write $(\bar{\alpha}, \alpha, \dot{\alpha}, \bar{\gamma}, r) \rhd_{\mathsf{C}} (\Gamma, e, S)$, iff

- the arity information is consistent, $(\bar{\alpha}, \alpha, \dot{\alpha}) \rhd (\Gamma, e, S) - r$,
- $\mathsf{dom}\, \bar{\alpha} = \mathsf{dom}\, \bar{\gamma}$,
- the cardinality information is correct, $\mathcal{C}_{(\bar{\alpha},\alpha,\dot{\alpha})}((\Gamma, e, S)) \sqsubseteq \bar{\gamma}$,
- many-called thunks are not going to be eta-expanded, i.e. $\bar{\alpha}\ x = 0$ for $x \in \mathsf{thunks}\, \Gamma$ with $\bar{\gamma}\ x = \infty$ and
- only bindings that are not going to be called ($\bar{\gamma}\ x = \bot$) are removed, i.e. $r \subseteq (\mathsf{dom}\, \Gamma \cup \#S) - \mathsf{dom}\, \bar{\gamma}$. ◇

Lemma 23
Assume $\mathcal{A}$ and $\mathcal{C}$ fulfil the specifications in Definitions 6 and 11.

If $(\Gamma, e, S) \Rightarrow^{*} (\Gamma', e', S')$ and $(\bar{\alpha}, \alpha, \dot{\alpha}, \bar{\gamma}, r) \rhd_{\mathsf{C}} (\Gamma, e, S)$, then there exists an arity annotation $(\bar{\alpha}', \alpha', \dot{\alpha}', \bar{\gamma}', r')$ such that $(\bar{\alpha}', \alpha', \dot{\alpha}', \bar{\gamma}', r') \rhd_{\mathsf{C}} (\Gamma', e', S')$, and $\mathsf{T}_{(\bar{\alpha},\alpha,\dot{\alpha})}((\Gamma, e, S) - r) \Rightarrow_{\#}^{*} \mathsf{T}_{(\bar{\alpha}',\alpha',\dot{\alpha}')}((\Gamma', e', S') - r')$. ◇

The lemma is an analogue to Lemma 18. The main difference, besides the extra data to keep track of, is that we produce an evaluation in the forgetful semantics, with some bindings removed.

Proof
by the individual steps of $\Rightarrow^*$. The preservation of the arity annotation consistency in the proof of Lemma 18 can be used here as well. Note that both the arity annotation requirement and the transformation are applied to $(\Gamma, e, S) - r$, so this goes well together. The correctness of the cardinality information (the second condition in Definition 13) follows easily from the inequalities in Definition 11.

I elaborate only on the interesting cases:

Case: VAR_1
We cannot have $\bar{\gamma}\ x = \bot$ because of (C-call).

If $\bar{\gamma}\ x = \infty$ we get $\bar{\alpha}\ x = 0$, as before, and nothing surprising happens.

If $\bar{\gamma}\ x = 1$, we know that this is the only call to x, so we set $r' = r \cup \{x\}$, $\bar{\gamma}' = \bar{\gamma} - x$ and use DROPUPD to get rid of the mention of $\#x$ on the stack.

Case: VAR_2
If $x \notin r$, proceed as before. If $x \in r$, then the transformed configurations are identical and the $\Rightarrow_{\#}^*$ judgement follows from reflexivity. ■

Corollary 24
The cardinality based arity analysis is safe for closed expressions, i.e. if $\mathsf{fv}\, e = \{\}$ and $([], e, []) \Rightarrow^* (\Gamma, v, [])$ then there exists Γ' and v' such that $([], \mathsf{T}_0(e), []) \Rightarrow^* (\Gamma', v', [])$ where Γ and Γ' contain the same number of bindings. ◇

Proof
We need $\mathsf{fv}\, e = \{\}$ to have $\mathcal{C}_{\bot,0,[]}(([], e, [])) = \bot$, so that $(\bot, 0, [], \bot, []) \triangleright_{\mathsf{c}} ([], e, [])$ holds. Now according to Lemma 23 there are $\bar{\alpha}$, α, $\dot{\alpha}$ and r so that $\mathsf{T}_{(\bot,0,[])}(([], e, [])) \Rightarrow_{\#}^* \mathsf{T}_{(\bar{\alpha},\alpha,\dot{\alpha})}((\Gamma, v, []) - r)$.

As the forgetful semantics only drops unused bindings, but does not otherwise behave any different than the real semantics, a technical lemma allows us to recover $\mathsf{T}_{(\bot,0,[])}(([], e, [])) \Rightarrow^* \mathsf{T}_{(\bar{\alpha},\alpha,\dot{\alpha})}((\Gamma', v, []))$ for a Γ' where $\overline{\mathsf{T}}_{\bar{\alpha}}(\Gamma) - r = \Gamma' - r'$. As $r \subseteq \Gamma$ and $r' \subseteq \Gamma'$, this concludes the proof of the corollary: Γ, $\overline{\mathsf{T}}_{\bar{\alpha}}(\Gamma)$ and Γ' all bind the same variables. ■

4.3.2 Trace tree cardinality analysis

In the second refinement, I look – still quite abstractly – at the implementation of the cardinality analysis. For the arity information, the type of the result required for the transformation ($\mathsf{Var} \to \mathbb{N}_\bot$) was sufficiently rich to be used in the analysis as well. This is unfortunately not the case for the cardinality analysis: Even if we know that an expression calls x and y each at most once, this does not tell us whether these calls can occur together (as in $e\ x\ y$) or whether they are exclusive (as in $e\,\mathbf{?}\,x : y$).

So I need a richer type that captures the future calls of an expression, that can distinguish different code paths and that maps easily to the type $\mathsf{Var} \to \mathsf{Card}$: This is the type TTree of (possibly infinite) trees, where each edge is labelled with a variable name, and a node has at most one outgoing edge for each variable name. The paths in the tree correspond to the possible executions and the labels on the edges record each occurring variable call. I use t for values of type TTree.

There are other, equivalent ways to interpret this type: Each TTree corresponds to a non-empty set of (finite) lists of variable names that is prefixed-closed (i.e. for every list in the set, its prefixes are also in the set). Each such list corresponds to a (finite) path in the tree. The function

$$\mathsf{paths} : \mathsf{TTree} \to 2^{[\mathsf{Var}]}$$

implements this correspondence.

Yet another view is given by the function

$$\mathsf{next} \colon \mathsf{Var} \to \mathsf{TTree} \to \mathsf{TTree}_\bot,$$

where $\mathsf{next}_x\, t = t'$ iff the root of t has an edge labelled x leading to t', and $\mathsf{next}_x\, t = \bot$ if the root of t has no edge labelled x. In that sense, TTree represents automata with labelled transitions, and we can actually define a trace trees t by specifying $\mathsf{next}_x\, t$ for all $x \in \mathsf{Var}$.

The basic operations on trees are $\oplus$, given by $\mathsf{paths}(t \oplus t') = \mathsf{paths}\, t \cup \mathsf{paths}(t')$, and $\otimes$, where $\mathsf{paths}(t \otimes t')$ is the set of all interleavings of lists from $\mathsf{paths}\, t$ with lists from $\mathsf{paths}(t')$. I write t^* for $t \otimes t \otimes t \otimes \cdots$. A tree is called *repeatable* if $t = t \otimes t = t^*$.

The partial order used on TTree is

$$t \sqsubseteq t' \iff \mathsf{paths}\, t \subseteq \mathsf{paths}\, t'.$$

I write $\bullet$ for the tree with no edges and simply x for $\bullet\!\xrightarrow{\;x\;}$, the tree with exactly one edge labelled x. The tree $t \setminus V$ is t with all edges with labels in V contracted, $t|_V$ is t with all edges but those labelled with variables in V contracted.

Example
Consider the two trees

$t_1 =$ 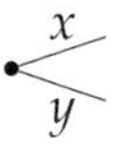

and $t_2 =$ 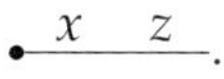

.

Then we have:

$t_1 \oplus t_2 =$ 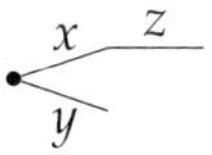

$t_1 \otimes t_2 =$ 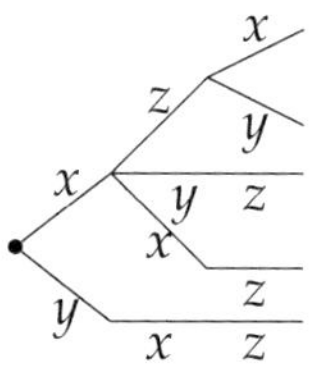

$t_1^* =$ 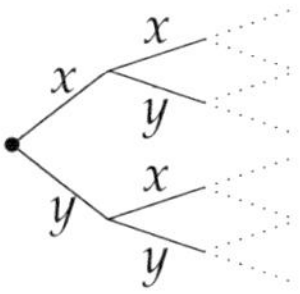

$(t_1 \otimes t_2) \setminus \{x\} = (t_1 \otimes t_2)|_{\{y,z\}} =$ 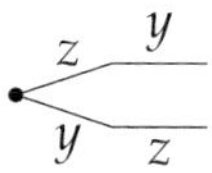

$\diamond$

Given a binding (Γ, e) where we have a TTree describing the calls done by e, and also one TTree for each expression bound in Γ, how can we combine that information into one tree describing the behaviour of the whole binding?

A first attempt might be a function

$$s\colon (\mathsf{Var} \to \mathsf{TTree}) \to \mathsf{TTree} \to \mathsf{TTree}$$

defined by

$$\mathsf{next}_x (s\; \bar{t}\; t) := \begin{cases} \bot & \text{if } \mathsf{next}_x\, t = \bot \\ s\; \bar{t}\; (t' \otimes \bar{t}\; x) & \text{if } \mathsf{next}_x\, t = t', \end{cases}$$

that traverses the tree t and upon every call interleaves the tree of the called name, $\bar{t}\; x$, with the remainder of t.

Example

Let $\bar{t}\ x = \bullet\xrightarrow{\ y\ }$, $\bar{t}\ y = \bullet\xrightarrow{\ z\ }$, $\bar{t}\ x = \bullet$ and $t = \bullet\xrightarrow{\ x\quad y\ }$. Then

$s\ \bar{t}\ t =$ 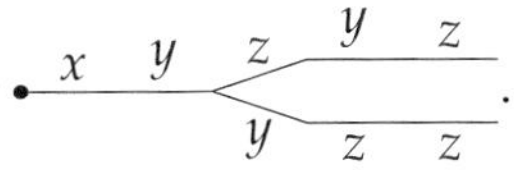

.
◇

This is a good start, but it does not cater for thunks, where the first call behaves differently than later calls. Therefore, we have to tell s which variables are bound to thunks, and give them special treatment: After a variable x referring to a thunk is evaluated, we pass on a modified map where $\bar{t}\ x = \bullet$.

Hence I extend the signature to

$$s\colon 2^{\mathsf{Var}} \to (\mathsf{Var} \to \mathsf{TTree}) \to \mathsf{TTree} \to \mathsf{TTree}$$

and the definition is now

$$\mathsf{next}_x(s_T\ \ \bar{t}\ \ t) \ := \ \begin{cases} \bot & \text{if } \mathsf{next}_x\, t = \bot \\ s_T\ \bar{t}\ (t' \otimes \bar{t}\ x) & \text{if } \mathsf{next}_x\, t = t',\, x \notin T \\ s_T\ (\bar{t}[x \mapsto \bullet])\ (t' \otimes \bar{t}\ x) & \text{if } \mathsf{next}_x\, t = t',\, x \in T. \end{cases}$$

The ability to define this function (relatively) easily is the main advantage of working with trace trees instead of co-call graphs at this stage.

As s is defined in terms of monotone operations, it is itself monotone in its arguments $\bar{t}$ and t.

Example

With the same arguments as above, for $T = \{y\}$ the effect of calling y, i.e. a call to z, happens only once, and we have

$s_T\ \bar{t}\ t =$ 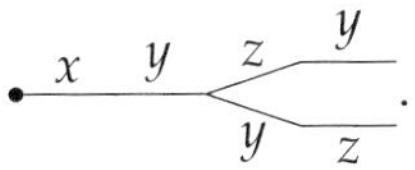

.
◇

We project a TTree to a value of type (Var $\to$ Card), as required for a cardinality analysis, using $c\colon \mathsf{TTree} \to (\mathsf{Var} \to \mathsf{Card})$ defined by

$$c(t)\ x := \begin{cases} \bot, & \text{if } x \text{ does not occur in } t \\ 1, & \text{if on each path in } t, x \text{ occurs at most once} \\ \infty, & \text{otherwise.} \end{cases}$$

From this definition it follows

Lemma 25
$c(\mathsf{next}_x\ t) \sqsubseteq c(t) - x.$ ◇

Specification

A tree cardinality analysis determines for every expression e and arity α the tree $\mathcal{T}_\alpha(e)$ of calls to free variables of e which are performed by evaluating e with α arguments and using the result in any way. As the resulting value might be passed to unknown code or stored in a data structure, we cannot assume anything about how often the resulting value is used. This justifies the arity parameter: We expect $\mathcal{T}_0(\lambda x.\, y) = y^*$ but $\mathcal{T}_1(\lambda x.\, y) = y$.

I write $\overline{\mathcal{T}_{\bar\alpha}}(\Gamma)$ for the analysis lifted to bindings, returning $\bot$ for variables not bound in Γ or mapped to $\bot$ in $\bar\alpha$.

I also need a variant $\mathcal{T}_\alpha(\Gamma, e)$ that, given bindings Γ, an expression e and an arity α, reports the calls on $\operatorname{dom}\Gamma$ performed by e and Γ with these bindings in scope.

I can now identify conditions on $\mathcal{T}$ that allow to satisfy the specifications in Definition 11.

Definition 14 (Tree cardinality analysis specification)
I expect the cardinality analysis to agree with the arity analysis on which variables are called at all:

$$\operatorname{dom} \mathcal{T}_\alpha(e) = \operatorname{dom} \mathcal{A}_\alpha(e) \qquad \text{(T-dom)}$$
$$\operatorname{dom} \mathcal{T}_\alpha(\Gamma, e) = \operatorname{dom} \mathcal{A}_\alpha(\Gamma, e) \qquad \text{(Th-dom)}$$

Inequalities for the syntactic constructs:

$$x^* \otimes \mathcal{T}_{\alpha+1}(e) \sqsubseteq \mathcal{T}_\alpha(e\ x) \qquad \text{(T-App)}$$

$$(\mathcal{T}_{\alpha-1}(e)) \setminus \{x\} \sqsubseteq \mathcal{T}_\alpha(\lambda x.\, e) \qquad \text{(T-Lam)}$$

$$\mathcal{T}_\alpha(e[y := x]) \sqsubseteq x^* \otimes (\mathcal{T}_\alpha(e)) \setminus \{y\} \qquad \text{(T-subst)}$$

$$x \sqsubseteq \mathcal{T}_\alpha(x) \qquad \text{(T-Var)}$$

$$\mathcal{T}_0(e) \otimes (\mathcal{T}_\alpha(e_\mathbf{t}) \oplus \mathcal{T}_\alpha(e_\mathbf{f})) \sqsubseteq \mathcal{T}_\alpha(e\,\mathbf{?}\,e_\mathbf{t} : e_\mathbf{f}) \qquad \text{(T-If)}$$

$$(s_{\mathsf{thunks}\,\Gamma}\ (\overline{\mathcal{T}}_{\mathcal{A}_\alpha(\Gamma,e)}(\Gamma))\ (\mathcal{T}_\alpha(e))) \setminus \mathsf{dom}\,\Gamma \sqsubseteq \mathcal{T}_\alpha(\mathbf{let}\ \Gamma\ \mathbf{in}\ e) \qquad \text{(T-Let)}$$

For values, analysed without arguments, the analysis is expected to return a repeatable tree:

$$\mathsf{isVal}\, e \implies \mathcal{T}_0(e) \text{ is repeatable} \qquad \text{(T-value)}$$

The specification for $\mathcal{A}_\alpha(\Gamma, e)$ is closely related to (T-Let):

$$(s_{\mathsf{thunks}\,\Gamma}\ (\overline{\mathcal{T}}_{\mathcal{A}_\alpha(\Gamma,e)}(\Gamma))\ (\mathcal{T}_\alpha(e)))|_{\mathsf{dom}\,\Gamma} \sqsubseteq \mathcal{T}_\alpha(\Gamma, e) \qquad \text{(Th-s)}$$

And finally, the connection to the arity analysis:

$$x \in \mathsf{thunks}\,\Gamma,\ c(\mathcal{T}_\alpha(\Gamma, e))\ x = \infty \implies (\mathcal{A}_\alpha(\Gamma, e))\ x = 0 \quad \text{(Th-}\infty\text{-thunk)}$$

◇

Safety

Given a tree cardinality analysis, I can define a cardinality analysis in the sense of the previous section. The definition for $\mathcal{C}_\alpha(\Gamma, e)$ is straight forward:

$$\mathcal{C}_\alpha(\Gamma, e) := c(\mathcal{T}_\alpha(\Gamma, e)).$$

In order to define $\mathcal{C}_{(\bar{\alpha},\alpha,\dot{\alpha})}((\Gamma, e, S))$ I need to fold the tree cardinality analysis over the stack:

$$\begin{aligned}
\dot{\mathcal{T}}__([]) &:= \bot \\
\dot{\mathcal{T}}_{\alpha\cdot\dot{\alpha}}((e_\mathbf{t} : e_\mathbf{f})\cdot S) &:= \dot{\mathcal{T}}_{\dot{\alpha}}(S) \otimes (\mathcal{T}_\alpha(e_\mathbf{t}) \oplus \mathcal{T}_\alpha(e_\mathbf{f})) \\
\dot{\mathcal{T}}_{\dot{\alpha}}(\$x\cdot S) &:= \dot{\mathcal{T}}_{\dot{\alpha}}(S) \otimes x^* \\
\dot{\mathcal{T}}_{\dot{\alpha}}(\#x\cdot S) &:= \dot{\mathcal{T}}_{\dot{\alpha}}(S).
\end{aligned}$$

With this I can define

$$\mathcal{C}_{(\bar{\alpha},\alpha,\dot{\alpha})}((\Gamma, e, S)) := c\big(s_{\mathsf{thunks}\,\Gamma}\ (\overline{\mathcal{T}}_{\bar{\alpha}}(\Gamma))\ (\mathcal{T}_{\alpha}(e) \otimes \dot{\mathcal{T}}_{\dot{\alpha}}(S))\big),$$

and set out to prove

Lemma 26
Given a tree cardinality analysis satisfying Definition 14, together with an arity analysis satisfying Definition 6, the derived cardinality analysis satisfies Definition 11. ◇

Proof
The conditions (C-dom) and (Ch-dom) follow directly from (T-dom) and (Th-dom) with (A-dom) and (Ah-dom).

The conditions (C-cong), (C-not-called) and (C-upd) follow directly from the definitions of $\overline{\mathcal{T}}$ and $\dot{\mathcal{T}}$

We have $x^* \sqsubseteq \dot{\mathcal{T}}_{\dot{\alpha}}(S)$ for $\$x \in S$, so (C-args) follows from

$$[x \mapsto \infty] = c(x^*) \sqsubseteq c(\dot{\mathcal{T}}_{\dot{\alpha}}(S)) \sqsubseteq (\mathcal{C}_{(\bar{\alpha},\alpha,\dot{\alpha})}((\Gamma, e, S))).$$

Similar calculations prove (C-call) using (T-Var), (C-App) using (T-App), (C-Lam) using (T-subst) and (T-Lam), (C-If_1) using (T-If).

Condition (C-If_2) is where the precision comes from, as we retain the knowledge that the two code paths are mutually exclusive. The proof is a direct consequence of $t \sqsubseteq t \oplus t'$.

The variable cases are interesting, as these interact with the heap, and hence with the s function.

We first show that ($\text{C-Var}'_1$) is fulfilled. Abbreviate $T := \mathsf{thunks}\,\Gamma$ and note that $x \notin T$. We have

$$\begin{aligned}
&\mathcal{C}_{(\bar{\alpha},\dot{\alpha}\ x,\dot{\alpha})}((\Gamma, e, S)) \\
&= c\big(s_T\ (\overline{\mathcal{T}}_{\bar{\alpha}}(\Gamma))\ (\mathcal{T}_{\bar{\alpha}\ x}(e) \otimes \dot{\mathcal{T}}_{\dot{\alpha}}(S))\big) \\
&= c\big(s_T\ (\overline{\mathcal{T}}_{\bar{\alpha}}(\Gamma))\ (\mathsf{next}_x\, x \otimes \mathcal{T}_{\bar{\alpha}\ x}(e) \otimes \dot{\mathcal{T}}_{\dot{\alpha}}(S))\big) && \{\text{ as } \mathsf{next}_x\, x = \bullet\,\} \\
&\sqsubseteq c\big(s_T\ (\overline{\mathcal{T}}_{\bar{\alpha}}(\Gamma))\ (\mathsf{next}_x(x \otimes \dot{\mathcal{T}}_{\dot{\alpha}}(S))) \otimes \mathcal{T}_{\bar{\alpha}\ x}(e))\big) \\
& && \{\text{ using } (\mathsf{next}_x\, t) \otimes t' \sqsubseteq \mathsf{next}_x(t \otimes t')\,\} \\
&= c\big(\mathsf{next}_x(s_T\ (\overline{\mathcal{T}}_{\bar{\alpha}}(\Gamma))\ (x \otimes \dot{\mathcal{T}}_{\dot{\alpha}}(S)))\big) && \{\text{ by the definition of } s\,\}
\end{aligned}$$

$$\begin{aligned}
&\sqsubseteq c\big(s_T\ (\overline{\mathcal{T}_{\bar{\alpha}}}(\Gamma))\ (x \otimes \dot{\mathcal{T}}_{\dot{\alpha}}(S))\big) - x && \{\text{ by Lemma 25 }\}\\
&\sqsubseteq c\big(s_T\ (\overline{\mathcal{T}_{\bar{\alpha}}}(\Gamma))\ (\mathcal{T}_{\alpha}(x) \otimes \dot{\mathcal{T}}_{\dot{\alpha}}(S))\big) - x && \{\text{ by (T-Var) and } s \text{ monotone }\}\\
&= \mathcal{C}_{(\bar{\alpha},\alpha,\dot{\alpha})}((\Gamma, x, S)) - x.
\end{aligned}$$

Condition (C-Var$_1$) represents the evaluation of a thunk. The proof is analogue, using $\overline{\mathcal{T}_{\bar{\alpha}}}(\Gamma)[x \mapsto \bullet] = \overline{\mathcal{T}_{\bar{\alpha}}}(\Gamma')$ in the step where the definition of s is unfolded.

For (C-Var$_2$) abbreviate $T := \mathsf{thunks}\,\Gamma = \mathsf{thunks}(\Gamma[x \mapsto e])$. We know $\mathsf{isVal}\,e$, so $\mathcal{T}_0(e)$ is repeatable, by (T-value). If a repeatable tree t is already contained in the second argument to s, then we can remove it from the range of the first argument:

$$s_T\ (\bar{t}[x \mapsto t])\ (t \otimes t') = s_T\ \bar{t}\ (t \otimes t')$$

Altogether, we show

$$\begin{aligned}
&\mathcal{C}_{(\bar{\alpha},0,\dot{\alpha})}((\Gamma[x \mapsto e], e, S))\\
&= c\big(s_T\ (\overline{\mathcal{T}_{\bar{\alpha}}}(\Gamma[x \mapsto e]))\ (\mathcal{T}_0(e) \otimes \dot{\mathcal{T}}_{\dot{\alpha}}(S))\big)\\
&= c\big(s_T\ (\overline{\mathcal{T}_{\bar{\alpha}}}(\Gamma)[x \mapsto \mathcal{T}_{\bar{\alpha}\ x}(e)])\ (\mathcal{T}_0(e) \otimes \dot{\mathcal{T}}_{\dot{\alpha}}(S))\big)\\
&\sqsubseteq c\big(s_T\ (\overline{\mathcal{T}_{\bar{\alpha}}}(\Gamma)[x \mapsto \mathcal{T}_0(e)])\ (\mathcal{T}_0(e) \otimes \dot{\mathcal{T}}_{\dot{\alpha}}(S))\big)\\
&= c\big(s_T\ (\overline{\mathcal{T}_{\bar{\alpha}}}(\Gamma))\ (\mathcal{T}_0(e) \otimes \dot{\mathcal{T}}_{\dot{\alpha}}(S))\big) && \{\text{ by } \mathcal{T}_0(e) \text{ repeatable }\}\\
&= \mathcal{C}_{(\bar{\alpha},0,\dot{\alpha})}((\Gamma, e, \#x \cdot S)).
\end{aligned}$$

Proving condition (C-Let) is for the most part a tedious calculation involving freshness of variables. We use that if the domain of $\bar{t}'$ is disjoint from the variables occurring in $\bar{t}$ (i.e. $\forall y.\, \forall x \in \bar{t}\ y.\, \bar{t}'\ x = \bullet$), then

$$s_T\ (\bar{t} \sqcup \bar{t}')\ t = s_T\ \bar{t}\ (s_T\ \bar{t}'\ t).$$

Abbreviating $T := \mathsf{thunks}\,\Gamma$ and $T' := \mathsf{thunks}\,\Delta$, we show:

$$\begin{aligned}
&\mathcal{C}_{(\mathcal{A}_\alpha(\Delta,e) \sqcup \bar{\alpha},\alpha,\dot{\alpha})}((\Delta \cdot \Gamma, e, S))\\
&= c\big(s_{T \cup T'}\ (\overline{\mathcal{T}}_{\mathcal{A}_\alpha(\Delta,e) \sqcup \bar{\alpha}}(\Gamma \cdot \Delta))\ (\mathcal{T}_\alpha(e) \otimes \dot{\mathcal{T}}_{\dot{\alpha}}(S))\big)\\
&= c\big(s_{T \cup T'}\ (\overline{\mathcal{T}_{\bar{\alpha}}}(\Gamma))\ (s_{T \cup T'}\ (\overline{\mathcal{T}}_{\mathcal{A}_\alpha(\Delta,e)}(\Delta))\ (\mathcal{T}_\alpha(e) \otimes \dot{\mathcal{T}}_{\dot{\alpha}}(S)))\big)\\
& && \{\text{ by the above equation }\}
\end{aligned}$$

$$
\begin{aligned}
&= c(s_T\ (\overline{\mathcal{T}}_{\bar\alpha}(\Gamma))\ (s_{T'}\ (\overline{\mathcal{T}}_{\mathcal{A}_\alpha(\Delta,e)}(\Delta))\ (\mathcal{T}_\alpha(e) \otimes \dot{\mathcal{T}}_{\dot\alpha}(S))))\\
&= c(s_T\ (\overline{\mathcal{T}}_{\bar\alpha}(\Gamma))\ (s_{T'}\ (\overline{\mathcal{T}}_{\mathcal{A}_\alpha(\Delta,e)}(\Delta))\ (\mathcal{T}_\alpha(e)) \otimes \dot{\mathcal{T}}_{\dot\alpha}(S)))\\
&\qquad\qquad\qquad\qquad \{\text{ as } \mathsf{dom}\,\Delta \text{ is fresh with regard to } S\ \}\\
&= c(s_T\ (\overline{\mathcal{T}}_{\bar\alpha}(\Gamma))\ (s_{T'}\ (\overline{\mathcal{T}}_{\mathcal{A}_\alpha(\Delta,e)}(\Delta))\ (\mathcal{T}_\alpha(e)) \otimes \dot{\mathcal{T}}_{\dot\alpha}(S)))|_{\mathsf{dom}\,\Delta} \sqcup\\
&\quad\ c(s_T\ (\overline{\mathcal{T}}_{\bar\alpha}(\Gamma))\ (s_{T'}\ (\overline{\mathcal{T}}_{\mathcal{A}_\alpha(\Delta,e)}(\Delta))\ (\mathcal{T}_\alpha(e)) \otimes \dot{\mathcal{T}}_{\dot\alpha}(S))) \setminus \mathsf{dom}\,\Delta\\
&= c(s_{T'}\ (\overline{\mathcal{T}}_{\mathcal{A}_\alpha(\Delta,e)}(\Delta))\ (\mathcal{T}_\alpha(e))|_{\mathsf{dom}\,\Delta}) \sqcup\\
&\quad\ c(s_T\ (\overline{\mathcal{T}}_{\bar\alpha}(\Gamma))\ (s_{T'}\ (\overline{\mathcal{T}}_{\mathcal{A}_\alpha(\Delta,e)}(\Delta))\ (\mathcal{T}_\alpha(e)) \setminus \mathsf{dom}\,\Delta \otimes \dot{\mathcal{T}}_{\dot\alpha}(S)))\\
&\sqsubseteq c(\mathcal{T}_\alpha(\Delta,e)) \sqcup c(s_T\ (\overline{\mathcal{T}}_{\bar\alpha}(\Gamma))\ (\mathcal{T}_\alpha(\textbf{let}\ \Delta\ \textbf{in}\ e) \otimes \dot{\mathcal{T}}_{\dot\alpha}(S)))\\
&\qquad\qquad\qquad\qquad \{\text{ by (Th-s) and (T-Let) }\}\\
&= \mathcal{C}_\alpha(\Delta,e) \sqcup \mathcal{C}_{(\bar\alpha,\alpha,\dot\alpha)}((\Gamma, \textbf{let}\ \Delta\ \textbf{in}\ e, S)).
\end{aligned}
$$

Finally, (Ah-∞-thunk) follows directly from (Th-∞-thunk). ∎

4.3.3 Co-call cardinality analysis

The preceding section provides a framework for a cardinality analysis, but the infinite nature of the TTree data type prevents an implementation on that level. Therefore, the concrete implementation uses a practically implementable data type which can serve as an approximation to trace trees: The co-call graphs introduced in Section 3.2.

We can convert such a graph to a TTree, using the function $t\colon \mathsf{Graph} \to \mathsf{TTree}$ given by

$$\mathsf{paths}(t(G)) := \{x_1 \cdots x_n \mid \forall i.\, x_i \in \mathsf{dom}\, G \wedge \forall j \neq i.\, x_i \text{—} x_j \in G\}.$$

Conversely, we can approximate a TTree by a Graph, as implemented by the function $g\colon \mathsf{TTree} \to \mathsf{Graph}$ where

$$g(t) := \bigsqcup\{\dot g(\dot x) \mid \dot x \in \mathsf{paths}\, t\}$$

which uses $\dot g\colon [\mathsf{Var}] \to \mathsf{Graph}$ given by

$$
\begin{aligned}
\mathsf{dom}\, \dot g(x_1 \cdots x_n) &= \{x_1, \ldots, x_n\}\\
\dot g(x_1 \cdots x_n) &:= \{x_i \text{—} x_j \mid i \neq j \leq n\}.
\end{aligned}
$$

The mappings t and g form a monotone Galois connection:

$$g(t) \sqsubseteq G \iff t \sqsubseteq t(G).$$

It even is a Galois insertion, as $g(t(G)) = G$.

Example
For

$t =$ 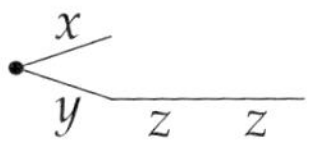

we have

$g(t) =$ 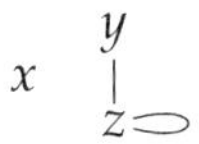

and

$t(g(t)) =$ 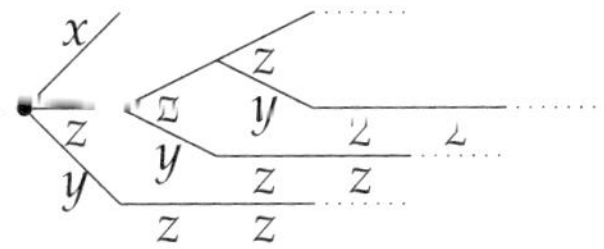

which shows that converting from trees to graphs and back loses information, in particular about whether something is called twice or more often, but the resulting tree still contains all the paths of the original tree. ◇

Specification

I proceed in the usual scheme, by giving a specification for a safe co-call cardinality analysis, connecting it to the tree cardinality analysis, and eventually proving that our implementation fulfils the specification.

A co-call cardinality analysis determines for each expression e and incoming arity α its co-call graph $\mathcal{G}_\alpha(e)$. As before, there is also a variant that analyses bindings, written $\mathcal{G}_\alpha(\Gamma, e)$. The conditions in the following definition are obviously designed to connect to Definition 14.

Definition 15 (Co-call cardinality analysis specification)
We want the co-call graph analysis to agree with the arity analysis on what is called at all:

$$\mathsf{dom}\, \mathcal{G}_\alpha(e) = \mathsf{dom}\, \mathcal{A}_\alpha(e) \qquad \text{(G-dom)}$$

As usual, we have inequalities for the syntactic constructs:

$$\mathcal{G}_{\alpha+1}(e) \sqcup (\{x\} \times \mathsf{fv}\,(e\ x)) \sqsubseteq \mathcal{G}_{\alpha}(e\ x) \tag{G-App}$$

$$\mathcal{G}_{\alpha-1}(e) \setminus \{x\} \sqsubseteq \mathcal{G}_{\alpha}(\lambda x.\, e) \tag{G-Lam}$$

$$\mathcal{G}_{\alpha}(e[y := x]) \setminus \{x, y\} \sqsubseteq \mathcal{G}_{\alpha}(e) \setminus \{x, y\} \tag{G-subst}$$

$$\mathcal{G}_0(e) \sqcup \mathcal{G}_{\alpha}(e_{\mathbf{t}}) \sqcup \mathcal{G}_{\alpha}(e_{\mathbf{f}}) \sqcup (\mathsf{dom}\,\mathcal{A}_0(e) \times (\mathsf{dom}\,\mathcal{A}_{\alpha}(e_{\mathbf{t}}) \cup \mathsf{dom}\,\mathcal{A}_{\alpha}(e_{\mathbf{f}})))$$
$$\sqsubseteq \mathcal{G}_{\alpha}(e\,\mathbf{?}\,e_{\mathbf{t}} : e_{\mathbf{f}}) \tag{G-If}$$

$$\mathcal{G}_{\alpha}(\Gamma, e) \setminus \mathsf{dom}\,\Gamma \sqsubseteq \mathcal{G}_{\alpha}(\mathbf{let}\ \Gamma\ \mathbf{in}\ e) \tag{G-Let}$$

$$\mathsf{isVal}\,e \implies \quad (\mathsf{fv}\,e)^2 \sqsubseteq \mathcal{G}_0(e) \tag{G-value}$$

The following conditions concern $\mathcal{G}_{\alpha}(\Gamma, e)$, which has to cater for the calls originating in e,

$$\mathcal{G}_{\alpha}(e) \sqsubseteq \mathcal{G}_{\alpha}(\Gamma, e), \tag{Gh-body}$$

the calls originating in the right-hand-sides,

$$(x \mapsto e') \in \Gamma \implies \quad \mathcal{G}_{\mathcal{A}_{\alpha}(\Gamma,e)\ x}(e') \sqsubseteq \mathcal{G}_{\alpha}(\Gamma, e), \tag{Gh-heap}$$

and finally the extra edges between what is called from the right-hand-side of a variable and whatever the variable is called with:

$$(x \mapsto e') \in \Gamma,\ \mathsf{isVal}(e') \implies$$
$$(\mathsf{fv}\,e') \times N_x(\mathcal{G}_a(\gamma, e)) \sqsubseteq \mathcal{G}_{\alpha}(\Gamma, e). \tag{Gh-extra}$$

For thunks, we can be slightly more precise: Only one call to them matters, so we can ignore a possible edge x—x:

$$(x \mapsto e') \in \Gamma,\ \neg\mathsf{isVal}(e') \implies$$
$$(\mathsf{fv}\,e') \times (N_x(\mathcal{G}_a(\gamma, e)) \setminus \{x\}) \sqsubseteq \mathcal{G}_{\alpha}(\Gamma, e) \tag{Gh-extra'}$$

Finally, we need to ensure that the cardinality analysis is actually used by the arity analysis when dealing with thunks. For recursive bindings, we never eta-expand thunks:

$$\mathsf{rec}\,\Gamma,\ x \in \mathsf{thunks}\,\Gamma,\ x \in \mathsf{dom}\,\mathcal{A}_{\alpha}(\Gamma, e) \implies$$
$$\mathcal{A}_{\alpha}(\Gamma, e) = 0 \tag{Rec-∞-thunk}$$

But for a non-recursive thunk, we only have to worry about thunks which are possibly called multiple times:

$$x \notin \mathsf{fv}\, e',\ \neg\mathsf{isVal}(e'),\ x\text{—}x \in \mathcal{G}_\alpha(\Gamma, e) \implies \mathcal{A}_\alpha([x \mapsto e'], e) = 0 \qquad \text{(Nonrec-}\infty\text{-thunk)}$$

◇

Safety

From a co-call analysis fulfilling Definition 15 we can derive a tree cardinality analysis fulfilling Definition 14, using

$$\mathcal{T}_\alpha(e) := t(\mathcal{G}_\alpha(e)).$$

The definition of $\mathcal{T}_\alpha(\Gamma, e)$ differs for non-recursive and recursive bindings.

- For a non-recursive binding $\Gamma = [x \mapsto e']$ we have $\mathcal{T}_\alpha(\Gamma, e) := t(\mathcal{G}_\alpha(e))|_{\mathsf{dom}\,\Gamma}$ and
- for recursive Γ we define $\mathcal{T}_\alpha(\Gamma, e) := t((\mathsf{dom}\,\mathcal{A}_\alpha(\Gamma, e))^2)$, i.e. the bound variables may call each other in any way.

Lemma 27
Given a co-call cardinality analysis satisfying Definition 15, together with an arity analysis satisfying Definition 6, the derived cardinality analysis satisfies Definition 14. ◇

Proof
Most conditions of Definition 14 follow by simple calculation from their counterpart in Definition 15 using the Galois connection

$$t \sqsubseteq t(G) \iff g(t) \sqsubseteq G$$

and identities such as $g(t \oplus t') = g(t) \sqcup g(t')$ and $g(t \otimes t') = g(t) \sqcup g(t') \sqcup (\mathsf{dom}\, t \times \mathsf{dom}\, t')$.

For (T-Let), we use (G-Let) with the following Lemma 28, instantiated with $T = \mathsf{thunks}\,\Gamma$, $\bar{t} = \overline{\mathcal{T}}_{\mathcal{A}_\alpha(\Gamma,e)}(\Gamma)$, $t = \mathcal{T}_\alpha(e)$ and $S = \mathsf{dom}\,\Gamma$. ■

Lemma 28
Given

- $g(t) \sqsubseteq G$,
- $\forall x \notin S.\, \bar{t}\, x = \bot$,
- $\forall x \in S.\, g(\bar{t}\, x) \sqsubseteq G$,
- $\forall x \in S,\, x \notin T.\, \mathsf{dom}\, (\bar{t}\, x) \times N_x(G) \sqsubseteq G$ and
- $\forall x \in S,\, x \in T.\, \mathsf{dom}\, (\bar{t}\, x) \times (N_x(G) \setminus \{x\}) \sqsubseteq G$

we have $g((s_T\, \bar{t}\, t) \setminus S) \sqsubseteq G$. ◇

Intuitively, this lemma describes how we can approximate the trace tree that is the result of integrating trace trees representing the bound expressions in a recursive binding with the trace tree describing the calls from the body. The conditions specify that

- the body is approximated by the graph G,
- the set S encompasses all bound variables,
- the effect of each individual bound trace tree is approximated by G,
- for a non-thunk x, for every edge x—$y \in G$, there is also an edge from y to anything that is called by x and
- similarly for a thunk x, but disregarding a possible loop x—$x \in G$.

The absence in G of an edge x—y for $x, y \in S$ does not indicate that calls to x are y are exclusive (they are mutually recursive, so typically both will be called, many times), but rather that in an infinite unwrapping of the recursive let, as explained on page 102, the recursion proceeds with either x or y. Therefore, the inequality in the conclusion of the lemma disregards variables from S.

Proof
In order to prove $g((s_T\, \bar{t}\, t) \setminus S) \sqsubseteq G$, we have to show that $\dot{g}(\dot{x} \setminus S) \sqsubseteq G$ for every path $\dot{x} \in \mathsf{paths}(s_T\; \bar{t}\; t)$. I write $\dot{x} \setminus S$ for the list $\dot{x}$ with all elements in S filtered out.

The behaviour of the function s can also be described as follows: In order to produce the path $\dot{x} \in \mathsf{paths}(s_T\; \bar{t}\; t)$, s picks a specific path $\dot{y} \in \mathsf{paths}\, t$ (and disregards t otherwise). Going through each entry x on $\dot{y}$, the function chooses a a specific path from $\bar{t}\, x$ and interleaves it into $\dot{y}$ after the entry x. This procedure then continues with the interleaved path, at the position following x.

In order to do a proof by induction, I strengthen the proposition, and keep track of two sets: The set V of variables not in S that have been called so far, and the set V_T that keeps track of the thunks that have been called. The assumptions of the strengthened proposition are

- $\dot{x}$ is a path produced by interleaving the trees from $\bar{t}$ into $\dot{y}$, as described above,
- $\dot{g}(\dot{y} \setminus V_T) \sqsubseteq G$,
- $V \times (\dot{y} \setminus V_T) \sqsubseteq G$,
- $V \cap S = \{\}$,
- $V_T \subseteq S$,
- $\forall x \in V_T, \bar{t}\, x = \bot$,

and we show not only $g(\dot{x} \setminus S) \sqsubseteq G$, but also $V \times (\dot{x} \setminus V_T) \sqsubseteq G$.

With $V = V_T = \{\}$, the assumptions are fulfilled, so by proving this proposition, we conclude the lemma.

The statement is trivial for $\dot{y} = \dot{x} = []$. Otherwise, $\dot{x}$ and $\dot{y}$ are necessarily headed by the same variable, so let $\dot{y} = x \cdot \dot{y}'$ and $\dot{x} = x \cdot \dot{x}'$, where $\dot{x}'$ is a path produced by interleaving the trees from $\bar{t}'$ into an interleaving of $\dot{y}'$ and $\dot{z}$, where $\dot{z}$ is a path in the tree $\bar{t}\, x$ and $\bar{t}'$ is $\bar{t}$ if $x \notin T$ and $\bar{t}[x \mapsto \bullet]$ otherwise (cf. the definition of s on page 153).

There are three cases to consider:

- If x refers to a thunk that we have seen before (i.e. $x \in V_T$), then $\bar{t}\, x$ is the empty tree. We invoke the inductive hypothesis with the same V and V_T and obtain $g(\dot{x}' \setminus S) \sqsubseteq G$ and $V \times (\dot{x}' \setminus V_T) \sqsubseteq G$. The assumptions are fulfilled, as $x \in V_T$ and $\dot{z} = []$, and the conclusion immediately implies the desired $g(\dot{x} \setminus S) \sqsubseteq G$ and $V \times (\dot{x} \setminus V_T) \sqsubseteq G$, as $x \in V_T$ and $x \in S$ due to $V_T \subseteq S$.

- Otherwise, if x is a recursive call (i.e. $x \in S$), we again invoke the inductive hypothesis, this time extending V_T by x if $x \in T$. To establish the assumptions, we first decompose what we have given:

  $$\dot{g}((x \cdot \dot{y}') \setminus V_T) = \{x\} \times (\dot{y}' \setminus V_T) \sqcup \dot{g}(\dot{y}' \setminus V_T).$$

  and

  $$V \times ((x \cdot \dot{y}') \setminus V_T) = V \times \{x\} \sqcup V \times (\dot{y}' \setminus V_T).$$

Furthermore, we note that $g(\dot{z} \setminus V_T) \sqsubseteq G$.

It remains to show that $V \times (\dot{z} \setminus V_T) \sqsubseteq G$. Above decomposition provides $V \times \{x\} \sqsubseteq G$, so all calls seen so far are adjacent to x in G, and thus $V \subseteq N_x(G) \setminus \{x\}$. Together with $\dot{z} \subseteq \mathsf{dom}\,(\bar{t}\ x)$ the assumption of the lemma provides the desired inequality.

We then obtain $g(\dot{x}' \setminus S) \sqsubseteq G$ and $V \times (\dot{x}' \setminus V_T) \sqsubseteq G$, which, together with $V \times \{x\} \sqsubseteq G$, implies the desired result.

- The remaining case is that of a call to something not in S, i.e. $x \notin S$. In this case, $\dot{z} = []$, so the above decompositions suffice to establish the assumptions of the inductive hypothesis. Here, we extend V with $\{x\}$ and obtain $g(\dot{x}' \setminus S) \sqsubseteq G$ and $(V \cup \{x\}) \times (\dot{x}' \setminus V_T) \sqsubseteq G$.

  This implies the desired result together with $V \times \{x\} \sqsubseteq G$ and $\{x\} \times (\dot{x}' \setminus S) \sqsubseteq G$, which follows from the second conclusion of the inductive hypothesis due to $V_T \subseteq S$. ∎

4.3.4 Call Arity, concretely

At last I can give the complete and concrete co-call analysis corresponding to GHC's Call Arity, and establish its safety via our chain of refinements, simply by checking the conditions in Definition 15. It is a slightly more concise reformulation of the specification given in Section 3.3.1, and adjusted to the restricted syntax where application arguments are always variables.

The arity analysis is:

$$
\begin{aligned}
\mathcal{A}_\alpha(x) &:= [x \mapsto \alpha] \\
\mathcal{A}_\alpha(e\ x) &:= \mathcal{A}_{\alpha+1}(e) \sqcup [x \mapsto 0] \\
\mathcal{A}_\alpha(\lambda x.\, e) &:= \mathcal{A}_{\alpha-1}(e) \setminus \{x\} \\
\mathcal{A}_\alpha(e\,?\,e_{\mathbf{t}} : e_{\mathbf{f}}) &:= \mathcal{A}_0(e) \sqcup \mathcal{A}_\alpha(e_{\mathbf{t}}) \sqcup \mathcal{A}_\alpha(e_{\mathbf{f}}) \\
\mathcal{A}_\alpha(\mathbf{C}_b) &:= \bot \qquad \text{for } b \in \{\mathbf{t}, \mathbf{f}\}
\end{aligned}
$$

The analysis of a let expression $\mathcal{A}_\alpha(\mathbf{let}\ \Gamma\ \mathbf{in}\ e)$ as well as the analysis of a binding $\mathcal{A}_\alpha(\Gamma, e)$ are defined differently for recursive and non-recursive bindings.

For a recursive Γ, we have $\mathcal{A}_\alpha(\textbf{let}\ \Gamma\ \textbf{in}\ e) := \bar{\alpha} \setminus \mathsf{dom}\,\Gamma$ and $\mathcal{A}_\alpha(\Gamma, e) := \bar{\alpha}\big|_{\mathsf{dom}\,\Gamma}$ where $\bar{\alpha}$ is the least fixed point defined by the equation[15]

$$\bar{\alpha} = \overline{\mathcal{A}}_{\bar{\alpha}}(\Gamma) \sqcup \mathcal{A}_\alpha(e) \sqcup [x \mapsto 0 \mid x \in \mathsf{thunks}\,\Gamma].$$

For a non-recursive binding $\Gamma = [x \mapsto e']$ we have $\mathcal{A}_\alpha(\textbf{let}\ \Gamma\ \textbf{in}\ e) := (\mathcal{A}_{\alpha'}(e') \sqcup \mathcal{A}_\alpha(e)) \setminus \mathsf{dom}\,\Gamma$ and $\mathcal{A}_\alpha(\Gamma, e) := [x \mapsto \alpha']$ where

$$\alpha' := \begin{cases} 0 & \text{if } \neg\mathsf{isVal}(e') \text{ and } x\text{—}x \in \mathcal{G}_\alpha(e) \\ \mathcal{A}_\alpha(e)\ x & \text{otherwise.} \end{cases}$$

We have $\mathsf{dom}\,\mathcal{G}_\alpha(e) = \mathsf{dom}\,\mathcal{A}_\alpha(e)$ and

$$\begin{aligned}
\mathcal{G}_\alpha(x) &:= \{\} \\
\mathcal{G}_\alpha(e\ x) &:= \mathcal{G}_{\alpha+1}(e) \sqcup (\{x\} \times \mathsf{fv}\,(e\ x)) \\
\mathcal{G}_0(\lambda x.\, e) &:= (\mathsf{fv}\,e)^2 \setminus \{x\} \\
\mathcal{G}_{\alpha+1}(\lambda x.\, e) &:= \mathcal{G}_\alpha(e) \setminus \{x\} \\
\mathcal{G}_\alpha(e\ \textbf{?}\ e_\mathbf{t} \textbf{:}\ e_\mathbf{f}) &:= \mathcal{G}_0(e) \sqcup \mathcal{G}_\alpha(e_\mathbf{t}) \sqcup \mathcal{G}_\alpha(e_\mathbf{f}) \sqcup \\
&\quad\ (\mathsf{dom}\,\mathcal{A}_0(e) \times (\mathsf{dom}\,\mathcal{A}_\alpha(e_\mathbf{t}) \cup \mathsf{dom}\,\mathcal{A}_\alpha(e_\mathbf{f}))) \\
\mathcal{G}_\alpha(\mathbf{C}_b) &:= \{\} \qquad \text{for } b \in \{\mathbf{t}, \mathbf{f}\} \\
\mathcal{G}_\alpha(\textbf{let}\ \Gamma\ \textbf{in}\ e) &:= \mathcal{G}_\alpha(\Gamma, e) \setminus \mathsf{dom}\,\Gamma
\end{aligned}$$

The analysis result for bindings is different for recursive and non-recursive bindings and uses the auxiliary function

$$\mathcal{G}_{\bar{\alpha};G}(x \mapsto e') := \begin{cases} (\mathsf{fv}(e'))^2 & \text{if } \mathsf{isVal}(e') \wedge x\text{—}x \in G \\ \mathcal{G}_{\bar{\alpha}\ x}(e') & \text{otherwise,} \end{cases}$$

which calculates the co-calls of an individual binding, adding the extra edges between multiple invocations of a bound variable, unless it is bound to a thunk and hence shared.

[15] The initial implementation of Call Arity did not include the third term in this equation, and thunks would erroneously be eta-expanded if they happened to be part of a linearly recursive bindings. Working towards this formalisation uncovered the bug (see GHC commit 306d255).

For recursive Γ we define $\mathcal{G}_\alpha(\Gamma, e)$ as the least fixed point fulfilling

$$\mathcal{G}_\alpha(\Gamma, e) = \mathcal{G}_\alpha(e) \sqcup \bigsqcup_{(x \mapsto e') \in \Gamma} \mathcal{G}_{\mathcal{A}_\alpha(\Gamma,e);\mathcal{G}_\alpha(\Gamma,e)}(x \mapsto e') \sqcup \bigsqcup_{(x \mapsto e') \in \Gamma} (\mathsf{fv}(e') \times N_x(\mathcal{G}_\alpha(\Gamma, e))).$$

For a non-recursive $\Gamma = [x \mapsto e']$, we have

$$\mathcal{G}_\alpha(\Gamma, e) = \mathcal{G}_\alpha(e) \sqcup \mathcal{G}_{\mathcal{A}_\alpha(\Gamma,e);\mathcal{G}_\alpha(e)}(x \mapsto e') \sqcup \begin{cases} \mathsf{fv}(e') \times (N_x(\mathcal{G}_\alpha(e)) \setminus \{x\}) & \text{if } \neg\mathsf{isVal}(e') \\ \mathsf{fv}(e') \times N_x(\mathcal{G}_\alpha(e)) & \text{if } \mathsf{isVal}(e'). \end{cases}$$

Theorem 5
Call Arity is safe (in the sense of Definition 5).

Proof
By straightforward calculation (and simple induction for (G-subst)), we can show that the analyses fulfil Definitions 6 and 15. So by Lemmas 27, 26 and 23 and Corollary 19, Call Arity is safe. ∎

4.4 The Isabelle formalisation

On their own, the proofs presented in the previous sections are involved, but otherwise rather standard. What sets them apart from similar work is that these proofs have been carried out in the interactive theorem prover Isabelle [NPW02]. This provides a level of assurance that is hard to reach using pen-and-paper-proofs.

4.4.1 Size and effort

But it also greatly increases the effort involved in obtaining a result like Theorem 5. The Isabelle development corresponding to this chapter, including the definitions of the syntax and the semantics (but excluding unrelated results from Chapter 2, such as correctness and adequacy of the semantics), contains roughly 12,000 lines of code with 1,200 lemmas (many small, some large) in 75 theories, created over the course of 9 months [Bre15d]. Much of the complexity is owed to the problem of bindings and to the handling of monotonicity and continuity of the analysis. See Section 2.6 for more information on the formalisation, especially how using Nominal logic, as discussed (Sections 1.6 and 2.6.1) and the HOLCF package (Section 1.7.3) has helped here.

So while the actual result shown here might not have warranted that effort on its own – after all, performance regressions due to bugs in the Call Arity analysis do not have very serious consequences – it lays ground towards formalising more and more parts of the core data structures and algorithms in our compilers.

4.4.2 Structure

The separation into individual theories (Isabelle's equivalent to Haskell's modules) as well as the use of *locales* ([Bal14], Isabelle's approximation to a module system) helps to gain insight into the structure of an otherwise very large proof, by ensuring a separation of concerns. For example, the proof of $[\![\mathsf{T}_0(e)]\!] = [\![e]\!]$ has only the conditions from Definition 6 available, which shows that the cardinality analysis is irrelevant for functional correctness.

4.4.3 The trace tree type implementation

Isabelle/HOL is a logic of total functions, and it is not a surprise that it has good support for inductive data types via the **datatype** command, where each element of the type has a finite size. But the type of trace trees introduced in Section 4.3.2 is not of that kind: To model program behaviour with recursion I need infinite trees as well.

Fortunately, it is possible to define such types in Isabelle/HOL, and there are actually a few options available:

- The HOLCF package can construct domains with an infinitely deep structure from a domain equation like

$$\mathsf{TTree} = \mathsf{Var} \to \mathsf{TTree}_\perp$$

which can be implemented as

domain $('a::countable)$ *tree'* = *Node* (**lazy** *next'* :: *'a discr* → *'a tree'*)
type_synonym *'a tree* = *'a discr* → *'a tree'*

- The **codatatype** command provides support for co-inductive data types, which can create the appropriate type directly:

  codatatype (*lset*: *'a*) *tree* = *Node* (*nxt* : *'a* ⇒ *'a tree option*)

- The type can be constructed "by hand" using the plain **typedef** command.

I have experimented with all three variants and found that the first two approaches would not provide me with the right tools (e.g. definition tools, induction principles) that allow me to efficiently define the required operation and prove the required lemmas, so I turned to the "by hand" construction.

To that end, I defined the notion of sets of lists where for every list, all its prefixes are in the set as well. These are the downward-closed sets under the prefix-order on lists:

definition *downset* :: *'a list set* ⇒ *bool* **where** TTree.thy
downset xss = $(\forall x\ n.\ x \in xss \longrightarrow take\ n\ x \in xss)$

Any non-empty downward-closed set is then such a trace tree:

typedef *'a ttree* = $\{xss :: 'a\ list\ set\ .\ [] \in xss \wedge downset\ xss\}$ **by** *auto*

A **typedef** is only admissible if the given set is not empty; this is the proof obligation solved automatically using **by** *auto*; the set $\{[]\}$, corresponding to the tree •, is one possible witness of that.

In Section 4.3.2 I describe two concrete interpretation of trace trees: As sets of traces and as automata with labelled transitions. The actual type definition is based on the first, so the function paths returns nothing but the representation of a tree based on that type definition. Using the helpful machinery of the lifting package [HK13], this function is thus defined to be the identity function, once the abstraction is removed:

lift_definition *paths* :: *'a ttree* ⇒ *'a list set* **is** (λ *x*. *x*).

The automata view is realised by the two functions *possible* and *nxt* which indicate what labels are present on the root's edges, and the corresponding child node.

lift_definition *possible* ::*'a ttree* ⇒ *'a* ⇒ *bool*
  is λ *xss x*. ∃ *xs*. *x#xs* ∈ *xss*.

lift_definition *nxt* ::*'a ttree* ⇒ *'a* ⇒ *'a ttree*
  is λ *xss x*. *insert* [] {*xs* | *xs*. *x#xs* ∈ *xss*}
  by (*auto simp add*: *downset_def take_Suc_Cons*[*symmetric*] *simp del*: *take_Suc_Cons*)

In order to make *nxt* a total function I add the empty list to the result, which only matters if there was no edge with the requested label in the given tree. The proof obligation following the definition ensures that the result of *nxt* is a valid tree, i.e. non-empty and downward closed.

The important operations on trees, ⊕ and ⊗, are defined in terms of set union and list interleavings. As the Isabelle theory for list interleavings already uses the latter symbol, I use ⊕⊕ resp. ⊗⊗ in my formalisation for the operations on trees:

lift_definition *either* :: *'a ttree* ⇒ *'a ttree* ⇒ *'a ttree* (**infixl** ⊕⊕ *80*)
  is *op* ∪
  by (*auto simp add*: *downset_def*)

lift_definition *both* :: *'a ttree* ⇒ *'a ttree* ⇒ *'a ttree* (**infixl** ⊗⊗ *86*)
  is λ *xss yss* . ⋃ {*xs* ⊗ *ys* | *xs ys*. *xs* ∈ *xss* ∧ *ys* ∈ *yss*}
  by (*force simp*: *ex_ex_eq_hint dest*: *interleave_butlast*)

Further operations include, for example, the function *without* that is defined in terms of *filter*:

lift_definition *without* :: *'a* ⇒ *'a ttree* ⇒ *'a ttree*
  is λ *x xss*. *filter* (λ *x'*. *x'* ≠ *x*) ' *xss*
  by (*auto intro*: *downset_filter*)(*metis filter.simps*(1) *imageI*)

Operations like this and the similar *ttree_restr* are partly the reason why using the existing infrastructure for co-inductive definitions failed, as filtering is a notoriously difficult problem here: The paper [LH14] discusses that problem in depth.

Most of the code in the Isabelle theory on trace trees is concerned with the s function (see page 153), which is defined as

$$\mathsf{next}_x(s_T\ \ \bar{t}\ \ t)\ :=\ \begin{cases}\bot & \text{if } \mathsf{next}_x\, t = \bot\\ s_T\ \bar{t}\ (t' \otimes \bar{t}\ x) & \text{if } \mathsf{next}_x\, t = t',\, x \notin T\\ s_T\ (\bar{t}[x \mapsto \bullet])\ (t' \otimes \bar{t}\ x) & \text{if } \mathsf{next}_x\, t = t',\, x \in T.\end{cases}$$

In the Isabelle formalisation, I first define a related predicate on traces (*substitute'*), by recursion on the trace, as I need to prove that predicate to be downward-closed before I can lift it to form the real *substitute* on trace trees:

definition *f_nxt* :: *('a ⇒ 'a ttree) ⇒ 'a set ⇒ 'a ⇒ ('a ⇒ 'a ttree)*
  where *f_nxt f T x = (if x ∈ T then f(x:=empty) else f)*

fun *substitute'* :: *('a ⇒ 'a ttree) ⇒ 'a set ⇒ 'a ttree ⇒ 'a list ⇒ bool* **where**
  substitute'_Nil: substitute' f T t [] ⟷ True
  | *substitute'_Cons: substitute' f T t (x#xs) ⟷*
    possible t x ∧ substitute' (f_nxt f T x) T (nxt t x ⊗⊗ f x) xs

lift_definition *substitute* :: *('a ⇒ 'a ttree) ⇒ 'a set ⇒ 'a ttree ⇒ 'a ttree*
  is *λ f T t. Collect (substitute' f T t)*
  by *(simp add: downset_substitute)*

Depending on the proposition that one wants to show, a different definition of *substitute* provides a more useful induction scheme. In this alternative definition, it is emphasised that every path in $s_T\ \bar{t}\ t$ comes from a specific path in t. I formalised this using the following inductive definition and equivalence proof:

inductive *substitute''* :: *('a ⇒ 'a ttree) ⇒ 'a set ⇒ 'a list ⇒ 'a list ⇒ bool* **where**
  substitute''_Nil: substitute'' f T [] []
  | *substitute''_Cons:*

$zs \in paths\ (f\,x) \Longrightarrow xs' \in interleave\ xs\ zs \Longrightarrow substitute''\ (f\_nxt\ f\ T\ x)\ T\ xs'\ ys$
$\Longrightarrow substitute''\ f\ T\ (x\#xs)\ (x\#ys)$

lemma *substitute_substitute''*:
$xs \in paths\ (substitute\ f\ T\ t) \longleftrightarrow (\exists\ xs' \in paths\ t.\ substitute''\ f\ T\ xs'\ xs)$

This alternative definition is used in one direction of the following lemma, which states that $s_T\ \bar{t}\ t|_S = s_T\ \bar{t}\ (t|_S)$ holds if all of $\bar{t}$, i.e. both its domain as well as all variables in its range, are in the set S.

lemma *ttree_rest_substitute2*:
assumes $\forall\ x.\ carrier\ (f\ x) \subseteq S$
assumes *const_on f* $(-S)$ *empty*
shows *ttree_restr S* $(substitute\ f\ T\ t) = substitute\ f\ T\ (ttree\_restr\ S\ t)$

This lemma, which I use implicitly without much ado in the proof on page 158, is a good example how much intuitivity and proof difficulty can differ:

It is quite obviously true, as s only acts on and adds edges with labels in S, which is completely ignored by $\_|_S$.

Nevertheless, the proof consists of more than 120 lines of Isar, not counting supporting definitions such as the alternative definition of s. The complexity is owed to the fact that on both sides of the equality, we have a filtered trees. Induction over a path of filtered tree is not very useful, as in one step of the induction, still many (filtered) edges can be traversed by s. So I need to get hold of the original, unfiltered tree, which in a way hides behind an existential quantifier, and working in Isabelle with such existentially quantified statement tends to require more explicit steps.

This also confirms the observation that combining filter-like operations and co-inductive definitions is tricky.

4.5 The formalisation gap

Every formalisation – whether hand-written or machine-checked – has a formalisation gap, i.e. a difference to the formalised artefact that is not (and often cannot) be formally bridged. Despite the effort that went into this formalisation, the gap is not very narrow, and has been wide enough to fall into.

4.5.1 Core vs. my syntax

The most obvious difference between formalisation and reality is the syntax of the language: GHC's Core (Fig. 2) is defined with 15 constructors, while the small lambda calculus that I use to represent Core has only six (Fig. 5 plus the two in Section 2.4.2). I argue that it is still a reasonable representation of Core: As I explain in Section 3.4, the additional syntactic constructs are irrelevant to our analysis: It either returns the trivial result (literals, types, coercions), or transparently looks through them (casts, ticks, type abstraction and applications).

A similar difference is that Core is typed. Nevertheless it is ok not to include types in the formalisation, as the Call Arity analysis ignores them anyways. One might now worry that the transformation might break type safety. This does not happen, as the type-ignorant Call Arity code does not actually transform the code: It merely annotates it, and the existing general-purpose simplifier then actually eta-expands it, if the types allow this. If they do not (which may be the case with type families), it will simply refuse to do so. This does not affect the safety results, as in my proofs I always only require a lower bound on the analysis result (i.e. an upper bound on the reported arity), so being less aggressive is always safe.

4.5.2 Core vs. my semantics

As mentioned in Section 1.4.1, there is no official operational semantics for GHC Core that captures its evaluation behaviour, besides the actual implementation. It is folklore and my own understanding of GHC inner workings that justify that I use Launchbury's semantics to model Core's evaluation behaviour.

This is not without pitfalls: Core allows arbitrary expressions as arguments, while my syntax follows Launchbury and restricts that to variables. The transformation is rather simple: Just replace $e_1\ e_2$ with **let** $z = e_2$ **in** $e_1\ z$ – this is essentially the first step of the Core-to-STG transformation as performed by GHC. But this is not the whole story: If the argument already is a variable, i.e. $e_1\ x$, then no extra let-binding is introduced.

This subtly changes the evaluation behaviour: While the evaluation of $e_1\ (x\ y)$ calls x at most once, the evaluation of $e_1\ x$ can call x multiple times. Therefore, the equation for $\mathcal{G}_\alpha(e_1\ e_2)$ in Fig. 12 has two cases.

Originally, the Call Arity code did not take that into account and would return a wrong result in such instances. Interestingly, this could not be observed: As the argument of an application $e_1\ x$ is always analysed with an incoming arity of 0, this would thus be the call arity of x, and no eta-expansion would happen. Furthermore, when concluding the analysis of the let-expression where x is bound, α_x is definitely 0 and then, according to the equations in Fig. 13 resp. Fig. 14, it does not matter whether x is called multiple times.

It would make a noticeable difference if the cardinality result is to be used elsewhere as well, e.g. to avoid the updating of thunks that are used at most once anyways (Section 3.7.2): Preliminary testing confirms that this leads to a huge increase of allocations and program run time if this corner case had not been taken care of.

In order to prove such update-avoidance based on my (or any) analysis to be correct, one could use a semantics that models these update flags explicitly. In [PB10] Pirog & Biernacki describe a big-step semantics for STG which is operationally very close to the GHC runtime, as from it they derive – formally verified(!) – a virtual machine equivalent to the STG machine (cf. Section 1.4.3).

But as Call Arity is a Core-to-Core analysis, this clearly shows that there is demand for a precise formal semantics for GHC's Core with enough detail to describe its evaluation and sharing behaviour. It would help to avoid such mistakes and can serve as a reference for developers coming up and implementing Core-to-Core transformations and other parts of the compiler.

4.5.3 Core's annotations

Identifiers in GHC's core are annotated with a wealth of additional information – inlining information, occurrence information, strictness signatures, demand information. As later phases rely on these information, they have to be considered part of the language, and should be included in a formal semantics.

This actually caused a nasty bug[16] that appeared in the third release candidate of GHC 7.10. The symptoms were weird: The program would skip over a call to error and simply carry on with the rest of the code. With Call Arity disabled, nothing surprising happened and the exception was raised as expression. What went wrong?

It boiled down to a function

```
f :: a → b
f x = error "..."
```

which the strictness analyser annotates with `<B,A>b`, indicating that once f is called with one argument, the result is definitely bottom.

In the code at hand, every call to f passes two arguments, i.e. **case** f x y **of** {...}. Therefore, Call Arity determines f's external arity to be 2, and changes the definition to

```
f x y = error "..." y
```

The strictness annotation on f, however, is still present, allowing the simplifier to change the code that contains the call to f to **case** f x **of** {}, as passing one argument is enough to cause the exception to be raised. It also removes all alternatives from the **case**, as the control flow will not return.

On their own, each transformation is correct; together, havoc is created: Due to the eta-expansion, the evaluation of f x does *not* raise an exception. Because the **case** expression has no alternatives any more, the execution of the final program continues at some other, undefined part of the program.

One way to fix this would be to completely remove annotations that might no longer be true after eta-expanding a function definition, losing

---

[16] https://ghc.haskell.org/trac/ghc/ticket/10176

the benefit that these annotations provide. The actual fix was more careful and capped the reported arity at the number of arguments with which, according to the strictness signature, the function is definitely bottom.

4.5.4 Implementation vs. formalisation

Clearly I have formalised and verified the algorithm behind Call Arity, but not the implementation. For example, the Isabelle code simply uses *fix* to calculate the least fixedpoint during the analysis of a recursive **let**, where the implementation has to explicitly iterate the analysis result, starting from bottom and stopping when a fixed point is reached. Termination of this implementation is not handled formally, and neither the correctness of the implementation with regard to its formal description here or in the Isabelle theories.

I currently do not see a practical way to do so: There are a few Haskell-specific formal methods, e.g. refinement types in the form of Liquid Haskell [VSJVP14], but they are not powerful enough to do such a full-fledged correctness proof with regard to a formal specification. Another approach would be to employ Isabelle to verify the implementation: As Haftmann writes [Haf10], this requires either a conversion of the Haskell implementation into Isabelle using the tool Haskabelle or to go the other way and using Isabelle's code generation features [Haf09] to produce the implementation from the Isabelle definition. Either direction would require formalising large parts of the existing GHC codebase itself – a daunting prospect.

Furthermore, GHC works with Haskell code that is structured in modules and packages; this naturally affects the implementation, which will, for example, not collect arity and co-call information for external identifiers, as they cannot be used anyways (see Section 3.4.1). This implementation short-cut is ignored here.

4.5.5 Performance and safety in the larger context

Call Arity is but one transformation in a large number of analyses and transformations performed by GHC, and the safety result established in this chapter does not immediately carry over to the whole thing. It is quite possible that a subsequent transformation works better on the original code e than on the transformed code $\mathcal{T}_0(e)$, and that this difference outweighs the improvement due to Call Arity. In that sense, the safety theorem is not composable.

The property that I would like to be able to assume about the other transformations is monotonicity: If e_2 is better than e_1 before the transformation, then the transformed e_2 is better than the transformed e_1, where "better" refers to the abstract performance measure used – in my case, the number of allocations. Then it would follow from my safety theorem that the insertion of Call Arity in the sequence of transformations will not make the end result perform worse.

In practice, this assumption is certainly "somewhat true", i.e. holds in common cases, as also shown by the empirical results. But it is unlikely true in a complete and rigorous sense, i.e. I expect that one can construct corner cases where it does not hold.

Finally, my formal notion of performance is of course just an approximation for real performance, justified by little more than the empirically observed good correlation between allocations and execution time. Formally capturing the actual runtime of a program on modern hardware with multiple cores, long instruction pipelines, branch prediction and complex caches is currently way out of reach.

4.6 Related work

This work connects arity and cardinality analyses with operational safety properties, using an interactive theorem prover to verify its claims; as such this is a first.

However, this is not the first compiler transformation proven correct in an interactive theorem prover. After all there is CompCert (e.g.

[Ler06; Ler12]), a complete verified optimising compiler for C implemented in Coq. Furthermore, a verified Java to Java bytecode compiler [Loc10] was written using Isabelle's code generation facilities, and the CakeML project has produced, among other things, a verified compiler from CakeML to CakeML bytecode, implemented in the HOL4 theorem prover [KMNO14]. The Vellvm project provides formal semantics for LLVM's intermediate representation and uses it for formal verification of compiler transformations [ZNMZ13]. These projects address functional correctness, though, and not (yet) performance.

Using a resource aware program logic for a subset of Java bytecode, which they have implemented in Isabelle, Aspinall, Beringer and Momigliano validate local optimisations [ABM07] to be indeed optimisations with regard to a variety of resource algebras. Following the precedent set by transformation validation, in this work the safety of the transformation is not proved once and for all, but rather for every conrete program a proof is constructed. The Isabelle formalisations of the proofs seem to be lost.

In the realm of functional programming languages, a number of formal treatments of compiler transformations exist, e.g. verification of the CPS transformation in Coq (e.g. [Chl10; DL07]), Twelf (e.g. [Tia06]) or Isabelle (e.g. [MO03]). As their focus lies on finding proper techniques for handling naming, their semantics do not express heap usage and sharing.

An approach that necessarily produces safe program transformations are generated transformations: Here, a large number of possible program transformations of a specific form are mechanically enumerated and checked if they are both semantics preserving and performance improving; these checks often build on SMT solvers. The selected concrete transformations are then safe by construction. Examples of this line of research include [JNR02], [BA06] and [Buc15].

Sand's *improvement theory* [San92] provides a general, inequational algebra to describe the effect of program transformations on performance. Its notion of improvement is similar to my notion of safety, while the more general notion of weak improvement allows performance regressions up to a constant factor. This theory was adapted for lazy languages, both for improvement of time [MS99] and space [GS99; GS01].

Recently, Hackett and Hutten [HH14] took up on Sands' work and built a general framework to prove *worker/wrapper transformations* time improving. And while neither that nor Sands's work have yet been machine-checked, at least the semantic correctness of Hutton's worker/ wrapper framework has been verified using Isabelle [Gam09].

Could I have built my results on theirs, especially as [HH14] uses almost the same abstract machine? Indeed, eta-expansion can be phrased as an instance of the worker/wrapper transformation, with abstraction and representation contexts $\mathsf{Abs} = []$ and $\mathsf{Rep} = (\lambda z_1 \ldots z_n.\, ([]\ z_1 \ldots\ z_n))$. Unfortunately, the assumptions of the worker/wrapper improvement theorem are not satisfied, and this is to be expected: Sands' notion of improvement – and hence Hackett and Hutton's theorems – guarantee improvement in *all* contexts, while in my case the eta-expansion is justified by an analysis of the actual context, and is generally unsafe in other contexts.

So in the current form, improvement theory is tailored to local transformations and, as Sands points out in [GS01], would require the introduction of context information to apply to whole-program transformations such as Call Arity. Such a grand unified improvement theory for call-by-need would be a tremendously useful thing to have.

Excuse me, but real programmers use butterflies.

Randall Munroe, xkcd #378

CHAPTER 5
Conclusion

In this work, I have spanned the arc from down-to-earth compiler transformations over formal semantics to machine-verified proofs of operational properties of the compiler transformation.

By introducing the Call Arity analysis into the Haskell compiler GHC, I made it practically possible to let an important class of list-consuming and -processing functions take part in the list fusion program transformation, which is an important mechanism to make idiomatic Haskell code perform well. This solves a long-standing open issue.

My key observation was that in the context of a lazy programming language, a good arity analysis requires the help of a precise cardinality analysis, and my key contribution is the novel cardinality analysis based on the notion of co-call graphs, which allows the compiler to get precise information about how often a variable is used, even if the call occurs from within a recursive function.

Empirical measurements show that introducing the analysis improves the performance of some programs in the standard benchmark suite. Furthermore, changing the definitions of list consumers with accumulators to now take part in list fusion provides a more significant performance boost to a number of existing programs, and a huge improvement to some programs. Thus it now allows performance-aware programmers to write more high-level code, instead of manually transforming their code into a less idiomatic form to make up for the compiler's previous inability to produce good code in these situations.

One can consider Call Arity to be a whole-program analysis, given that it works best if all occurrences of a function are known. I have shown that a compiler employing separate compilation can still make good use of such a transformation, as inlining in some cases gives the analysis the chance to see all use-sites of a function's definition.

To pave the way to a formal treatment of such analyses and transformations of lazy functional programs, I created a formalisation of Launchbury's natural semantics, of Sestoft's mark-1 abstract machine and of related denotational semantics in the interactive theorem prover Isabelle. These reusable artefacts extend the growing library of formalisations and lower the barrier of entry for formalising further research on programming languages in a machine-checked setting.

The formalisation contains a proof of the adequacy of Launchbury's natural semantics with regard to a standard denotational semantics. The original paper only sketches this proof, and the sketch has so far resisted attempts to complete it with rigour. By slightly deviating from the path outlined in the proof sketch, I found a more elegant and more direct proof of adequacy, which is also machine-checked. This does not shake the foundations a large swathes of research, as the adequacy theorem holds as expected, but it fortifies them instead.

My formalisation builds on relatively new mechanisms for dealing with names and binders in Isabelle, namely the Isabelle package Nominal2, and constitutes one of the largest developments using this technology. It is also the first to combine it with domain theory in the form of the HOLCF package.

Finally, I used these formalised semantics to model the Call Arity analysis and transformation and proved not only functional correctness, but also – and especially – safety: The performance of the program is not reduced by applying the Call Arity transformation.

I chose to measure performance by counting the number of dynamic allocations, and I explain why this measure is suitable to ensure that the

Call Arity analysis does not go wrong, and that it is a good compromise between formal tractability and "real" performance.

I introduced the notion of trace trees as a suitable abstract type to think and reason about cardinality analyses. My proof is modularised using Isabelle's *locales*, making it possible to re-use just parts of it. This should make similar formalisation endeavours, such as a safety proof of the other arity and cardinality related analyses in GHC, more tractable.

As with most formalisation attempts, by pursuing it I have improved the understanding of how and why the analysis works, sharpened its specification and rooted out bugs that the conventional test suite did not find.

Operational properties of compiler transformations, such as safety, are rarely investigated on a formal level, especially not with the rigour provided by a theorem prover. I have demonstrated that such a feat is possible, with an effort that may be justified in certain high-stake use cases.

There are limits to the applicability of my safety theorem, as Call Arity is but one step in a large sequence of other analyses and transformations performed by the compiler. Therefore, the no-regression result does not transfer to the complete compiler in complete universality: For example, if subsequent transformations were not monotonous, then the introduction of Call Arity could have an overall negative effect on some programs. I elaborate on this and other aspects of the "formalisation gap" immanent in such formal work.

To overcome some of the formalisation gap, it would be desirable to formalise GHC's Core in Isabelle. Using Isabelle's code generation to Haskell and GHC's plugin architecture, even verified implementations of Core-to-Core transformations in GHC would appear to be within reach. This would be a milestone on the way to formally verified compilation of Real-World-Haskell.

All in all, this thesis exhibits an approach to the design and development of compiler transformations that is supported by formal methods. I hope that it will inspire more researchers in this field to dare to not only test their claims, but actually prove them, and to even do that with the rigour provided by machine-checked proofs.

Honk iff you love formal logic.

Randall Munroe, xkcd #1033

APPENDIX A

Formal definitions and main theorems

Polemically speaking, formal proofs are irrelevant – only their existence matters. Once a proposition has been proved, and the proof has been checked by the theorem prover, this is all that matters to a reader interested in just the assurance that the proof is fine.

The same cannot be said for definitions and theorems: The machine cannot check whether these really state what the author claims them to state! Therefore, this appendix reproduces the Isabelle formulation of the main theorems of this thesis, together with all definitions required to understand them.

The intention is to enable the reader to check the formal results precisely, without reaching out for the actual Isabelle sources. Naturally, this does not protect against malice on the side of the author. To rule that out, you'd not only have to process the Isabelle sources yourself, but also verify each line of code for tricks such as introducing new axioms, using other unchecked commands or messing with the parser and printer to obtain misleading results. There is a certain level of assurance that this is not the case, as my work has been accepted in the Archive of Formal Proofs [Bre13; Bre15d].

The listings reproduce the Isabelle code as typed, and hence do not benefit from Isabelle's pretty-printing abilities; the name of the Isabelle theory file that contains the code is printed next to the listing, unless the previous listing is from the same file.

For a few functions, not the actual, technical definition is given here, but rather a proposition involving the function that completely describes it. In these cases, the definition that one intuitively wants is not accepted by the definitory command (e.g. using **definition** to define a function in HOLCF's type of continuous functions) or the proof obligations produced by such a command are hard to discharge, and a different formulation is easier to work with, and can later be shown to be equivalent to the desired formulation (e.g. with **nominal_function**'s equivariance obligations). Also, in the cases where I use locales to abstract over similar definitions, reproducing the locale interface, the abstract function definition and the actual instantiation of the locale would obscure the view, so I describe the resulting function as if I had defined it directly.

In the end, in Isabelle/HOL, it does not matter whether a function is define with one set of equations or another: As long as they fully describe the function (i.e. if they are exhaustive and terminating), the resulting constant is identical for all purposes.

A.1 Terms

The definition of the type of terms requires that the type of variables are defined first. In order to use the Nominal machinery, I need to declare that type using the **atom_decl** command. To us, the resulting type is abstract, and all that we know about it is that it is countably infinite:

atom_decl *var* Vars.thy

Based on that, I define our type of lambda expressions is defined as follows. See Section 2.6.1 for an explanation of this construction:

nominal_datatype *exp* = Terms.thy
  Var var

| *App exp var*
| *LetA as::assn body::exp* **binds** *bn as* **in** *body as*
| *Lam x::var body::exp* **binds** *x* **in** *body* (*Lam* [_]. _ [100, 100] 100)
| *Bool bool*
| *IfThenElse exp exp exp* (((_)/ ? (_)/ : (_)) [0, 0, 10] 10)
and *assn* =
ANil | *ACons var exp assn*
binder
bn :: *assn* ⇒ *atom list*
where *bn ANil* = [] | *bn* (*ACons x t as*) = (*atom x*) # (*bn as*)

The function *atom* is provided by the Nominal package. It embeds our type *var* into the type *atom* encompassing all possible name types, but as we use only one such type in our formalisation, one can assume *var* and *atom* to be isomorphic.

Only lambda abstractions and Booleans are considered to be values, as characterised by the following function:

nominal_function *isVal* :: *exp* ⇒ *bool* **where**
isVal (*Var x*) = *False* |
isVal (*Lam* [*x*]. *e*) = *True* |
isVal (*App e x*) = *False* |
isVal (*Let as e*) = *False* |
isVal (*Bool b*) = *True* |
isVal (*scrut* ? *e1* : *e2*) = *False*

The type *heap* that occurs in some of the listing is but a type abbreviation:

type_synonym *heap* = (*var* × *exp*) *list*

The domain of such a heap is the set of variables that are bound to some expression:

definition *domA* AList-Utils.thy
where *domA h* = *fst* ‘ *set h*

As explained in Section 2.6.1, the type *assn* is but a work-around, and we'd really like the *Let* constructor to have such an *heap* as the parameter.

Therefore, I define a conversion function and define *Let* in terms of that; from then on, *LetA* is not used:

fun *heapToAssn* :: *heap* ⇒ *assn* Terms.thy
 where *heapToAssn* [] = *ANil*
 | *heapToAssn* ((*v*,*e*)#Γ) = *ACons v e* (*heapToAssn* Γ)

definition *Let* :: *heap* ⇒ *exp* ⇒ *exp*
 where *Let* Γ *e* = *LetA* (*heapToAssn* Γ) *e*

We will use substitution of one variable for another, in variables, expressions and heaps. For variables, this is easily defined:

fun Substitution.thy
 subst_var :: *var* ⇒ *var* ⇒ *var* ⇒ *var* (_[_::v=_] [1000,100,100] 1000)
where *x*[*y* ::*v*= *z*] = (*if x* = *y then z else x*)

For expressions and heaps, due to them being mutually recursive, the definition is more involved. In particular, I had to jump through a few hoops to be able to discharge the proof obligations produced by **nominal_function**; the complex *default* and *invariant* annotations were required for that:

nominal_function (*default case_sum* (λ*x*. *Inl undefined*) (λ*x*. *Inr undefined*),
 invariant λ *a r* . (∀ Γ *y z* . ((*a* = *Inr* (Γ, *y*, *z*) ∧ *atom* ‘ *domA* Γ ♯∗ (*y*, *z*))
⟶ *map* (λ*x* . *atom* (*fst x*)) (*Sum_Type.projr r*) = *map* (λ*x* . *atom* (*fst x*)) Γ)))
 subst :: *exp* ⇒ *var* ⇒ *var* ⇒ *exp* (_[_::=_] [1000,100,100] 1000)
and
 subst_heap :: *heap* ⇒ *var* ⇒ *var* ⇒ *heap* (_[_::h=_] [1000,100,100] 1000)
where
 (*Var x*)[*y* ::= *z*] = *Var* (*x*[*y* ::*v*= *z*])
 | (*App e v*)[*y* ::= *z*] = *App* (*e*[*y* ::= *z*]) (*v*[*y* ::*v*= *z*])
 | *atom* ‘ *domA* Γ ♯∗ (*y*,*z*) ⟹
 (*Let* Γ *body*)[*y* ::= *z*] = *Let* (Γ[*y* ::*h*= *z*]) (*body*[*y* ::= *z*])
 | *atom x* ♯ (*y*,*z*) ⟹ (*Lam* [*x*].*e*)[*y* ::= *z*] = *Lam* [*x*].(*e*[*y*::=*z*])
 | (*Bool b*)[*y* ::= *z*] = *Bool b*
 | (*scrut* ? *e1* : *e2*)[*y* ::= *z*] = (*scrut*[*y* ::= *z*] ? *e1*[*y* ::= *z*] : *e2*[*y* ::= *z*])
 | [][*y* ::*h*= *z*] = []
 | ((*v*,*e*)# Γ)[*y* ::*h*= *z*] = (*v*, *e*[*y* ::= *z*])# (Γ[*y* ::*h*= *z*])

A.2 Semantics

A.2.1 Natural semantics

Launchbury's natural semantics is defined as an inductive predicate:

inductive Launchbury.thy

```
  reds :: heap ⇒ exp ⇒ var list ⇒ heap ⇒ exp ⇒ bool
  (_ : _ ⇓_ _ : _ [50,50,50,50] 50)
where
   Lambda:
    Γ : (Lam [x]. e) ⇓L Γ : (Lam [x]. e)
 | Application: ⟦
    atom y ♯ (Γ,e,x,L,Δ,Θ,z) ;
    Γ : e ⇓L Δ : (Lam [y]. e');
    Δ : e'[y ::= x] ⇓L Θ : z
  ⟧ ⟹
    Γ : App e x ⇓L Θ : z
 | Variable: ⟦
    map_of Γ x = Some e; delete x Γ : e ⇓x#L Δ : z
  ⟧ ⟹
    Γ : Var x ⇓L (x, z) # Δ : z
 | Let: ⟦
    atom ‘ domA Δ ♯* (Γ, L);
    Δ @ Γ : body ⇓L Θ : z
  ⟧ ⟹
    Γ : Let Δ body ⇓L Θ : z
 | Bool:
    Γ : Bool b ⇓L Γ : Bool b
 | IfThenElse: ⟦
    Γ : scrut ⇓L Δ : (Bool b);
    Δ : (if b then e1 else e2) ⇓L Θ : z
  ⟧ ⟹
    Γ : (scrut ? e1 : e2) ⇓L Θ : z
```

The denotational semantics maps expressions to a denotational domain, which is defined using the HOLCF machinery:

domain *Value* = *Fn* (**lazy** *Value* → *Value*) | *B* (**lazy** *bool discr*) Value.thy

fixrec *Fn_project* :: *Value* → *Value* → *Value*
where $Fn\_project\cdot(Fn\cdot f) = f$

abbreviation *Fn_project_abbr* (**infix** ↓*Fn* 55)
where $f \downarrow Fn\ v \equiv Fn\_project\cdot f\cdot v$

A.2.2 Small-step semantics

Sestoft's mark-1 abstract machine is defined via the **inductive** command, which is convenient even if there is no recursion. I also introduce some nicer syntax for the transitive reflexive closure.

inductive *step* :: *conf* ⇒ *conf* ⇒ *bool* (**infix** ⇒ 50) **where** Sestoft.thy
app_1: $(\Gamma, App\ e\ x, S) \Rightarrow (\Gamma, e\ , Arg\ x\ \#\ S)$
| app_2: $(\Gamma, Lam\ [y].\ e, Arg\ x\ \#\ S) \Rightarrow (\Gamma, e[y ::= x]\ , S)$
| var_1: $map\_of\ \Gamma\ x = Some\ e \Longrightarrow (\Gamma, Var\ x, S) \Rightarrow (delete\ x\ \Gamma, e\ , Upd\ x\ \#\ S)$
| var_2: $x \notin domA\ \Gamma \Longrightarrow isVal\ e \Longrightarrow (\Gamma, e, Upd\ x\ \#\ S) \Rightarrow ((x,e)\#\ \Gamma, e\ , S)$
| let_1: $atom\ `\ domA\ \Delta\ \sharp{*}\ \Gamma \Longrightarrow atom\ `\ domA\ \Delta\ \sharp{*}\ S$
$\Longrightarrow (\Gamma, Let\ \Delta\ e, S) \Rightarrow (\Delta@\Gamma, e\ , S)$
| if_1: $(\Gamma, scrut\ ?\ e1 : e2, S) \Rightarrow (\Gamma, scrut, Alts\ e1\ e2\ \#\ S)$
| if_2: $(\Gamma, Bool\ b, Alts\ e1\ e2\ \#\ S) \Rightarrow (\Gamma, if\ b\ then\ e1\ else\ e2, S)$

abbreviation *steps* (**infix** $\Rightarrow^*$ 50) **where** $steps \equiv step^{**}$

The type *conf* in the signature of *step* is also but a type synonym:

type_synonym *conf* = (*heap* × *exp* × *stack*) SestoftConf.thy

A.2.3 Denotational semantics

The denotational semantics is defined by instantiating a more abstract locale, as explained in Section 2.6.3. The following equations fully describe the result, though.

abbreviation Denotational.thy
$ESem\_syn'' :: exp \Rightarrow (var => Value) \Rightarrow Value$ ($[\![\ \_\ ]\!]\_$ [60,60] 60)
where $[\![\ e\ ]\!]_\varrho \equiv ESem\ e \cdot \varrho$

lemma *ESem_simps*:
$[\![\ Lam\ [x].\ e\ ]\!]_\varrho = Fn\cdot(\Lambda\ v.\ [\![\ e\ ]\!]_{\varrho(x := v)})$
$[\![\ App\ e\ x\ ]\!]_\varrho = [\![\ e\ ]\!]_\varrho \downarrow Fn\ \varrho\ x$
$[\![\ Var\ x\ ]\!]_\varrho = \varrho\ x$
$[\![\ Bool\ b\ ]\!]_\varrho = B\cdot(Discr\ b)$
$[\![\ (scrut\ ?\ e_1 : e_2)\ ]\!]_\varrho = B\_project\cdot([\![\ scrut\ ]\!]_\varrho)\cdot([\![\ e_1\ ]\!]_\varrho)\cdot([\![\ e_2\ ]\!]_\varrho)$
$[\![\ Let\ \Gamma\ body\ ]\!]_\varrho = [\![body]\!]_{\{\!|\Gamma|\!\}\varrho}$

Towards defining the recursive heap semantics, the function *evalHeap* maps a given evaluation function (e.g. the *HSem* above) over the heap, producing a function from variable names to values. As this definition is yet abstract in the choices of expression and value types, its signature contains lots of type variables:

fun EvalHeap.thy
$evalHeap :: ('var \times 'exp)\ list \Rightarrow ('exp \Rightarrow 'value{::}\{pure,pcpo\}) \Rightarrow 'var \Rightarrow 'value$
where
$evalHeap\ []\ \_ = \bot$
$|\ evalHeap\ ((x,e)\#h)\ eval = (evalHeap\ h\ eval)\ (x := eval\ e)$

I introduce nicer syntax for this operation and then define the heap semantics using the fixed-point operator from HOLCF:

abbreviation *HSem_syn* ($\{\!|\ \_\ |\!\}\_$ [0,60] 60) HeapSemantics.thy
where $\{\!|\Gamma|\!\}\varrho \equiv HSem\ \Gamma \cdot \varrho$

lemma *HSem_def'*: $\{\!|\Gamma|\!\}\varrho = (\mu\ \varrho'.\ \varrho\ {+}{+}_{domA\ \Gamma}\ [\![\Gamma]\!]_{\varrho'})$

The following listings will mention the restriction of an environment to a set, which is defined as follows:

definition $env\_restr :: 'a\ set \Rightarrow ('a \Rightarrow 'b{::}pcpo) \Rightarrow ('a \Rightarrow 'b)$ Env.thy
where $env\_restr\ S\ m = (\lambda\ x.\ if\ x \in S\ then\ m\ x\ else\ \bot)$

abbreviation *env_restr_rev* (**infixl** $f|'$ 110)
where $env\_restr\_rev\ m\ S \equiv env\_restr\ S\ m$

A.3 Correctness and adequacy theorems

The main results from Chapter 2 are the correctness and adequacy of the natural semantics with regard to the standard denotational semantics.

The correctness theorem (Theorem 2) is as follows. Note that the assumption of closedness is written out explicitly.

theorem *correctness*: CorrectnessOriginal.thy
assumes $\Gamma : e \Downarrow_L \Delta : v$
and $fv\ (\Gamma, e) \subseteq set\ L \cup domA\ \Gamma$
shows $[\![e]\!]_{\{\!|\Gamma|\!\}\varrho} = [\![v]\!]_{\{\!|\Delta|\!\}\varrho}$
and $(\{\!|\Gamma|\!\}\varrho)\ f|'\ domA\ \Gamma = (\{\!|\Delta|\!\}\varrho)\ f|'\ domA\ \Gamma$

The adequacy theorem (Theorem 3) corresponds even closer to the original formulation. Note that the set S of variables to avoid is unconstrained, i.e. the theorem can produce a judgement for every choice of S. This only works because the set is represented as a list in the formalisation, otherwise finiteness of the set would have to be required explicitly.

theorem *adequacy*: Adequacy.thy
assumes $[\![e]\!]_{\{\!|\Gamma|\!\}} \neq \bot$
shows $\exists\ \Delta\ v.\ \Gamma : e \Downarrow_S \Delta : v$

A.4 Call Arity

For the formalisation of Chapter 4, I introduce a few custom data types.

A.4.1 Arities

I define the type *Arity* as an isomorphic copy the type of naturals:

typedef $Arity = UNIV :: nat\ set$ Arity.thy
morphisms *Rep_Arity to_Arity* **by** *auto*

Having a dedicated type for arities allows me to define the partial order required here. Note that it swaps the arguments of $\leq$:

instantiation *Arity* :: *po*
begin
lift_definition *below_Arity* :: *Arity* ⇒ *Arity* ⇒ *bool* **is** $\lambda\ x\ y\ .\ y \leq x$.

On the other hand, this additional abstraction layers requires me to lift a few definitions from the naturals, in particular zero and the predecessor and successor functions. The latter are defined in two steps: First lifting the function to *Arity*, and then into *HOLCF*'s type of continuous functions:

instantiation *Arity* :: *zero*
begin
lift_definition *zero_Arity* :: *Arity* **is** *0*.
instance..
end

lift_definition *inc_Arity* :: *Arity* ⇒ *Arity* **is** *Suc*.
lift_definition *pred_Arity* :: *Arity* ⇒ *Arity* **is** $(\lambda\ x\ .\ x - 1)$.

definition *inc* :: *Arity* → *Arity* **where**
  $inc = (\Lambda\ x.\ inc\_Arity\ x)$

definition *pred* :: *Arity* → *Arity* **where**
  $pred = (\Lambda\ x.\ pred\_Arity\ x)$

The type *AEnv* of arity environments is simply $var \Rightarrow Arity_{\bot}$. The following functions provide some useful operations on such and similar environments: The domain of an environments, singleton environments, and removal of one entry.

definition *edom* :: (*'key* ⇒ *'value::pcpo*) ⇒ *'key set* Env.thy
  where $edom\ m = \{x.\ m\ x \neq \bot\}$

lemma *esing_simps*[*simp*]:
  $(esing\ x \cdot n)\ x = n$
  $x' \neq x \Longrightarrow (esing\ x \cdot n)\ x' = \bot$

definition *env_delete* :: *'a* ⇒ (*'a* ⇒ *'b*) ⇒ (*'a* ⇒ *'b::pcpo*)
  where $env\_delete\ x\ m = m(x := \bot)$

A.4.2 Co-call graphs

The type *CoCalls* of co-call Graphs is defined to be isomorphic to the set of symmetric relations on *var*:

typedef *CoCalls* = {*G* :: (*var* × *var*) *set*. *sym G*} CoCallGraph.thy
morphisms *Rep_CoCall Abs_CoCall*
by (*auto intro*: *exI*[**where** *x* = {}] *symI*)

setup_lifting *type_definition_CoCalls*

The relevant operations are the calculation of the field of the relation, the member relation, the removal of a node from the graph, the restriction to a set, the Cartesian products and the set of neighbours.

lift_definition *ccField* :: *CoCalls* ⇒ *var set* **is** *Field*.

lift_definition
inCC :: *var* ⇒ *var* ⇒ *CoCalls* ⇒ *bool* (_−−_∈_ [*1000, 1000, 900*] *900*)
is λ *x y s*. (*x*,*y*) ∈ *s*.

abbreviation
notInCC :: *var* ⇒ *var* ⇒ *CoCalls* ⇒ *bool* (_−−_∉_ [*1000, 1000, 900*] *900*)
where *x*−−*y*∉*S* ≡ ¬ *x*−−*y*∈*S*

lift_definition *cc_delete* :: *var* ⇒ *CoCalls* ⇒ *CoCalls*
is λ *z*. *Set.filter* (λ (*x*,*y*) . *x* ≠ *z* ∧ *y* ≠ *z*)

lift_definition *cc_restr* :: *var set* ⇒ *CoCalls* ⇒ *CoCalls*
is λ *S*. *Set.filter* (λ (*x*,*y*) . *x* ∈ *S* ∧ *y* ∈ *S*)

lift_definition *ccProd* :: *var set* ⇒ *var set* ⇒ *CoCalls* (**infixr** *G*× *90*)
is λ *S1 S2*. *S1* × *S2* ∪ *S2* × *S1*
by (*auto intro*!: *symI elim*: *symE*)

definition *ccSquare* (_^{2} [*80*] *80*)
where S^2 = *ccProd S S*

lift_definition *ccNeighbors* :: *var* ⇒ *CoCalls* ⇒ *var set*
is λ *x G*. {*y* .(*y*,*x*) ∈ *G* ∨ (*x*,*y*) ∈ *G*}.

A.4.3 The Call Arity analysis

The equations for the arity analysis are mutually recursive with a few auxiliary functions to handle the heap.

lemma *Aexp_simps[simp]:* CoCallAnalysisImpl.thy

$\mathcal{A}_a(\mathit{Var}\ x) = \mathit{esing}\ x\cdot(\mathit{up}\cdot a)$

$\mathcal{A}_a(\mathit{Lam}\ [x].\ e) = \mathit{env\_delete}\ x\ (\mathcal{A}_{\mathit{pred}\cdot a}\ e)$

$\mathcal{A}_a(\mathit{App}\ e\ x) = \mathit{Aexp}\ e\cdot(\mathit{inc}\cdot a) \sqcup \mathit{esing}\ x\cdot(\mathit{up}\cdot 0)$

$\neg\ \mathit{nonrec}\ \Gamma \Longrightarrow \mathcal{A}_a(\mathit{Let}\ \Gamma\ e) =$

$(\mathit{Afix}\ \Gamma\cdot(\mathcal{A}_a\ e \sqcup (\lambda\_.\mathit{up}\cdot 0)\ f|^{\prime}\ \mathit{thunks}\ \Gamma))\ f|^{\prime}\ (-\ \mathit{domA}\ \Gamma)$

$x \notin \mathit{fv}\ e' \Longrightarrow \mathcal{A}_a(\mathit{let}\ x\ \mathit{be}\ e'\ \mathit{in}\ e) =$

$\mathit{env\_delete}\ x\ (\mathcal{A}^{\perp}{}_{\mathit{ABind\_nonrec}\ x\ e'\cdot(\mathcal{A}_a\ e,\ \mathcal{G}_a\ e)}\ e' \sqcup \mathcal{A}_a\ e)$

$\mathcal{A}_a(\mathit{Bool}\ b) = \perp$

$\mathcal{A}_a(\mathit{scrut}\ ?\ e1 : e2) = \mathcal{A}_0\ \mathit{scrut} \sqcup \mathcal{A}_a\ e1 \sqcup \mathcal{A}_a\ e2$

lemma *CCexp_simps[simp]:*

$\mathcal{G}_a(\mathit{Var}\ x) = \perp$

$\mathcal{G}_0(\mathit{Lam}\ [x].\ e) = (\mathit{fv}\ (\mathit{Lam}\ [x].\ e))^2$

$\mathcal{G}_{\mathit{inc}\cdot a}(\mathit{Lam}\ [x].\ e) = \mathit{cc\_delete}\ x\ (\mathcal{G}_a\ e)$

$\mathcal{G}_a\ (\mathit{App}\ e\ x) = \mathcal{G}_{\mathit{inc}\cdot a}\ e \sqcup \{x\}\ G{\times}\mathit{insert}\ x\ (\mathit{fv}\ e)$

$\neg\ \mathit{nonrec}\ \Gamma \Longrightarrow \mathcal{G}_a\ (\mathit{Let}\ \Gamma\ e) =$

$(\mathit{CCfix}\ \Gamma\cdot(\mathit{Afix}\ \Gamma\cdot(\mathcal{A}_a\ e \sqcup (\lambda\_.\mathit{up}\cdot 0)\ f|^{\prime}\ \mathit{thunks}\ \Gamma),\ \mathcal{G}_a\ e))\ \mathrm{G}|^{\prime}\ (-\ \mathit{domA}\ \Gamma)$

$x \notin \mathit{fv}\ e' \Longrightarrow \mathcal{G}_a\ (\mathit{let}\ x\ \mathit{be}\ e'\ \mathit{in}\ e) =$

$\mathit{cc\_delete}\ x$

$(\mathit{ccBind}\ x\ e'\ \cdot(\mathit{Aheap\_nonrec}\ x\ e'\cdot(\mathcal{A}_a\ e,\ \mathcal{G}_a\ e),\ \mathcal{G}_a\ e)$

$\sqcup\ \mathit{fv}\ e'\ G{\times}\ (\mathit{ccNeighbors}\ x\ (\mathcal{G}_a\ e) - (\mathit{if}\ \mathit{isVal}\ e'\ \mathit{then}\ \{\}\ \mathit{else}\ \{x\})) \sqcup \mathcal{G}_a\ e)$

$\mathcal{G}_a\ (\mathit{Bool}\ b) = \perp$

$\mathcal{G}_a\ (\mathit{scrut}\ ?\ e1 : e2) =$

$\mathcal{G}_0\ \mathit{scrut} \sqcup (\mathcal{G}_a\ e1 \sqcup \mathcal{G}_a\ e2) \sqcup$

$\mathit{edom}\ (\mathcal{A}_0\ \mathit{scrut})\ G{\times}\ (\mathit{edom}\ (\mathcal{A}_a\ e1) \cup \mathit{edom}\ (\mathcal{A}_a\ e2))$

A superscripted $\perp$ indicates that the function is lifted to $\mathit{Arity}_{\perp}$:

abbreviation *Aexp_bot_syn* ($\mathcal{A}^{\perp}\_$) ArityAnalysisSig.thy
where $\mathcal{A}^{\perp}{}_a\ e \equiv \mathit{fup}\cdot(\mathit{Aexp}\ e)\cdot a$

abbreviation *ccExp_bot_syn* ($\mathcal{G}^{\perp}\_$) CoCallAnalysisSig.thy
where $\mathcal{G}^{\perp}{}_a \equiv (\lambda e.\ \mathit{fup}\cdot(\mathit{ccExp}\ e)\cdot a)$

The function *Afix*, building on *ABinds* and *ABind*, implements the fix-pointing in the arity analysis:

lemma *ABind_eq[simp]*: $ABind\ v\ e \cdot ae = \mathcal{A}^{\perp}{}_{ae\ v}\ e$ ArityAnalysisAbinds.thy

fun *ABinds* :: $heap \Rightarrow (AEnv \rightarrow AEnv)$
  where $ABinds\ [] = \perp$
  $|\ ABinds\ ((v,e)\#binds) = ABind\ v\ e \sqcup ABinds\ (delete\ v\ binds)$

lemma *Afix_eq*: $Afix\ \Gamma \cdot ae = (\mu\ ae'.\ (ABinds\ \Gamma \cdot ae') \sqcup ae)$ ArityAnalysisFix.thy

In the non-recursive case, the function *ABind_nonrec* is used; this is where the arity analysis depends on the co-call cardinality analysis.

lemma *ABind_nonrec_eq*: CoCallFix.thy
$ABind\_nonrec\ x\ e \cdot (ae,G) = (if\ isVal\ e \vee x{-}{-}x \notin G\ then\ ae\ x\ else\ up \cdot 0)$

The fixed-point calculation of the co-call-graph is defined similarly:

lemma *ccBind_eq*: CoCallAnalysisBinds.thy
$ccBind\ v\ e \cdot (ae,\ G) = (if\ v{-}{-}v \notin G \vee \neg\ isVal\ e\ then\ \mathcal{G}^{\perp}{}_{ae\ v}\ e\ G|'\ fv\ e\ else\ (fv\ e)^2)$

lemma *ccBinds_eq*:
$ccBinds\ \Gamma \cdot i = (\bigsqcup v \mapsto e \in map\_of\ \Gamma.\ ccBind\ v\ e \cdot i)$

lemma *ccBindsExtra_eq*: $ccBindsExtra\ \Gamma \cdot (ae,G) =$
$G \sqcup ccBinds\ \Gamma \cdot (ae,G) \sqcup (\bigsqcup x \mapsto e \in map\_of\ \Gamma.\ fv\ e\ G \times ccNeighbors\ x\ G)$

lemma *CCfix_eq*: CoCallFix.thy
$CCfix\ \Gamma \cdot (ae,G) = (\mu\ G'.\ ccBindsExtra\ \Gamma \cdot (ae,\ G') \sqcup G)$

Finally, the actual transformation, which uses the arity analysis, is

lemma *transform_simps*: ArityTransform.thy
$\mathcal{T}_a\ (App\ e\ x) = App\ (\mathcal{T}_{inc \cdot a}\ e)\ x$

$\mathcal{T}_a$ (*Lam* [*x*]. *e*) = *Lam* [*x*]. $\mathcal{T}_{pred \cdot a}$ *e*
$\mathcal{T}_a$ (*Var x*) = *Var x*
$\mathcal{T}_a$ (*Let* Γ *e*) = *Let* (*map_transform Aeta_expand* (*Aheap* Γ *e·a*) (*map_transform* (*λa.* $\mathcal{T}_a$) (*Aheap* Γ *e·a*) Γ)) ($\mathcal{T}_a$ *e*)
$\mathcal{T}_a$ (*Bool b*) = *Bool b*
$\mathcal{T}_a$ (*scrut ? e1 : e2*) = ($\mathcal{T}_0$ *scrut ?* $\mathcal{T}_a$ *e1* : $\mathcal{T}_a$ *e2*)

where the auxiliary function *map_transform* applies a transformation of type *Arity* ⇒ *exp* ⇒ to an Arity environment and a *heap*:

lemma *lift_transform_simps*[*simp*]: TransformTools.thy
lift_transform t ⊥ *e* = *e*
lift_transform t (*up·a*) *e* = *t a e*

definition
map_transform :: (*'a::cont_pt* ⇒ *exp* ⇒ *exp*) ⇒ (*var* ⇒ $'a_\bot$) ⇒ *heap* ⇒ *heap*
where *map_transform t ae* = *map_ran* (λ *x e* . *lift_transform t* (*ae x*) *e*)

A.4.4 Call Arity theorems

The Call Arity transformation is functionally correct, i.e. does not change the semantics (Theorem 4):

corollary *Arity_transformation_correct'*: ArityAnalysisCorrDenotational.thy
$[\![\mathcal{T}_0\ e]\!]_\varrho = [\![e]\!]_\varrho$

The main safety theorem for Call Arity (Theorem 5) reads as follows:

theorem *end2end_closed*: CallArityEnd2EndSafe.thy
assumes *closed*: *fv e* = ({} :: *var set*)
assumes ([], *e*, []) ⇒* (Γ,*v*,[]) **and** *isVal v*
obtains Γ' **and** *v'*
where ([], $\mathcal{T}_0$ *e*, []) ⇒* (Γ',*v'*,[]) **and** *isVal v'*
and *card* (*domA* Γ') ≤ *card* (*domA* Γ)

It's like someone took a transcript of a couple arguing at IKEA and made random edits until it compiled without errors.

Randall Munroe, xkcd #1513

APPENDIX B

Call Arity code

This appendix lists the actual implementation of Call Arity, as it is shipped in GHC 7.10.3, which is also the version that I produced the benchmarks in Section 3.5.3 with. I give the code without modifications besides

- the removal of comments and notes and
- whitespace-only changes to better fit the page format and to produce nicer alignment.

The mild pretty-printing and code alignment is performed using lhs2Tex [HL15].

B.1 Co-call graphs

```
module UnVarGraph
  ( UnVarSet
  , emptyUnVarSet, mkUnVarSet, varEnvDom,
  , unionUnVarSet, unionUnVarSets
  , delUnVarSet
  , elemUnVarSet, isEmptyUnVarSet
  , UnVarGraph
  , emptyUnVarGraph
```

```
  , unionUnVarGraph, unionUnVarGraphs
  , completeGraph, completeBipartiteGraph
  , neighbors
  , delNode
  ) where
import Id
import VarEnv
import UniqFM
import Outputable
import Data.List
import Bag
import Unique

import qualified Data.IntSet as S

newtype UnVarSet = UnVarSet (S.IntSet)
  deriving Eq

k :: Var → Int
k v = getKey (getUnique v)

emptyUnVarSet :: UnVarSet
emptyUnVarSet = UnVarSet S.empty

elemUnVarSet :: Var → UnVarSet → Bool
elemUnVarSet v (UnVarSet s) = k v ‘S.member‘ s

isEmptyUnVarSet :: UnVarSet → Bool
isEmptyUnVarSet (UnVarSet s) = S.null s

delUnVarSet :: UnVarSet → Var → UnVarSet
delUnVarSet (UnVarSet s) v = UnVarSet $ k v ‘S.delete‘ s

mkUnVarSet :: [Var] → UnVarSet
mkUnVarSet vs = UnVarSet $ S.fromList $ map k vs
```

```
varEnvDom :: VarEnv a → UnVarSet
varEnvDom ae = UnVarSet $ ufmToSet_Directly ae

unionUnVarSet :: UnVarSet → UnVarSet → UnVarSet
unionUnVarSet (UnVarSet set1) (UnVarSet set2)
  = UnVarSet (set1 'S.union' set2)

unionUnVarSets :: [UnVarSet] → UnVarSet
unionUnVarSets = foldr unionUnVarSet emptyUnVarSet

instance Outputable UnVarSet where
  ppr (UnVarSet s) = braces $
    hcat $ punctuate comma [ppr (getUnique i) | i ← S.toList s]

data Gen = CBPG UnVarSet UnVarSet
         | CG   UnVarSet
newtype UnVarGraph = UnVarGraph (Bag Gen)

emptyUnVarGraph :: UnVarGraph
emptyUnVarGraph = UnVarGraph emptyBag

unionUnVarGraph :: UnVarGraph → UnVarGraph → UnVarGraph
unionUnVarGraph (UnVarGraph g1) (UnVarGraph g2)
  = UnVarGraph (g1 'unionBags' g2)

unionUnVarGraphs :: [UnVarGraph] → UnVarGraph
unionUnVarGraphs = foldl' unionUnVarGraph emptyUnVarGraph

completeBipartiteGraph :: UnVarSet → UnVarSet → UnVarGraph
completeBipartiteGraph s1 s2
  = prune $ UnVarGraph $ unitBag $ CBPG s1 s2

completeGraph :: UnVarSet → UnVarGraph
completeGraph s = prune $ UnVarGraph $ unitBag $ CG s

neighbors :: UnVarGraph → Var → UnVarSet
```

```
neighbors (UnVarGraph g) v
  = unionUnVarSets $ concatMap go $ bagToList g
  where
    go (CG s)         = (if v `elemUnVarSet` s  then [s]  else [])
    go (CBPG s1 s2) = (if v `elemUnVarSet` s1 then [s2] else []) ++
                        (if v `elemUnVarSet` s2 then [s1] else [])

delNode :: UnVarGraph → Var → UnVarGraph
delNode (UnVarGraph g) v = prune $ UnVarGraph $ mapBag go g
  where
    go (CG s)         = CG (s `delUnVarSet` v)
    go (CBPG s1 s2) = CBPG (s1 `delUnVarSet` v) (s2 `delUnVarSet` v)

prune :: UnVarGraph → UnVarGraph
prune (UnVarGraph g) = UnVarGraph $ filterBag go g
  where
    go (CG s)         = not (isEmptyUnVarSet s)
    go (CBPG s1 s2) = not (isEmptyUnVarSet s1) &&
                        not (isEmptyUnVarSet s2)

instance Outputable Gen where
  ppr (CG s)          = ppr s <> char '2'
  ppr (CBPG s1 s2)    = ppr s1 <+> char 'x' <+> ppr s2
instance Outputable UnVarGraph where
  ppr (UnVarGraph g) = ppr g
```

B.2 The Call Arity analysis

```
module CallArity (callArityAnalProgram, callArityRHS) where

import VarSet
import VarEnv
import DynFlags (DynFlags)
```

```
import BasicTypes
import CoreSyn
import Id
import CoreArity (typeArity)
import CoreUtils (exprIsHNF, exprIsTrivial)
import UnVarGraph
import Demand

import Control.Arrow (first, second)

callArityAnalProgram :: DynFlags → CoreProgram → CoreProgram
callArityAnalProgram _dflags binds = binds'
  where
    (_, binds') = callArityTopLvl [] emptyVarSet binds

callArityTopLvl :: [Var] → VarSet → [CoreBind] →
                   (CallArityRes, [CoreBind])
callArityTopLvl exported _ []
    = ( calledMultipleTimes $
        (emptyUnVarGraph, mkVarEnv $ [(v, 0) | v ← exported])
      , [])
callArityTopLvl exported int1 (b : bs)
    = (ae2, b' : bs')
  where
    int2        = bindersOf b
    exported'   = filter isExportedId int2 ++ exported
    int'        = int1 `addInterestingBinds` b
    (ae1, bs')  = callArityTopLvl exported' int' bs
    (ae2, b')   = callArityBind (boringBinds b) ae1 int1 b
callArityRHS :: CoreExpr → CoreExpr
callArityRHS = snd . callArityAnal 0 emptyVarSet

callArityAnal :: Arity → VarSet → CoreExpr → (CallArityRes, CoreExpr)
callArityAnal _ _ e@(Lit _)
  = (emptyArityRes, e)
```

```
callArityAnal _     _   e@(Type _)
  = (emptyArityRes, e)
callArityAnal _     _   e@(Coercion _)
  = (emptyArityRes, e)

callArityAnal arity int (Tick t e)
  = second (Tick t) $ callArityAnal arity int e
callArityAnal arity int (Cast e co)
  = second (λe → Cast e co) $ callArityAnal arity int e

callArityAnal arity int e@(Var v)
  | v ‘elemVarSet‘ int
  = (unitArityRes v arity, e)
  | otherwise
  = (emptyArityRes, e)

callArityAnal arity int (Lam v e) | not (isId v)
  = second (Lam v) $ callArityAnal arity (int ‘delVarSet‘ v) e

callArityAnal 0     int (Lam v e)
  = (ae', Lam v e')
 where
   (ae, e') = callArityAnal 0 (int ‘delVarSet‘ v) e
   ae'      = calledMultipleTimes ae

callArityAnal arity int (Lam v e)
  = (ae, Lam v e')
 where
   (ae, e') = callArityAnal (arity − 1) (int ‘delVarSet‘ v) e

callArityAnal arity int (App e (Type t))
  = second (λe → App e (Type t)) $ callArityAnal arity int e
```

```
callArityAnal arity int (App e1 e2)
  = (final_ae, App e1' e2')
  where
    (ae1, e1') = callArityAnal (arity + 1) int e1
    (ae2, e2') = callArityAnal 0           int e2

    ae2' | exprIsTrivial e2 = calledMultipleTimes ae2
         | otherwise        = ae2
    final_ae   = ae1 `both` ae2'

callArityAnal arity int (Case scrut bndr ty alts)
  = (final_ae, Case scrut' bndr ty alts')
  where
    (alt_aes, alts')     = unzip $ map go alts
    go (dc, bndrs, e)    = let (ae, e') = callArityAnal arity int e
                           in (ae, (dc, bndrs, e'))
    alt_ae               = lubRess alt_aes
    (scrut_ae, scrut')   = callArityAnal 0 int scrut

    final_ae             = scrut_ae `both` alt_ae

callArityAnal arity int (Let bind e)
  = (final_ae, Let bind' e')
  where
    int_body             = int `addInterestingBinds` bind
    (ae_body, e')        = callArityAnal arity int_body e
    (final_ae, bind')    = callArityBind (boringBinds bind) ae_body int bind
isInteresting :: Var -> Bool
isInteresting v = 0 < length (typeArity (idType v))

interestingBinds :: CoreBind -> [Var]
interestingBinds = filter isInteresting . bindersOf

boringBinds :: CoreBind -> VarSet
boringBinds = mkVarSet . filter (not . isInteresting) . bindersOf
```

```
addInterestingBinds :: VarSet → CoreBind → VarSet
addInterestingBinds int bind
  = int ‘delVarSetList‘    bindersOf bind
        ‘extendVarSetList‘ interestingBinds bind
callArityBind ::
    VarSet → CallArityRes → VarSet → CoreBind →
    (CallArityRes, CoreBind)
callArityBind boring_vars ae_body int (NonRec v rhs)
    | otherwise
  = (final_ae, NonRec v' rhs')
  where
    is_thunk = not (exprIsHNF rhs)

    boring = v ‘elemVarSet‘ boring_vars

    (arity, called_once)
                | boring           = (0, False)
                | otherwise        = lookupCallArityRes ae_body v
    safe_arity  | called_once      = arity
                | is_thunk         = 0
                | otherwise        = arity

    trimmed_arity = trimArity v safe_arity

    (ae_rhs, rhs') = callArityAnal trimmed_arity int rhs

    ae_rhs'     | called_once      = ae_rhs
                | safe_arity == 0  = ae_rhs
                | otherwise        = calledMultipleTimes ae_rhs

    called_by_v = domRes ae_rhs'
    called_with_v
                | boring           = domRes ae_body
                | otherwise        = calledWith ae_body v ‘delUnVarSet‘ v
```

```
    final_ae = addCrossCoCalls called_by_v called_with_v
           $ ae_rhs' `lubRes` resDel v ae_body

    v' = v `setIdCallArity` trimmed_arity

callArityBind boring_vars ae_body int b@(Rec binds)
  = (final_ae, Rec binds')
  where
    any_boring       = any (`elemVarSet` boring_vars) [i | (i, _) ← binds]

    int_body         = int `addInterestingBinds` b
    (ae_rhs, binds') = fix initial_binds
    final_ae         = bindersOf b `resDelList` ae_rhs

    initial_binds    = [(i, Nothing, e) | (i, e) ← binds]

    fix :: [(Id, Maybe (Bool, Arity, CallArityRes), CoreExpr)] →
        (CallArityRes, [(Id, CoreExpr)])
    fix ann_binds
        | any_change = fix ann_binds'
        | otherwise  = (ae, map (λ(i, _, e) → (i, e)) ann_binds')
      where
        aes_old = [(i, ae) | (i, Just (_, _, ae), _) ← ann_binds]
        ae = callArityRecEnv any_boring aes_old ae_body

        rerun (i, mbLastRun, rhs)
          | i `elemVarSet` int_body &&
            not (i `elemUnVarSet` domRes ae)
          = (False, (i, Nothing, rhs))

          | Just (old_called_once, old_arity, _) ← mbLastRun
          , called_once == old_called_once
          , new_arity == old_arity
          = (False, (i, mbLastRun, rhs))
```

```
      | otherwise
      = let is_thunk = not (exprIsHNF rhs)

            safe_arity | is_thunk = 0
                       | otherwise = new_arity

            trimmed_arity = trimArity i safe_arity

            (ae_rhs, rhs') = callArityAnal trimmed_arity
                                           int_body rhs

            ae_rhs' | called_once       = ae_rhs
                    | safe_arity == 0 = ae_rhs
                    | otherwise         = calledMultipleTimes ae_rhs

        in (True, (i `setIdCallArity` trimmed_arity,
                   Just (called_once, new_arity, ae_rhs'), rhs'))
     where
       (new_arity, called_once) | i `elemVarSet` boring_vars
                                = (0, False)
                                | otherwise
                                = lookupCallArityRes ae i

    (changes, ann_binds') = unzip $ map rerun ann_binds
    any_change = or changes
callArityRecEnv ::
  Bool → [(Var, CallArityRes)] → CallArityRes → CallArityRes
callArityRecEnv any_boring ae_rhss ae_body
  = ae_new
 where
  vars = map fst ae_rhss

  ae_combined = lubRess (map snd ae_rhss) `lubRes` ae_body
```

```
    cross_calls
      | any_boring           = completeGraph (domRes ae_combined)
      | length ae_rhss > 25 = completeGraph (domRes ae_combined)
      | otherwise            = unionUnVarGraphs $ map cross_call ae_rhss
    cross_call (v, ae_rhs)
      = completeBipartiteGraph called_by_v called_with_v
     where
      is_thunk = idCallArity v == 0

      ae_before_v | is_thunk
                    = lubRess (map snd $ filter ((/ =v) . fst) ae_rhss)
                        `lubRes` ae_body
                  | otherwise
                    = ae_combined

      called_with_v
        = unionUnVarSets $ map (calledWith ae_before_v) vars
      called_by_v = domRes ae_rhs

    ae_new = first (cross_calls `unionUnVarGraph`) ae_combined
trimArity :: Id -> Arity -> Arity
trimArity v a = minimum [a, max_arity_by_type, max_arity_by_strsig]
  where
    max_arity_by_type = length (typeArity (idType v))
    max_arity_by_strsig
      | isBotRes result_info = length demands
      | otherwise = a

    (demands, result_info) = splitStrictSig (idStrictness v)


type CallArityRes = (UnVarGraph, VarEnv Arity)

emptyArityRes :: CallArityRes
emptyArityRes = (emptyUnVarGraph, emptyVarEnv)
```

```
unitArityRes :: Var → Arity → CallArityRes
unitArityRes v arity = (emptyUnVarGraph, unitVarEnv v arity)

resDelList :: [Var] → CallArityRes → CallArityRes
resDelList vs ae = foldr resDel ae vs

resDel :: Var → CallArityRes → CallArityRes
resDel v (g, ae) = (g ‘delNode‘ v, ae ‘delVarEnv‘ v)

domRes :: CallArityRes → UnVarSet
domRes (_, ae) = varEnvDom ae

lookupCallArityRes :: CallArityRes → Var → (Arity, Bool)
lookupCallArityRes (g, ae) v
  = case lookupVarEnv ae v of
       Just a    → (a, not (v ‘elemUnVarSet‘ (neighbors g v)))
       Nothing → (0, False)

calledWith :: CallArityRes → Var → UnVarSet
calledWith (g, _) v = neighbors g v

addCrossCoCalls :: UnVarSet → UnVarSet → CallArityRes → CallArityRes
addCrossCoCalls set1 set2
  = first (completeBipartiteGraph set1 set2‘unionUnVarGraph‘)

calledMultipleTimes :: CallArityRes → CallArityRes
calledMultipleTimes res
  = first (const (completeGraph (domRes res))) res

both :: CallArityRes → CallArityRes → CallArityRes
both r1 r2
  = addCrossCoCalls (domRes r1) (domRes r2) $ r1 ‘lubRes‘ r2
```

```
lubRes :: CallArityRes → CallArityRes → CallArityRes
lubRes (g1, ae1) (g2, ae2)
  = (g1 `unionUnVarGraph` g2, ae1 `lubArityEnv` ae2)

lubArityEnv :: VarEnv Arity → VarEnv Arity → VarEnv Arity
lubArityEnv = plusVarEnv_C min

lubRess :: [CallArityRes] → CallArityRes
lubRess = foldl lubRes emptyArityRes
```

Bibliography

[Abr90] Samson Abramsky. *The lazy lambda calculus*. Research topics in functional programming. Ed. by David A. Turner. Addison-Wesley, 1990. Chap. 4.

[AO93] Samson Abramsky and Chih-Hao Luke Ong. *Full Abstraction in the Lazy Lambda Calculus*. Information and Computation 105.2 (1993). DOI: 10.1006/inco.1993.1044.

[ABM07] David Aspinall, Lennart Beringer and Alberto Momigliano. *Optimisation Validation*. Compiler Optimisation Meets Compiler Verification (COCV) 2006. Vol. 176-3. ENTCS. 2007. DOI: 10.1016/j.entcs.2006.06.017.

[BKHT99] Clem Baker-Finch, David King, Jon Hall and Phil Trinder. *An Operational Semantics for Parallel Call-by-Need*. Tech. rep. 99/1. Faculty of Mathematics and Computing, The Open University, 1999.

[BKT00] Clem Baker-Finch, David King and Phil Trinder. *An Operational Semantics for Parallel Lazy Evaluation*. International Conference on Functional Programming (ICFP). ACM, 2000. DOI: 10.1145/351240.351256.

[Bal14] Clemens Ballarin. *Locales: A Module System for Mathematical Theories*. Journal of Automated Reasoning 52.2 (2014). DOI: 10.1007/s10817-013-9284-7.

[BA06] Sorav Bansal and Alex Aiken. *Automatic Generation of Peephole Superoptimizers*. Architectural Support for Programming Languages and Operating Systems (ASPLOS). ACM, 2006. DOI: 10.1145/1168857.1168906.

[Bir89] Richard Simpson Bird. *Algebraic Identities for Program Calculation*. Computer Journal 32.2 (1989). DOI: 10.1093/comjnl/32.2.122.

[Bre13] Joachim Breitner. *The Correctness of Launchbury's Natural Semantics for Lazy Evaluation*. Archive of Formal Proofs (Jan. 2013). URL: http://afp.sf.net/entries/Launchbury.shtml.

[Bre15a] Joachim Breitner. *Call Arity*. Trends in Functional Programming (TFP) 2014. Vol. 8843. LNCS. Springer, 2015. DOI: 10.1007/978-3-319-14675-1_3.

[Bre15b] Joachim Breitner. *Formally proving a compiler transformation safe*. Haskell Symposium. ACM, 2015. DOI: 10.1145/2804302.2804312.

[Bre15c] Joachim Breitner. *The Adequacy of Launchbury's Natural Semantics for Lazy Evaluation*. preprint, submitted to the Journal of Functional Programming. 2015. URL: http://joachim-breitner.de/publications/LaunchburyAdequacy-preprint.pdf.

[Bre15d] Joachim Breitner. *The Safety of Call Arity*. Archive of Formal Proofs (Feb. 2015). URL: http://afp.sf.net/entries/Call_Arity.shtml.

[Bre16] Joachim Breitner. *Lazy Evaluation: From natural semantics to a machine-checked compiler transformation*. Ph.D. thesis. Karlsruhe Institute of Technology, 2016. DOI: 10.5445/IR/1000054251.

[BEPW14] Joachim Breitner, Richard A. Eisenberg, Simon Peyton Jones and Stephanie Weirich. *Safe Zero-cost Coercions for Haskell*. International Conference on Functional Programming (ICFP). ACM, 2014. DOI: 10.1145/2628136.2628141.

[BHMS13] Joachim Breitner, Brian Huffman, Neil Mitchell and Christian Sternagel. *Certified HLints with Isabelle/HOLCF-Prelude*. Haskell and Rewriting Techniques (HART). 2013. arXiv: 1306.1340.

[Buc15] Sebastian Buchwald. *Optgen: A Generator for Local Optimizations*. Compiler Construction. Vol. 9031. LCNS. Springer, 2015. DOI: 10.1007/978-3-662-46663-6_9.

[Chl10] Adam Chlipala. *A Verified Compiler for an Impure Functional Language*. Principles of Programming Languages (POPL). ACM, 2010. DOI: 10.1145/1706299.1706312.

[Coq04] The Coq development team. *The Coq proof assistant reference manual*. Version 8.0. LogiCal Project. 2004. URL: http://coq.inria.fr.

[Cou10] Duncan Coutts. *Stream Fusion: Practical shortcut fusion for coinductive sequence types*. Ph.D. thesis. University of Oxford, 2010.

[CLS07] Duncan Coutts, Roman Leshchinskiy and Don Stewart. *Stream Fusion. From Lists to Streams to Nothing at All*. International Conference on Functional Programming (ICFP). ACM, 2007. DOI: 10.1145/1291151.1291199.

[CB13] Charlie Curtsinger and Emery D. Berger. *STABILIZER: Statistically Sound Performance Evaluation*. Architectural Support for Programming Languages and Operating Systems (ASPLOS). ACM, 2013. DOI: 10.1145/2451116.2451141.

[DL07] Zaynah Dargaye and Xavier Leroy. *Mechanized Verification of CPS Transformations*. Logic for Programming, Artificial Intelligence, and Reasoning (LPAR). Vol. 4790. LNCS. Springer, 2007. DOI: 10.1007/978-3-540-75560-9_17.

[EM04] Marko van Eekelen and Maarten de Mol. *Mixed lazy/strict graph semantics*. Tech. rep. NIII-R0402. Radboud University Nijmegen, Jan. 2004.

[Eis15] Richard Eisenberg. *System FC, as implemented in GHC*. Version 414e20b. 2015. URL: https://github.com/ghc/ghc/blob/master/docs/core-spec/core-spec.pdf (visited on 04/24/2015).

[FHG14] Andrew Farmer, Christian Höner zu Siederdissen and Andrew John Gill. *The HERMIT in the Stream: Fusing Stream Fusion's concatMap*. Partial Evaluation and Program Manipulation (PEPM). ACM, 2014. DOI: 10.1145/2543728.2543736.

[Gam09] Peter Gammie. *The Worker/Wrapper Transformation*. Archive of Formal Proofs (Oct. 2009). URL: http://afp.sf.net/entries/WorkerWrapper.shtml.

[Gil96] Andrew John Gill. *Cheap deforestation for non-strict functional languages*. Ph.D. thesis. University of Glasgow, 1996.

[GLP93] Andrew John Gill, John Launchbury and Simon Peyton Jones. *A Short Cut to Deforestation*. Functional Programming Languages and Computer Architecture (FPCA). ACM, 1993. DOI: 10.1145/165180.165214.

[GS99] Jörgen Gustavsson and David Sands. *A Foundation for Space-Safe Transformations of Call-by-Need Programs*. Higher Order Operational Techniques in Semantics (HOOTS). Vol. 26. ENTCS. 1999. DOI: 10.1016/S1571-0661(05)80284-1.

[GS01] Jörgen Gustavsson and David Sands. *Possibilities and Limitations of Call-by-Need Space Improvement*. International Conference on Functional Programming (ICFP). ACM, 2001. DOI: 10.1145/507635.507667.

[HH14] Jennifer Hackett and Graham Hutton. *Worker/Wrapper/Makes It/Faster*. International Conference on Functional Programming (ICFP). ACM, 2014. DOI: 10.1145/2628136.2628142.

[Haf09] Florian Haftmann. *Code Generation from Specifications in Higher Order Logic*. Ph.D. thesis. Technische Universität München, 2009.

[Haf10] Florian Haftmann. *From Higher-order Logic to Haskell: There and Back Again*. Partial Evaluation and Program Manipulation (PEPM). ACM, 2010. DOI: 10.1145/1706356.1706385.

[HHM07] Jurriaan Hage, Stefan Holdermans and Arie Middelkoop. *A generic usage analysis with subeffect qualifiers*. International Conference on Functional Programming (ICFP). ACM, 2007. DOI: 10.1145/1291151.1291189.

[HL15] Ralf Hinze and Andres Löh. *lhs2tex: Preprocessor for typesetting Haskell sources with LaTeX*. Version 1.19. Apr. 2015. URL: http://hackage.haskell.org/package/lhs2tex-1.19.

[Huf12] Brian Huffman. *HOLCF '11: A Definitional Domain Theory for Verifying Functional Programs*. Ph.D. thesis. Portland State University, 2012.

[HK13] Brian Huffman and Ondřej Kunčar. *Lifting and Transfer: A Modular Design for Quotients in Isabelle/HOL*. Certified Programs and Proofs (CPP). Vol. 8307. LCNS. Springer, 2013. DOI: 10.1007/978-3-319-03545-1_9.

[JNR02] Rajeev Joshi, Greg Nelson and Keith Randall. *Denali: A Goal-directed Superoptimizer*. ACM, 2002. DOI: 10.1145/512529.512566.

[KMNO14] Ramana Kumar, Magnus O. Myreen, Michael Norrish and Scott Owens. *CakeML: A Verified Implementation of ML*. Principles of Programming Languages (POPL). ACM, 2014. DOI: 10.1145/2535838.2535841.

[Lau93] John Launchbury. *A Natural Semantics for Lazy Evaluation*. Principles of Programming Languages (POPL). ACM, 1993. DOI: 10.1145/158511.158618.

[Ler06] Xavier Leroy. *Formal certification of a compiler back-end, or: programming a compiler with a proof assistant*. Principles of Programming Languages (POPL). ACM, 2006. DOI: 10.1145/1111037.1111042.

[Ler12] Xavier Leroy. *Mechanized Semantics for Compiler Verification*. Asian Symposium on Programming Languages and Systems (APLAS). Vol. 7705. LNCS. Invited talk. Springer, 2012. DOI: 10.1007/978-3-642-35182-2_27.

[Loc10] Andreas Lochbihler. *Verifying a Compiler for Java Threads*. European Symposium on Programming (ESOP). Vol. 6012. LNCS. Springer, 2010. DOI: 10.1007/978-3-642-11957-6_23.

[LH14] Andreas Lochbihler and Johannes Hölzl. *Recursive Functions on Lazy Lists via Domains and Topologies*. Interactive Theorem Proving (ITP). Vol. 8558. LNCS (LNAI). Springer, 2014. DOI: 10.1007/978-3-319-08970-6_22.

[Mar10] Simon Marlow, ed. *Haskell 2010 Language Report*. 2010.

[MP06] Simon Marlow and Simon Peyton Jones[17]. *Making a fast curry: push/enter vs. eval/apply for higher-order languages*. Journal of Functional Programming 16.4-5 (2006). DOI: 10.1017/S0956796806005995.

[MP12] Simon Marlow and Simon Peyton Jones[17]. *The Glasgow Haskell Compiler*. The Architecture of Open Source Applications, Volume II. Ed. by Amy Brown and Greg Wilson. Lulu, 2012. Chap. 5.

[Mid12] Jan Midtgaard. *Control-flow Analysis of Functional Programs*. ACM Computing Surveys (CSUR) 44.3 (June 2012). DOI: 10.1145/2187671.2187672.

[MO03] Yasuhiko Minamide and Koji Okuma. *Verifying CPS Transformations in Isabelle/HOL*. Mechanized Reasoning About Languages with Variable Binding (MERLIN). ACM, 2003. DOI: 10.1145/976571.976576.

[17] famously known as "The Simons"

[MS99] Andrew K. Moran and David Sands. *Improvement in a Lazy Context: An Operational Theory for Call-By-Need*. Principles of Programming Languages (POPL). ACM, 1999. DOI: 10.1145/292540.292547.

[MDHS09] Todd Mytkowicz, Amer Diwan, Matthias Hauswirth and Peter F. Sweeney. *Producing Wrong Data Without Doing Anything Obviously Wrong!* Architectural Support for Programming Languages and Operating Systems (ASPLOS). ACM, 2009. DOI: 10.1145/1508284.1508275.

[Nak10] Keiko Nakata. *Denotational semantics for lazy initialization of letrec: black holes as exceptions rather than divergence*. Fixed Points in Computer Science (FICS). 2010.

[NH09] Keiko Nakata and Masahito Hasegawa. *Small-step and big-step semantics for call-by need*. Journal of Functional Programming 19.6 (2009). DOI: 10.1017/S0956796809990219.

[NS07] Nicholas Nethercote and Julian Seward. *Valgrind: A Framework for Heavyweight Dynamic Binary Instrumentation*. Programming Language Design and Implementation (PLDI). ACM, 2007. DOI: 10.1145/1273442.1250746.

[Nip02] Tobias Nipkow. *Structured Proofs in Isar/HOL*. Types for Proofs and Programs (TYPES). Vol. 2646. LNCS. Springer, 2002. DOI: 10.1007/3-540-39185-1_15.

[NPW02] Tobias Nipkow, Lawrence C. Paulson and Markus Wenzel. *Isabelle/HOL – A Proof Assistant for Higher-Order Logic*. Vol. 2283. LNCS. Springer, 2002. DOI: 10.1007/3-540-45949-9.

[OSu15] Bryan O'Sullivan. *criterion: Robust, reliable performance measurement and analysis*. Version 1.1.0.0. Mar. 2015. URL: http://hackage.haskell.org/package/criterion-1.1.0.0.

[Par93] Will Partain. *The nofib Benchmark Suite of Haskell Programs*. Functional Programming 1992. Workshops in Computing. Springer, 1993. DOI: 10.1007/978-1-4471-3215-8_17.

[Pey92] Simon Peyton Jones. *Implementing Lazy Functional Languages on Stock Hardware: The Spineless Tagless G-Machine*. Journal of Functional Programming 2.2 (1992). DOI: 10.1017/S0956796800000319.

[Pey03] Simon Peyton Jones, ed. *Haskell 98 Language and Libraries – The Revised Report*. Journal of Functional Programming 13.1 (2003).

[PM02] Simon Peyton Jones and Simon Marlow[17]. *Secrets of the Glasgow Haskell Compiler Inliner*. Journal of Functional Programming 12.5 (2002). DOI: 10.1017/S0956796802004331.

[PTH01] Simon Peyton Jones, Andrew Tolmach and Tony Hoare. *Playing by the rules: rewriting as a practical optimisation technique in GHC*. Haskell Workshop. 2001.

[PVWW06] Simon Peyton Jones, Dimitrios Vytiniotis, Stephanie Weirich and Geoffrey Washburn. *Simple Unification-based Type Inference for GADTs*. International Conference on Functional Programming (ICFP). ACM, 2006. DOI: 10.1145/1159803.1159811.

[PB10] Maciej Pirog and Dariusz Biernacki. *A Systematic Derivation of the STG Machine Verified in Coq*. Haskell Symposium. ACM, 2010. DOI: 10.1145/1863523.1863528.

[Pit03] Andrew M. Pitts. *Nominal logic, a first order theory of names and binding*. Vol. 186. Information and Computation 2. Elsevier, 2003. DOI: 10.1016/S0890-5401(03)00138-X.

[RDP10] Norman Ramsey, João Dias and Simon Peyton Jones. *Hoopl: A Modular, Reusable Library for Dataflow Analysis and Transformation*. Haskell Symposium. ACM, 2010. DOI: 10.1145/1863523.1863539.

[RH15] Tobias Rittweiler and Florian Haftmann. *Haskabelle – converting Haskell source files to Isabelle/HOL theories*. 2015. URL: http://isabelle.in.tum.de/haskabelle.html.

[SHO10] Lidia Sánchez-Gil, Mercedes Hidalgo-Herrero and Yolanda Ortega-Mallén. *An Operational Semantics for Distributed Lazy Evaluation*. Trends in Functional Programming (TFP) 2009. Intellect, 2010.

[SHO11] Lidia Sánchez-Gil, Mercedes Hidalgo-Herrero and Yolanda Ortega-Mallén. *Relating function spaces to resourced function spaces*. Symposium on Applied Computing (SAC). ACM, 2011. DOI: 10.1145/1982185.1982469.

[SHO12] Lidia Sánchez-Gil, Mercedes Hidalgo-Herrero and Yolanda Ortega-Mallén. *A Locally Nameless Representation for a Natural Semantics for Lazy Evaluation*. Theoretical Aspects of Computing (ICTAC). Vol. 7521. LNCS. Springer, 2012. DOI: 10.1007/978-3-642-32943-2_8.

[SHO14] Lidia Sánchez-Gil, Mercedes Hidalgo-Herrero and Yolanda Ortega-Mallén. *Launchbury's semantics revisited: On the equivalence of context-heap semantics (Work in progress)*. XIV Jornadas sobre Programación y Lenguajes (2014).

[SHO15] Lidia Sánchez-Gil, Mercedes Hidalgo-Herrero and Yolanda Ortega-Mallén. *The role of indirections in lazy natural semantics*. Perspectives of System Informatics (PSI) 2014. Vol. 8974. LNCS. Springer, 2015. DOI: 10.1007/978-3-662-46823-4_24.

[San92] David Sands. *Operational Theories of Improvement in Functional Languages (Extended Abstract)*. Glasgow Workshop on Functional Programming 1991. Workshops in Computing. Springer, 1992. DOI: 10.1007/978-1-4471-3196-0_24.

[SPCS08] Tom Schrijvers, Simon Peyton Jones, Manuel M. T. Chakravarty and Martin Sulzmann. *Type Checking with Open Type Functions*. International Conference on Functional Programming (ICFP). ACM, 2008. DOI: 10.1145/1411204.1411215.

[SVP14] Ilya Sergey, Dimitrios Vytiniotis and Simon Peyton Jones. *Modular, Higher-order Cardinality Analysis in Theory and Practice*. Principles of Programming Languages (POPL). ACM, 2014. DOI: 10.1145/2535838.2535861.

[Ses97] Peter Sestoft. *Deriving a lazy abstract machine*. Journal of Functional Programming 7.03 (1997). DOI: 10.1017/S0956796897002712.

[SCPD07] Martin Sulzmann, Manuel M. T. Chakravarty, Simon Peyton Jones and Kevin Donnelly. *System F with type equality coercions*. Types in Languages Design and Implementation (TLDI). ACM, 2007. DOI: 10.1145/1190315.1190324.

[Sve02] Josef Svenningsson. *Shortcut Fusion for Accumulating Parameters & Zip-like Functions*. International Conference on Functional Programming (ICFP). ACM, 2002. DOI: 10.1145/581478.581491.

[Tak14] Akio Takano. *Worker-Wrapper Fusion*. Prototype. 2014. URL: https://github.com/takano-akio/ww-fusion (visited on 02/02/2014).

[Tia06] Ye Henry Tian. *Mechanically Verifying Correctness of CPS Compilation*. Computing: The Australasian Theory Symposium (CATS). Vol. 51. CRPIT. ACS, 2006, pp. 41–51.

[UK12] Christian Urban and Cezary Kaliszyk. *General Bindings and Alpha-Equivalence in Nominal Isabelle*. Logical Methods in Computer Science 8.2 (2012). DOI: 10.2168/LMCS-8(2:14)2012.

[UT05] Christian Urban and Christine Tasson. *Nominal Techniques in Isabelle/HOL*. Automated Deduction – CADE-20. Vol. 3632. LNCS. Springer, 2005. DOI: 10.1007/11532231_4.

[VSJVP14] Niki Vazou, Eric L. Seidel, Ranjit Jhala, Dimitrios Vytiniotis and Simon Peyton Jones. *Refinement types for Haskell*. Iternational conference on Functional programming (ICFP). ACM, 2014. DOI: 10.1145/2628136.2628161.

[WVPZ11] Stephanie Weirich, Dimitrios Vytiniotis, Simon Peyton Jones and Steve Zdancewic. *Generative type abstraction and type-level computation*. Principles of Programming Languages (POPL). ACM, 2011. DOI: 10.1145/1926385.1926411.

[XP05] Dana N. Xu and Simon Peyton Jones. *Arity Analysis*. Working notes. 2005.

[ZNMZ13] Jianzhou Zhao, Santosh Nagarakatte, Milo M.K. Martin and Steve Zdancewic. *Formal Verification of SSA-based Optimizations for LLVM*. ACM, 2013. DOI: 10.1145/2491956.2462164.

Index

The following is a combined index and glossary. For each listed symbol, function or term it references the page of its first occurrence and often gives a brief explanation.

Symbols

Defined Terms

Glossary

arity 17
arity annotation 137
atom 20
a name (nominal logic)
balanced execution 71
blackholing 37
build 13
list fusion interface for list producers
closed judgement 38
configuration 69
heap, expression and stack (small-step semantics)
consitent 137
arity annotation with regard to a configuration
de-Bruijn index 19
equivariance 23
commutes with name permutations (nominal logic)
eta-expansion 17
fixed-point induction 30